Enigma Books

Also published by Enigma Books

Charles Weiss

Closing the Books

Jewish Insurance Claims
from
the Holocaust

Foreword by
Abraham Foxman

Enigma Books

Enigma Books
New York, NY
www.enigmabooks.com

ISBN 978-1-929631-83-4

Printed in the United States of America

Publisher's Cataloging-In-Publication Data

Weiss, Charles (Charles B.), 1928-
  Closing the books : Jewish insurance claims from the Holocaust / Charles
Weiss ; foreword by Abraham Foxman.

  p. ; cm.

  Includes index.
  ISBN: 978-1-929631-83-4

1. Holocaust survivors--Economic aspects. 2. Holocaust, Jewish (1939-1945)-
-Reparations. 3. Jewish property--Europe--Claims. 4. International
Commission on Holocaust Era Insurance Claims. 5. Banks and banking--
Corrupt practices--Switzerland--History--20th century. I. Foxman, Abraham
H. II. Title.

D804.7.E26 W45 2008
940.531/814/4

Table of Contents

This book recounts the story of an attempt to right a small part of the injustices perpetrated by the Nazis. It is dedicated to those whose selfless devotion to the task made the long-delayed insurance payments to thousands of beneficiaries possible.

Foreword

by

Abraham H. Foxman

Closing the Books: Jewish Insurance Claims from the Holocaust by Charles Weiss details a long and painful saga. In the wake of the landmark 1998 settlement of $1.25 billion agreed to by Swiss banks to compensate Holocaust survivors whose wartime accounts had not been honored, a whole backlog of material losses began to be recalculated. This was a half-century or more after survivors had resettled in Jewish refugee communities in Israel, America, Western Europe, and Australia, and other corners of the globe.

Interested parties on the one side included survivors and their heirs, American Jewish organizations, high-profile lawyers, and politicians in the United States with significant Jewish constituencies. On the other side were European banks and insurance companies who had profited from the desperation of

Jews who sought to protect their means, however small or great, while frantically trying to save their lives as the Nazi menace spread across the continent. By 1998, whether on one side or the other, it was clearly the eleventh hour for the dwindling number of Holocaust survivors. As law suits by policy holders against German and Italian insurance companies reopened old and still festering wounds, the complexities and complications of calculating the right amount of money for disbursement could only be seen as a substitute for the real moral reckoning which had yet to take place.

As a Holocaust survivor myself, I am not a disinterested party, for I am linked to all survivors, however different our experiences. And as the head of an organization that combats anti-Semitism, I am peculiarly sensitive to the centuries-old canards that *a priori* equate Jews with money, Jews with financial success, and Jews with sharp business practices. In 1998, after the Swiss banks reached their settlement and the tide turned to investigations of other countries, corporations, insurance companies, and art museums, I feared that legitimate claims for restitution might become the main focus of activity regarding the Holocaust without regard for the consequences. I did not want the century's last word on the Holocaust to be that Jews died not because they were Jews, but because they had bank accounts, beautiful art, and valuable real estate holdings. Nor did I want those with legitimate claims to be used as political footballs or meal tickets for ambulance chasers.

The matter of Holocaust restitution remains a vexing one in the history of justice denied, for there is no absolute justice nor can there be an absolute price for seeking it. No actuarial chart can assign a dollar amount to the life of a Jewish child whom the Swiss turned back at the border because, in the classic phrase of the period, "the boat is full." We can only hope for a measure of justice, a symbolic justice that demonstrates a willingness to face responsibility and attempt some accounting for the past.

Closing the Books illuminates the ethical, diplomatic, legislative, and financial issues that proceeded from the Swiss banking settlement and moved on to the German insurance companies, ultimately to be negotiated through the creation of the International Commission on Holocaust Era Insurance Claims (ICHEIC), a non-profit agency registered in Switzerland which was headed by the former United States Secretary of State, Lawrence Eagleburger. The establishment of ICHEIC enabled half-a-dozen European insurance companies, and subsequently, all German insurance companies, to join in the exhaustive process of tracking down unpaid policies, against a promise of safe haven from class action lawsuits or regulatory sanctions.

To completely understand the complex and competing forces that were engaged in adjudicating Holocaust restitution claims is a crucial undertaking, and thankfully, Charles Weiss has given voice to survivors whose individual stories reveal the way material grievance has its moral dimensions.

I remain persuaded after reading *Closing the Books* that pressing cases for Holocaust restitution teaches us something on the level of both *realpolitik* and ethics. For one, it is clear that too many nations and individuals do not do the right thing of their own volition. Political pressure must be applied. The Swiss government and banking system had to be put under the uncomfortable glare of the media spotlight to even begin to face matters that were half a century old.

Secondly, in seeking justice, the core moral issues of the Holocaust must not be forgotten. The Nazis sought to eradicate the Jewish people because they were Jews, not because of what they owned. The systematic pillaging of Jewish property went hand-in-hand with appropriating Jewish assets, but in the end, rich and poor alike were marched to the gas chambers. Thus, any effort to recover the funds that rightfully belonged to Jews and their families but were stolen during and after the war must not obscure for future generations the pure evil of religious and race prejudice that animated the Final Solution.

Thirdly, the particular Jewish character of Holocaust restitution will too often reveal and even provoke the anti-Semitism that still lives in nations called to account, so that all parties to these disputes must find ways to mitigate manifestations of anti-Semitism. As a phenomenon, anti-Semitism has little to do with Jews and more to do with the fears, prejudices, and insecurities of other groups and nations. Home countries in restitution disputes—Switzerland, Germany, et al.—need to set an example of respect and probity in their dealings with Jewish individuals and institutions. They must take a leading role in dealing forthrightly and publicly with residual anti-Semitism, and in discouraging anti-Semitic displays and gestures in the course of negotiations.

Complementary actions by the American Jewish community, which has taken the principal role in pressing these claims, should include closer consultation with those local Jewish communities in home countries which will be directly affected by resurgent anti-Semitism.

That said, it is key that the Jewish community as a whole reach agreed upon goals beforehand and present a united front in such negotiations. This requires a healthy consultative process, bearing in mind that representative Jewish agencies must never lose sight of the tragedy of the Shoah and the memory of the six million Jews who died.

Finally, we must acknowledge that it is because of the American commitment to promoting justice, democratic values, and human rights throughout the world that the rights of Jews, here and elsewhere, can be assured of continued monitoring and protection. From the end of the Second World War to the present, American administrations, Democratic and Republican alike, have time and again proven their commitment both to Israel and to the fight against homegrown anti-Semitism. We can not overestimate the changed climate towards Jews between the America of the 1930s and 1940s and today. It has been the willingness of American administrations, their representatives, and a bi-partisan Congress to deal with Holocaust-related issues that has enabled skilled, sensitive intermediaries to engage in delicate restitution negotiations in a manner that respects both sides. American Jews, Holocaust survivors and their families, feel enormous gratitude to this country whose ideals of equality and justice under the law encourage all minorities to feel safe and respected on these shores.

After an exhaustive and sometimes contentious nine-year process, described so well by Weiss, the ICHEIC under Chairman Eagleburger reached a complicated compensation formula that also allowed for the distribution of residual funds through the Conference on Material Claims Against Germany to institutions that provide social welfare services to Holocaust survivors everywhere in the world, as well as to Holocaust-related education programs run by Yad Vashem in Israel and the Jewish Agency. This conforms to my own sense that disbursements must take into account survivors in need, especially in Eastern Europe, and in Israel, which has the largest survivor community in the world. But as we learn in the Epilogue to *Closing the Books*, the issue has not ended there. The ICHEIC has all along had its detractors, criticizing it for a lack of transparency, among other perceived shortcomings.

So *Closing the Books* is, as it were, a work in progress, but a vital one in mapping the issues, recreating the atmospherics, providing profiles of the dramatis personae, and doing so within fair and high journalistic standards. The issue of Holocaust restitution is one that will not go away—not, alas, until every survivor is gone from the scene and every survivor's heir has passed on as well.

In the meantime, *Closing the Books* serves to help us get our facts straight, for this is a significant chapter in the history of the Holocaust. It tells us much about our continuing search for the truth, and for justice.

History, too, has its claims.

Abraham H. Foxman is National Director of the Anti-Defamation League and a Holocaust survivor. He is the author of *The Deadliest Lies: The Israel Lobby and the Myth of Jewish Control* and *Never Again? The Threat of the New Anti-Semitism.*

Introduction

During the late 1990s, the evils perpetrated by the Third Reich had a revival on the world stage, this time in the form of demands for compensation for what victims of the Nazis suffered. Spurred on by the billion and a quarter dollars that the Swiss banks put up to settle accusations that they had defrauded Holocaust-era depositors, teams of eager lawyers and a number of Jewish organizations turned their attention to the whole universe of German companies. Here, Deutsche Bank could be accused of despoiling Jewish depositors, Daimler Benz of exploiting slave labor, and Allianz Insurance of not honoring Jewish policies. Not only did the targets of the claims have very deep pockets, but, on the face of it, they appeared obviously liable.

But were they?

Germany, or West Germany at the time, had, under pressure from the victorious Allies, assumed financial responsibility for the depredations of the Nazis. Beginning in 1952 and all through the 1960s, 1970s, and 1980s, it had made a comprehensive, good faith effort to seek out those who had suffered and try to compensate them for what they had lost. There was no money that could bring back to life the more than six million Jews from all over Europe who had been murdered, but for the survivors and heirs, restitution payments often represented an opportunity to start anew. Payments were intended to cover actual property that was stolen, insurance policies that were seized, schooling that a person had been deprived of, pension rights never realized. Each loss was assessed and what at the time was regarded as a fair price was awarded as compensation. In addition, billions of dollars were given to the State of Israel and the Jewish Claims Conference as the legal heirs of the nameless murdered.

It was a national effort funded by a guilt-ridden, postwar West Germany intended to show that the German people had done something to atone for the evils of the Third Reich.

Then, in the 1990s, lawsuits began to proliferate against subsidiaries of German insurance companies in the United States. The parent companies, who had been persuaded that the question of unsettled outstanding policies had all been dealt with through the various state restitution programs, were taken by surprise. It was also a rude awakening on another level. More than 50 years after the war, German companies found themselves again in the dock of public opinion, accused of profiting from the very same crimes they had been accused of then. Germans saw themselves as Germans. For a large segment of American Jews, however, they were Nazis masquerading as repentant Germans.

It was as if nothing had happened in the intervening half a century. A generation of Germans who were not tainted by the Nazi curse had taken over, yet were nevertheless being saddled with guilt for the sins of their fathers.

Given the depravity of what the Nazis had actually done, it was an easy sell to say that a giant German insurance company had prospered in the post-War era thanks to the policies it had sold to Jews before the war and never paid off. Companies were a priori guilty simply for having the same name as the company that did in fact collaborate with the rulers of the Third Reich.

What emerged was a clash between the assumption that a terrible injustice had been perpetrated that had to be rectified and the much more mundane facts of what was due and what could be done. The lawyers, who normally work on a contingency basis in lawsuits against insurance companies, naturally tended to exaggerate claims of what was owed. The companies themselves, like all insurance companies, took the contrary position, first asserting that there were no unpaid policies or uncompensated policies, and then allowing that while there may a handful of policies still outstanding, claiming that they were for relatively small sums.

Where did the facts, as marshaled by the people who thought the German companies owed billions, intersect with the companies' stand that the few policies that may have gone unpaid represented only very small amounts?

Where did the truth lie? When the Swiss banks agreed to a settlement of more than a billion dollars it became the benchmark. The expectation was that unpaid insurance policies would be worth much more.

Elan Steinberg was at the time Executive Director of the World Jewish Congress, a New York-based group that had been trying to determine exactly how much money the Nazis stole from the Jews. He put the figure at $150 billion in present-day values and suggested that insurance, which he described as "the poor man's Swiss bank account," was one of the larger components, second only to real estate.

Shortly after the first class action lawsuit seeking billions of dollars from a selection of European insurance companies was filed in New York in 1997, State insurance commissioners stepped forward to seek justice for beneficiaries in their respective states. New York, California and Florida, with their large Jewish populations, led the way. The commissioners felt they could force the companies to pay up by threatening to lift the licenses of whatever businesses they might have in the United States. With law suits pending in New York and Los Angeles, bills drafted for a number of state legislatures and growing public pressure from Jewish organizations, insurance commissioners in key states proposed a way of consolidating the restitution process and speeding it up. The National Association of Insurance Commissioners (NAIC) rallied around the idea and joined in applying pressure on the companies. Their collective efforts eventually gave birth to the International Commission on Holocaust Era Insurance Claims (ICHEIC), a non-profit agency registered in Switzerland with offices in London and Washington and headed by former U.S. Secretary of State Lawrence Eagleburger.

In August 1998, six European insurance companies, together with representatives of U.S. insurance regulators and international Jewish organizations, signed a Memorandum of Understanding (MOU) to establish ICHEIC. The companies pledged "to cooperate fully with the Commission to expeditiously resolve all unpaid claims, provide full access to all of their relevant files and archives, and contribute to the establishment of a humanitarian fund and help pay for the expense of looking for unpaid policies." In return, the fact of their membership in ICHEIC gave them a promise of a "safe haven" from legal action.

A new dimension was added in 2000, with the establishment of the German Foundation, "Remembrance, Responsibility, and Future." Its DM 10 billion fund was intended to tie up all the loose ends of material damage caused by the Third Reich, and it was only natural that insurance claims would also be covered. The Foundation made ICHEIC a partner in its operation, and assigned it DM 550 million to resolve unpaid claims and for general humanitarian purposes. The German Insurance Association, the GDV, was charged with seeing that its members—including those who had already joined ICHEIC—authenticated the claims against them.

In its eight years of operation, ICHEIC has done quite a credible job of canvassing for unpaid policies and seeing that payment went out to beneficiaries. The process has not gone smoothly, however. All the principals, the state insurance commissioners, the Jewish organizations, and the companies, are united in their scathing criticism of the expense that the search entailed.

Moreover, the companies' argument at the outset that relatively few policies remained unpaid seems to have been borne out, and expectations that "billions of dollars" were involved proved greatly inflated. Driven by an abiding suspicion that the companies were guilty of concealing a treasure trove of unpaid policies, comprehensive audits were conducted at considerable expense in the archives of 15 of the companies that ICHEIC had picked out. In addition, teams of ICHEIC and Israeli accountants were charged with seeing that the companies did a thorough job of researching and processing claims.

One of ICHEIC's chief concerns was devoted of course to how German Jews fared with the German insurance industry. While Germany did not have the largest Jewish community on the Continent, it is where Hitler's atrocities began. It was here that the Nazis test drove their plans to dispossess the Jews, then expelled them, and eventually murdered them.

The German insurance industry has had a long and prosperous history. It was already well established when King William I of Prussia was proclaimed Emperor of a united Germany in the Hall of Mirrors in Versailles in January 1871, a landmark event that propelled German business onto the world stage. The Reich he ruled as constitutional monarch had replaced a loose confederation of tiny and often warring grand duchies, duchies, minor kingdoms, and principalities. Prussia, with the "Iron Chancellor," Otto von Bismarck, the power behind the Kaiser, was very much the first among equals in the federation. Over the next 40 years of peace in Europe, the insurance companies prospered as Germany introduced what, for the time, was quite progressive labor legislation. Bismarck is credited with pioneering the concept of universal social security.

The first comprehensive laws establishing state supervision over the conduct of the insurance business throughout the German Reich were introduced at the turn of the 20th Century. Companies were now required to obtain a license to sell insurance and the state could lay down rules on how they did it. In those first years, the German companies had to cope with fierce competition from many foreign companies—mainly Austrian and Swiss, and later on, English and North American as well. As the German economy grew stronger, the foreigners' market share decreased, and, at the same time, German life insurance companies grew more attractive, and some branched out into new fields, often through their own agencies abroad.

All this came to an end with the outbreak of war in 1914. The Entente countries (Britain, France and Russia), the enemy from the German point of view, immediately abrogated all insurance contracts with German companies. Hostilities ended four years and 11 million dead later with an armistice. Under the Treaty of Versailles that formally ended the war and came into force on January 10, 1920, Germany had to cede approximately 13 percent of its territory to the victors. Overall, the treaty put 10 percent of the prewar population of Germany outside its borders.

The extensive territorial changes had a profound effect on the German insurance industry. In addition to having to re-structure how business was conducted domestically, the companies also had to cope with the fact that a large part of what they had been doing abroad over the last decades was destroyed while great chunks of pre-World War I Germany (and consequently, the respective insurance business) now belonged to foreign countries.

The considerable impact the political changes had on development of foreign insurance business was most evident in the territory of the now defunct Austro-Hungarian Empire. German companies now had to apply for new permits to operate in all the countries that had emerged. For example, an independent foreign business had to be created not only in Hungary, but also in Romania, to service clients in the former Hungarian territories that Romania had taken over. Independent national insurance companies began to emerge in each country, and German companies had to comply with a host of new regulations. They could no longer sell insurance from their home base but had to issue policies in the country itself, subject to local jurisdiction. Premium reserves had to be kept in the country in which the policy was sold under local laws governing investment.

And that was not the only damage that the German name had suffered in former enemy countries. There was also the total collapse of the German mark twice in the course of the first decade after the War. First, there was the inflation which whipsawed the country in 1923 and 1924, when a loaf of bread sold for four billion marks. Then, Germany was devastated by the Great Depression that began on Wall Street in 1929.

The hyperinflation of 1923 rendered life insurance policies, like all other intangible assets, absolutely worthless and the industry had to start again from scratch. Only the introduction of a new currency in 1923, the Reichsmark, brought the runaway inflation to a halt. Gradually, anti-German sentiment died down, and even some German assets that had been seized in the course of the war were returned. The prerequisites for a slow revival of the insurance business were in place.

Whatever gains that were achieved after 1924 were almost wiped out from the end of the 1920s through the early 1930s. Business fell off dramatically as policies were cancelled or surrendered and repurchased prior to 1933 because the policy-holders hit by the Great Depression, could no longer afford the premiums.

In December 1931, the Reichsmark was decreed no longer convertible, further complicating doing insurance businesses abroad. Then political events intervened that affected every aspect of German life. In January of 1933, Adolf Hitler became Chancellor, and a 12-year-long nightmare of brutal excess began. In order to survive, insurance companies, like every other sector of German business, had no choice but to go along with Nazi decrees. It was not a part of their history they are proud of.

Closing the Books

Jewish Insurance Claims
from
the Holocaust

Chapter I

The Swiss Banks

In the mid-1990s, the conscience of the world was stirred by an old story that had taken on a new immediacy, a new topicality. Swiss banks were accused of appropriating assets that had been entrusted to them by Jews who sought a safe place for their possessions in the turbulent years before and during World War II. According to plaintiffs' lawyers, when the Jews failed to come back from the death camps and claim their money, the banks just kept it.

The Nazis of the Third Reich had been guilty of pillaging Jews for all they were worth, and anything they were accused of was credible. For Switzerland, on the other hand, the probity of its banking system was as famous as its ski slopes or its clocks. To allege that they had been willing accomplices of the Nazis was a real shocker. The lawyers estimated that as much as $7 billion was at stake.

Throughout the post-War years, there had been attempts to seek some kind of restitution for the atrocities and looting committed by the Nazis. The most successful and most comprehensive program was instituted by West Germany in the early 1950s at the behest of the American occupying powers. Called *Bundesentschädigungsgesetz*, or BEG for short, it purported to settle all legal claims against Germany for crimes committed by Hitler's Third Reich. (Other restitution programs included the *Bundesrückerstattungsgesetz* (real estate, etc.), the *Lastenausgleichsgesetz* as well as compensation laws that provided for life long pension payments. (See Chapter II for details).

While not all the victims were satisfied, few tried to get more through the courts, and those that did were very rarely successful. Moreover, it was a strictly German program, and the emphasis was on compensating victims of German crimes who had some residential connection to Germany (and then, only those who lived outside of Communist countries, to which currency transfers were barred).

Then along came the Swiss bank case. It was the first major attempt in years to recover what was stolen from the Jews solely because they were Jews.

What had started out as a scattershot attack on the banks based on random anecdotal evidence was given shape and form, not to mention publicity, by international Jewish organizations. By the time a final settlement was painstakingly hammered out, several governments were involved, legal precedents were established, and the media carried the story around the world.

While there was no direct connection, it was no coincidence that the success with the banks inspired the same cast of characters to assume central roles in the subsequent legal actions against German insurance companies, manufacturing concerns and banks.

In the case of Switzerland, the plaintiffs' lawyers employed a combination of diligent historical research, and persuasive public relations, to win a settlement of one and a quarter billion dollars from the Swiss banks. The money would go to a wide array of causes, most of them related to assisting Holocaust survivors. Payments also went to the class of people on whose behalf the suits were originally filed, the individuals who could show some sort of documentation that they themselves or a relative had deposited money in that bastion of financial integrity, a Swiss bank. Naturally, the lawyers also profited.

When the charges were first made public, the banks denied any wrongdoing. They argued that after the War they had carried out a thorough audit of accounts of foreign depositors that had lain dormant. Then, and in subsequent audits, they had turned up fewer than eight hundred accounts, with a total value of just over 38 million Swiss francs (about $22m).

Here the public relations aspect took over. Israel Singer, the executive head of the World Jewish Congress (WJC), worked tirelessly to involve powerful forces in Washington, including officials in Bill Clinton's administration, in what he claimed was the pursuit of justice. Singer, an ordained rabbi, together with the Chairman of the WJC, the billionaire Edgar Bronfman, first got New York Republican Senator Alphonse D'Amato to take the issue under his wing. Many of D'Amato's supporters lived in predominantly Jewish neighborhoods in Brooklyn, and he was only too happy to advance a cause that was sure to appeal to this loyal constituency. These same principals would also play important roles in making German insurance companies pay up, and getting German industry to concede its debt to former forced and slave laborers.

The Swiss banks had many large holdings in the United States and were particularly vulnerable to bad publicity. In March 1996, D'Amato convened a hearing of the Senate Banking Committee, of which he was Chairman, to look into the banks' wartime behavior. It proved a public relations disaster for the Swiss.

Ever the showman, D'Amato called as his first witness a retired tourist guide from the borough of Queens in New York. She was Greta Beer, who was born Greta Beligdisch in pre-War Romania. Her father was a well-to-do textile manufacturer who traveled widely on business throughout Europe. Before his death from natural causes in 1940, he told his family that he had deposited all the money they might ever need in a bank in Switzerland.

The Beligdisch family spent the war years in hiding and got to Switzerland only in the 1960s, long after the cessation of hostilities. While the deposit slips and even the name of the bank had vanished in the wartime turmoil, they went from bank to bank to press their claim. The reply was always the same: accounts are identified by number, not by name, and that banks are barred by law and time-hallowed custom from disclosing the contents to anyone who does not have that magic number.

Ms. Beligdisch concluded her testimony before the Senate committee with the plea, "I do hope that the Swiss banks will see the light—so many people have died in the meantime—and will see the light to correct what has been done."

Even if the issues involved dealt with events that had occurred many years before, reports of the manifest injustice that was beginning to emerge from the hearings made headlines across the country. The Swiss were identifiably the villains in a case in which the United States could only be regarded as the knight in shining armor. With President Clinton's open support, the United States took the lead in pressing for an independent audit of the accounts. He also assigned a senior State Department official, Stuart Eizenstat, to oversee the various American efforts to achieve a modicum of justice for those who had suffered in the Holocaust.

It was an informed choice. Clinton had appointed Eizenstat, an observant Jew, U.S. Ambassador to the European Union, where he engaged in negotiating the return of Jewish communal property in Western Europe. Afterwards, he continued his pursuit of stolen Jewish property at the Commerce Department, until the President gave him the personal rank of ambassador in charge of the Holocaust portfolio. It was in this capacity that he dealt with the Swiss banking issue, and, later on, with unpaid Holocaust insurance policies and compensation for slave labor.

It was largely through his intervention that the Swiss banks agreed that the former chairman of the U.S. Federal Reserve Bank, Paul Volcker, head a panel of "eminent persons" to search the bank archives. For the purposes of the investigation, the traditional secrecy rules were suspended for relevant accounts.

At about this time, the Swiss were blindsided by an incident which made the banks appear to be bent on destroying documents before they could be examined. A 28-year-old watchman, Christoph Meili, had been making his rounds at the Zurich headquarters of Union Bank of Switzerland (UBS), on the morning of January 8, 1997, when he came across two large plastic carts loaded with old documents destined for the shredder. In one of them he found a heavy, clothbound volume labeled 1920–1926, and another labeled Real Estate going back to 1930.

Meili's suspicions were aroused. Swiss newspapers had been full of reports of the investigation looking for Holocaust accounts, and he took the books home to examine them. After he and his wife saw what they contained, he handed them over to the Zurich Jewish community.

When the police stepped in to accuse Meili of stealing bank property, he became an instant martyr in the American media, and once again the banks were cast as the villains. Fearing arrest, however, the young watchman took his family and fled to the United States, where he immediately applied for asylum. Congress rose to the occasion and passed a special law to make him a citizen, which President Bill Clinton promptly signed.

As Meili would later testify before D'Amato's committee, "I was convinced that the documents were being destroyed illegally… [and wanted] to make the documents and actions known to the public. I also wanted the oppressed Jewish population, the Holocaust victims, to get justice."

Shortly afterwards Eizenstat, Clinton's point man on Holocaust issues, dropped another bombshell. On May 7, 1997, he called a news conference to read out a report on efforts to recover property wrongfully expropriated by the Nazis and restore it to its original owners. Once again, the Swiss were cast as the villains. Eizenstat accused the Swiss National Bank in Bern of accepting shipments of gold from Nazi Germany, that far exceeded Germany's known gold reserves at the outbreak of the war, and which the bank should have realized was stolen.

Speaking before television cameras, he methodically refuted Swiss claims after the war that they had never received looted gold. "The Swiss National Bank and the Swiss bankers knew as the war progressed that the Reichsbank's own coffers had been depleted and that the Swiss were handling vast sums of looted gold." He quoted from one receipt retrieved from the Reichsbank's microfilm archives which recorded that a shipment contained, "…on behalf of the Reich Finance Ministry, 854 rings, one trunk of silver objects, one trunk of dental gold, 29,996 grams." The "dental gold" was presumably pried out of the mouths of murdered Jews and smelted to look like bullion.

"Whatever their motivation," Eizenstat summed up, "the fact that they pursued vigorous trade with the Third Reich had the clear effect of supporting and prolonging Nazi Germany's capacity to wage war." This blunt appeal to patriotism allayed whatever hesitations Americans might have about attacking Switzerland for keeping money that belonged to Jews.

Meanwhile, the Meili affair had another, unforeseen, effect. The lawyers who had been preparing to sue Switzerland and the banks now had a valid pretext not to wait for the Volcker Commission to conclude its search of bank files.

If they did not quickly get into court, they argued, the banks would shred the evidence, and no one would get anything.

Initiating the campaign was Ed Fagan, a lawyer from New Jersey, whose client, Gizella Weisshaus, was the only member of her family to survive Auschwitz. Like Greta Beer, her father had told her he had saved money for the family in Switzerland but, like Greta, she had been unable to locate it. Fagan filed his complaint, Weisshaus v. Union Bank of Switzerland et al., in Brooklyn, demanding $20 million in damages. The suit, assigned to District Court Judge Edward Korman, generated wide media coverage.

It also sparked a rough and tumble fight among the lawyers who had been painstakingly documenting their own cases against some Swiss banks. Many of them represented the most prestigious legal firms in the country, and they did not take kindly to the arrival on the scene of Fagan, whom they saw as an upstart. Eventually, however, they were all combined into one class action suit before Judge Korman.

The Swiss were reluctant for the case to go to trial. Their American lawyers had warned them of the risks should a jury be called upon to assess damages in a case as emotionally fraught as this one. However, early negotiations to arrive at a settlement quickly broke down, when it became clear that what the plaintiffs had in mind was far more than what the banks were prepared to even contemplate.

In their book *The Victim's Fortune,* John Authers and Richard Wolffe describe a scene in which the plaintiffs' lead lawyer, Mel Weiss, asks his opposite number, Roger Witten, the kind of numbers the banks are willing to pay, adding that he assumed they were thinking of terms of "multiple billions." Witten was aghast. "Did you say billions with a 'b'?" he asked. With tongue in cheek, another plaintiffs' lawyer, Michael Hausfeld, pointed out that this was progress.

"We've argued him up from the end of the alphabet. He had started with a 'z'."

At the same time, it was becoming clear to the banks that if there was to be an out-of-court settlement, they had best conclude it quickly. The WJC's Israel Singer was moving on another front, drawing up plans to threaten the banks where it would hurt them most, their business interests in the United States. He hoped the threat of sanctions would make them more amenable to a deal with the Jews.

For this, he turned to Alan Hevesi, an old friend, who was then the Comptroller of New York City. The city was one of the biggest borrowers in the world, and such loan transactions earned investment banks huge fees. Hevesi had the authority to select the lender. When he wrote to the three largest Swiss banks to express concern about what was coming out of Senator D'Amato's committee and asking for their comment, he did not mention the possibility of denying them access to New York's business, but assumed that they understood the message.

In October 1997 New York announced that it was looking to borrow a sizeable sum, and invited the big investment banks to underwrite a letter of credit to the city. The syndicate that offered the best deal, however, was led by UBS. In Hevesi's eyes, it was the most extreme of the "big three" banks contesting

Jewish claims, and he balked at approving a contract. The loan was eventually negotiated with the same syndicate, but minus UBS. While the deal was consummated without publicity, the message was clear.

It was further reinforced after New York Governor George Pataki called for an investigation into whether there was evidence of any dormant accounts in the archives of the major Swiss banks in New York City. The State Superintendent of Banks, Elizabeth McCaul, issued what is known as a "consent order" against Swiss Bank Corporation (SBC), giving her the power to conduct an independent audit. Another such order was subsequently issued against UBS. That type of order is generally one step short of rescinding a bank's license to do business.

In the meantime, Alan Hevesi had convened a meeting of more than 150 financial officers from across the country to talk about what to do about the Swiss banks. It was a topic that had caught public and media attention. The first speaker was Israel Singer. He prefaced his remarks by saying, "we don't like boycotts of any kind… but we understand those who believe economic pressure is effective in bringing results." He recommended giving the Swiss banks 90 days "to resolve every last issue."

The delegates had been primed to push for sanctions, and they adopted the three-month moratorium by acclamation. Singer, who regarded the threat of sanctions as far more important in getting the Swiss banks to act than their actual imposition, was pleased. The State Department, which saw sanctions by local agencies as interfering in the conduct of American foreign policy, and had made its opposition clear, was mollified by the three months' grace that was included in the resolution.

The case against the Swiss banks was quickly coalescing onto three planes. Together, they were a formidable combination, but they did not necessarily function in unison. One was the courtroom, another was the threat of economic sanctions, and a third was a government-mediated agreement. The plaintiff's lawyers were understandably wedded to trying the cases in court, and letting a judge and jury decide. Israel Singer, and his allies in the financial world, believed they could coerce the banks into action through economic pressure. Stuart Eizenstat hoped he could broker an out-of-court agreement between the lawyers and the banks, but without involving Singer and his World Jewish Congress in the negotiations.

The Swiss, who had already spent a lot of money on the Volcker Commission's search for dormant accounts, saw no reason why they should not wait for the results to appear, and then pay what they owed. The Commission itself was bogged down by the sheer enormity of the task it had undertaken. At the outset, the members had little idea what it was they were looking for or even how to go about it. The prospect of painstakingly going through literally millions of files made the search for a needle in a haystack seem simple. For their part, the Swiss were in no hurry.

An event that was to define the shape of the eventual agreement came on March 26th, the day before the 90 day moratorium on sanctions was due to expire. The five-man steering committee on sanctions that Alan Hevesi had set up was going over its options of what to do next when a delegation of Swiss bankers appeared. They carried a one paragraph letter signed by the CEOs of the three major Swiss banks committing them to seek a global settlement that would ensure "legal peace for Switzerland." It stipulated that the agreement would have to be with Singer and the WJC under the auspices of Stuart Eizenstat, not a judge. Hevesi's steering committee on sanctions gave the Swiss another three months, until July 1.

Several weeks later Eizenstat convened what, in diplomatic parlance, are called "proximity talks" in his Washington office.

In one room he gathered the plaintiffs' lawyers and Israel Singer, and in the other the Swiss bankers. The only communication between the sides was through Eizenstat, who shuttled from room to room. This first round of negotiations ended with the sides sharply divided over how much money would be involved.

The Washington talks were upstaged by Senator D'Amato, who was insisting that New York's Superintendent of Banking hold up the merger between UBS and SBC. The merged company needed the State Banking Commission's approval to do business on Wall Street, and Superintendent Elizabeth McCaul simply refused to put the merger on the Commission's agenda. The Commission met once a month, and she had already held up the merger for consecutive months. The Swiss responded by boycotting the Washington talks so long as the approval was not forthcoming.

Eizenstat had to find a way out, and he did. He called Singer on the phone and told him that he had a firm commitment from the Swiss to pursue a resolution of the dispute, once the merger had been cleared. Singer assumed they were offering something in the range of what the plaintiffs' lawyers had mentioned, between one and three billion, and he let it be known on the eve of the June meeting of the Commission, that he wanted the merger to proceed. The Commission approved it by the narrowest of margins.

The "proximity talks" reconvened in New York the following day. When Singer learned from Eizenstat the sub-stance of what the banks were offering, $450 million, he was enraged. The proposal was less than half of what he had set as a minimum. He went back to Alan Hevesi and the sanctions option. A frustrated Eizenstat formally withdrew from further negotiations.

As expected, Hevesi and his steering committee, in the face of what they saw as a "stone-like impasse" in the negotiations, adopted a resolution imposing escalating sanctions. From September, 1998, first pension funds would be barred from making overnight deposits with Swiss banks, nor could they borrow from them through bond offerings. From November 15th, city and state investment managers would no longer be able to trade through Swiss firms. If still in effect on January 1, 1999, Swiss banks would no longer be eligible to manage pension funds.

Judge Korman, in whose courtroom the lawsuits against the banks had originally been filed, had built up a reputation over the years of trying to get litigants who appeared before him to agree to settle without a trial, and he undertook to try where Stuart Eizenstat had failed. He invited Singer and 19 of the lawyers in the case for dinner at a Brooklyn restaurant on the night before the hearings were to begin. Only the Swiss government was not represented.

The judge pointed out that at issue were events that had occurred on another continent more than 50 years ago, and said he did not believe a courthouse in Brooklyn was the proper venue to adjudicate them. On the other hand, he went on, both the Holocaust survivors and the Swiss people had a great deal to gain from a just settlement of the issue. In the course of a discussion which went on for several hours, Mel Weiss made a suggestion that pointed the way to the eventual agreement. He said that if Credit Suisse and UBS were to offer a sizeable enough amount, it would cover the obligations owed by the National Bank and all pending claims against Swiss companies and the government.

Before the dinner party broke up, Judge Korman suggested two possible settlement figures: $1.25 billion, to be paid in installments, that would cover all liabilities, or $1 billion plus compensation for any dormant accounts the Volcker Commission might uncover. Both sides left the restaurant confident that they were on to something, and that a settlement was at hand.

Everyone spent the next two days in Judge Korman's Brooklyn courthouse hammering out the details of a settlement. Witten got clearance from the heads of both UBS and Credit Suisse that they could agree to $1.25 billion, but stipulated that whatever the Volcker Commission found would have to be deducted from that sum. The banks' offer, in effect, made the commission's findings of purely academic interest, and that after spending $500 million on the two-year audit of all the records, what it turned up would have no bearing on what the banks would eventually have to pay.

The amount they were talking about was the figure that everyone agreed to in the end, but much had to be ironed out first. For one thing, Witten wanted the agreement to afford blanket legal protection for all Swiss wartime culpability, including insurance claims. For another, he wanted the $70 million the banks had paid into a humanitarian fund deducted as well. After tough bargaining, it was agreed that compensation for wartime refugees turned back at the Swiss border and slave laborers employed by Swiss-owned companies, would also come out of the $1.25 billion pool.

The question of insurance was a tougher issue. Two of the lawyers in the room had cases pending against Winterthur, a subsidiary of Credit Suisse, and did not want to forego what they saw as an additional source of big revenue. The lawyers finally agreed that the blanket immunity would cover insurance as well, but with the exception of Winterthur, Zurich and Basler Leben. (These three companies eventually sought protection from legal action by becoming founding members of a new entity, the International Commission on Holocaust Era Insurance Claims (ICHEIC)).

The banks had also won agreement to pay off the sum in installments, but a last minute breakdown in communications over the question of what interest would be charged threatened to derail the deal. Overnight, D'Amato and Singer had met and agreed that the sum was the important issue, and that bickering over interest on the installments was counterproductive. In the morning, D'Amato called Witten to say that the Jewish side waived the interest. The problem was, D'Amato had not cleared his offer beforehand with the lawyers, and they were furious. The lead attorneys, Hausfeld and Weiss, said flatly they would not sign.

By nightfall, however, a compromise was reached. The sides settled on using the money market rate published daily in the *Wall Street Journal.* It was 3.78 percent that day. Witten and Hausfeld informed Judge Korman that they had finally reached a deal.

When the Volcker Commission finally issued its report, summing up what it had found in its four years of investigating the archives and vaults of the world's most secretive banking system, it came as something of an anti-climax.

It claimed to have found about 21,000 dormant and closed accounts that had a "probable" connection to a Holocaust victim, and an additional 15,000 with a "possible" connection. It drew no conclusions about the value of the assets "probably" or "possibly" involved. At the Commission' request, the Swiss Bankers' Association authorized publication of the names associated with the "probables."

The fruits of its labor: the Claims Resolution Tribunal that authorized the Volcker Commission certified about 3,000 awards that could be traced to Holocaust victims' accounts, amounting to about $250 million.

Judge Korman's work did not end with the agreement on a global sum. He also had to divide up whatever remained after depositors and their heirs were located and paid. Here he called on a prominent New York attorney, Judah Gribetz, and appointed him Special Master to oversee who got what.

Generally, the agreement stipulated that the banks would pay $1.25 billion to settle all the claims of depositors or their heirs, as well as claims of people who suffered because of what the plaintiffs said was the cooperation of Swiss institutions with the Nazis. The lion's share, $800 million, was earmarked for depositors, though it quickly became clear that this would far exceed whatever claims would be submitted. In the end, most of the funds earmarked for compensating depositors went unclaimed.

While Judge Korman said it was still too soon to say that it was time to hand out the remaining money, he had the un-enviable task of having to decide who would get the $200 million the settlement made available for humanitarian aid. He would have to rule among a number of very deserving groups. The most prominent were Jewish Holocaust survivor groups from Israel, the former Soviet Union and the United States, as well as a representative of the gypsies who had also been persecuted by the Nazis.

Judge Korman said he was guided by his perception of where the greatest need existed. He ruled that 75 percent of this class of funds should go to impoverished Jewish survivors in the former Soviet Union, four percent to needy American survivors and the rest to Israel and the rest of the world. His announcement touched off what one witness, Thane Rosenbaum, a son of survivors, described as a "dog-eat-dog" mood in the packed Brooklyn courtroom.

Rosenbaum had earlier addressed the court to press the case that would make more money available for destitute survivors in the United States. People classified as survivors in the U.S., he said, really went through the concentration camps, while Jews in the Soviet Union had fled there to escape going to the camps. They were not entitled to the money, which, he said, was obtained to compensate direct victims. He called Judge Korman's approach "an affront to the living and a desecration of the dead."

An appeal against the Judge's ruling was later dismissed by a Federal appeals court, and the distribution of funds continues.

A comment about this last-minute bickering came from Abe Foxman, a prominent Jewish leader, and head of the influential Anti-Defamation League. He expressed what many people felt. A Holocaust survivor himself, he said: "Six million Jews died because they were Jews, not because they had money or bank accounts. Ninety-nine percent did not have Swiss bank accounts, didn't have gold, didn't have jewelry, didn't have art. They perished because of who they were. This debate, this discussion, as important as it is, skews the whole message, the lesson, the truth of the Holocaust. I do not want the last sound bite of the history of the Twentieth Century to be about Jews and their money."

What the Swiss bank case did was to bring two elements together that opened the floodgates of claims for other injuries suffered by the Jews. On the one hand, there was recognition that Jews had been dispossessed, and, on the other, that the money had not disappeared but that it could be recovered. There is also a postscript which presages the outcome of the search for unpaid insurance policies. In the end, most of the funds set aside to compensate account holders had to be diverted to other purposes: there were simply too few legitimate claims.

Chapter II

German Reparations for Victims of the Nazis

The vehemence of the class action suits that blossomed in the late 1990s accusing German companies of profiting from Nazi persecution conveyed the impression that Nazi victims had never received any compensation for material losses or that Germany had done nothing since the end of the Second World War to provide some measure of justice for the personal losses suffered by millions of plundered and murdered European Jews. It was a misleading picture.

There had been—and continues to be—a comprehensive German restitution and compensation program for victims of Nazi persecution. It was set up right after the war under the auspices of the Allied occupation forces, and so far, has paid out more than DM 120 billion, i.e., more than $100 billion in current values.[1] To a certain extent, this amount covers material losses, including insurance policies that were surrendered under duress or confiscated by the Nazi regime, but most of the money goes into ongoing payments to compensate for personal and physical injury, impaired health, loss of freedom, or loss of opportunities for professional or economic advancement.

What characterizes the whole program however—and in part, this may be why it is relatively little known—is the glaring asymmetry between the beneficiaries. Although over 90 percent of the Nazis' victims were foreign nationals (of the more than six million murdered Jews, approximately 165,000 had lived as German citizens in Germany)—Jewish victims who lived in the former communist states in central and eastern Europe or the former Soviet Union received only 10 percent of the payments. On the other hand, German or other west European citizens, both Jews and non-Jews, who were victimized by the Nazis but managed to get out of Germany in time or emigrated after the war and subsequently became citizens of other countries, notably Israel and the United States and who could show some residential relation with the German Reich, received the lion's share, about 90 percent of the allocations.[2]

This sharp disparity between western and eastern victims was a by-product of the Cold War. The indemnification of Nazi victims is inextricably linked to political decisions that mirrored the edge of the East-West confrontation. Compensation for Nazi crimes did not reflect the reality of Nazi persecution throughout German dominated Europe[3] so much as the power

---

1. In current values DM 212 billion as of 1999. Bundestagspräsident Wolfgang Thierse in his letter to the editor of the "Blätter für deutsche und internationale Politik," 1999, p. 125, quoted in Hans-Günter Hockerts, Christiane Kuller (eds.), *Nach der Verfolgung. Wiedergutmachung nationalsozialistischen Unrechts* (Göttingen 2003), p. 29 FN

2. Hans-Günter Hockerts (Ed.), *Grenzen der Weidergutmchung. Die Entschädigung für NS-verfolgte in West- und Osteuropa 1945–2000* (Göttingen, 2006) pp. 7f.

3. For a typology of Nazi-persecution and its dimensions see Dieter Pohl, *Verfolgung und Massenmord in der NS-Zeit 1933–1945* (Darmstadt, 2003).

structure that was established after the war and its geopolitical ramifications. Its basic features were defined by the U.S. administration, which was to become the driving political force behind the restitution and compensation endeavor.

This is why the question is not so much whether there was any indemnification at all, but rather who got what under the circumstances prevailing in the second half of the 20th century? What were the conditions and criteria under which the German restitution and compensation program, the so called *"Wiedergutmachung"* (literally "making good again"), evolved? What were the limitations and shortcomings of a program that the world came to regard as the political and moral touchstone for Germany's return to the community of nations and that today is being referred to more and more as a model of how to manage the material side of the transition from tyranny to democracy.

The German program rests on two pillars: restitution of property and compensation for personal injury. The basic features of just who would be entitled to raise claims were developed by the U.S. State Department even before the end of the war and were very much influenced by America's own experience in coping with tens of thousands of refugees from Europe. Persons who had to flee Nazi persecution on religious, racial, and political grounds were the core definition in all subsequent restitution and compensation legislation.[4]

The Role of the United States

As early as January 1943, the Allies made a point of declaring that any dispossession committed in German-occupied Europe

---

4. Constantin Goschler, *Schuld und Schulden. Die Politik der Wiedergutmachung für NS-Verfolgte* seit 1945 (Göttingen, 2005), pp. 47ff.

would have to be restored after the war and that no one should be able to profit from the spoliation of property.[5] Under classic international law, restitution of property is regarded as part of the broader issue of reparations. According to this scenario, German reparations payments would enable the states concerned to indemnify their despoiled citizens.

Shortly after the war ended and the disastrous consequences of the German conquest became clear, the Potsdam Agreement gave expression to the Allies' shared conviction that Germany should be forced "to provide compensation to the greatest extent possible for the losses and suffering that it caused to the Allied nations and for which the German people cannot avoid responsibility."[6] Theoretically this included all forms of Nazi persecution and not just the restitution of property. The amount of compensation was, of course, limited by Germany's ability to pay, a criterion that is ultimately subject to political calculations and priorities.

Another important decision was taken at Potsdam. It concerned the division of future reparations into two parts: those owed to the East, satisfying the reparation claims of the Soviet Union and Poland (Eastern reparations pool) and those owed to the West, which should cover the claims of the Western Allies

The quotas for each of the Western countries were fixed at the Inter-Allied Reparations Agreement negotiated in Paris at the end of 1945.[7] While the Paris conference decided on the

---

5. Inter-Allied Declaration Against Acts of Dispossession Committed in Territories Under Enemy Occupation or Control, 5.1.1943, in: FRUS 1943 I, pp. 443f. The Declaration was signed by 18 allied States.
6. Potsdam Agreement of August 2, 1945, Section IV, reprinted in Ingo von Münch (ed.), *Dokumente des geteilten Deutschland* (1968). (United States, Great Britain, France) and another 15 countries (Western reparations pool).
7. The signatories also included Australia, Belgium, Canada, Czechoslovakia, Denmark, Egypt, Greece, India, Italy, Luxembourg, Netherlands, New Zealand, Norway, South African Union, and Yugoslavia. 8105 United Nations Treaty Series 1946.

allocation formula, it left the total amount and timetable of the payments open. Since the countries were expected to subsume all their reparation claims arising from war and persecution under their respective quotas, the picture of what each would receive remained vague.

An estimated $2.5 to $3 billion were distributed from the "Western reparation pool." A very small part of it, around $30 million, was set aside for an international fund for those Nazi victims who had no state to turn to, such as stateless refugees from Germany and Austria or former concentration camp inmates who could not be repatriated to their once-occupied homelands.[8] The money was intended to facilitate the rehabilitation and resettlement of Jewish victims regardless of possible individual claims they might have against the former German Reich.

The American Joint Distribution Committee and the Jewish Agency for Palestine, who were charged with actually paying out the money, perceived it as an acknowledgement in principle of a collective Jewish claim. The Allies hoped to use the fund to alleviate the international refugee problem and at the same time cut back on what it was costing them by delving into not only Germany's external assets, but mainly heirless Jewish property in neutral countries as well as gold plundered by the Nazis that had been seized by the Allies in Germany.[9]

The problem of stateless persons could be dealt with through ad hoc solutions and foreign nationals were theoretically covered by their own states.

---

8. Final Act and Annex of the Paris Conference on Reparation, Part I, Art.: "Allocation of a Reparation Share to Non-Repatriable Victims of German Action," in: *Department of State Bulletin*, BD. XIV, 21.1.1946, p. 118f. Details were agreed upon between the USA, Great Britain, France, Czechoslovakia, and Yugoslavia later that year. Agreement Pertaining to Reparation Funds for Non-Repatriable Victims of German Action, 14.6.1946, in: *Department of State Bulletin*, Bd. XV, July–Dec. 1946, p. 71ff.
9. Goschler, 2005, pp. 55f.

Under international law, however, German victims of Nazi persecution had no prospect of being compensated by their own state.

Even during the war, the U.S. administration was already looking ahead to the indemnification of former German citizens. The property issue stood out clearly. At the same time, U.S. policy focused on making sure that reparations payments of any kind would not jeopardize Germany's economic recovery and the stabilization of democratic rule. Determined not to make the mistake that had been made at Versailles, where the crushing reparations burdens imposed on Germany set the stage for the rise of Hitler, many of the administration's far-reaching compensation plans for German victims of the Nazis were reduced to "restitution of property in the American occupation zone that had been taken away on racial, religious or political grounds."[10] Within the context of overall postwar planning, however, the compensation question remained a peripheral one.

To the other Allies, the restitution of German victims' property was even less important. For the Soviet Union, which as a nation had suffered major destruction, the reparation of war loss and damage had absolute priority, while individual restitution of property was an ideological no-no. Central for de Gaulle's France, besides its own reparations claims, were the consequences of Nazi persecution on French territory. For the British, restitution was not only a question of principle but also a pragmatic way of financing the return of refugees.

Attempts to achieve a concerted Allied policy towards compensating German victims ultimately did not go beyond the repeal of discriminatory acts and the declared intention to see to

---

10. The Joint Chiefs of Staff Directive 1067 signed by President Harry S. Truman on April 26, 1945, printed in Wilhelm Cornides, Hermann Wolle (eds.), *Um den Frieden mit Deutschland. Dokumente zum Problem der deutschen Friedensordnung 1948*, Oberursel, 1948, pp. 58–73; here § 48 p. 72.

the moral rehabilitation and compensation of those who were persecuted on racial, religious, and political grounds.[11] The issue of restitution touched off a controversy among the Allies hinging on three main points. The first concerned the question as to which Jewish property loss should be regarded as the result of an unjust act, i.e., whether coercion was a factor in the transfer of Jewish property in the early years of the National Socialist regime?

The second point dealt with the establishment of a supreme Allied restitution jurisdiction. A third was the demand of American Jewish organizations to transfer title of heirless Jewish property to Jewish successor organizations that were dedicated to rebuilding Jewish life outside Germany, especially in Palestine.

Restitution

The far-reaching ideas of the American Military Government, which were heavily influenced by the concerted effort of American and international Jewish organizations[12] and were personally supported by the American Military Governor, General Lucius D. Clay, did not sit well with the other Allies. The Soviets wanted the question of support for Nazi victims living abroad to be discussed solely in terms of Germany's external assets. The French and British rejected any confessional affiliation of successor organizations. The authorities in the German Länder (states), who in any case had little room for political maneuver, were only too happy to saddle the occupying powers with responsibility for a restitution program.

---

11. Proclamations No. 1 and No. 2 of the Allied Control Council, September 20, 1945.
12. These organizations were the World Jewish Congress, the American Joint Distribution Committee, the Jewish Agency for Palestine, the American Jewish Committee, and the American Jewish Conference.

In late 1947, the U.S. unilaterally proclaimed a comprehensive restitution law that set the standard for all subsequent German restitution legislation.[13] It was followed almost immediately by a British version, and, in 1949 by a French one. While the common features were the principle of territoriality, the exclusion of foreign nationals and the inclusion of German emigrants, the laws differed in their attitude towards who should benefit from heirless property.

While the Jewish Restitution Successor Organization (JRSO) was already installed in the American zone in 1948, other successor organizations could press claims for heirless property in the British and French zones only years later. In 1950, the Jewish Trust Corporation (JTC) was introduced as successor organization for heirless Jewish property in the British occupation zone and, in 1951, in the French zone. In the French zone, heirless property went into a fund that first compensated victims who lived in the zone, but this affected the barely five percent of the Jewish population that returned. At that time it was not unusual to divert the proceeds of heirless Jewish property to the state budget but earmarking the funds to providing direct assistance to Jewish victims who would otherwise have to be supported by taxpayers' money. It took some time for the Western Allies to acknowledge a collective Jewish claim, something they had opposed till then on geopolitical grounds, or acknowledge the distinct ethnic makeup of persecuted groups.

---

13. Law No. 59 (Rückerstattung feststellbarere Vermögensgegenstände an Opfer der nationalsozialistischen Unterdrückungsmaßnahmen) der Militärregierung Deutschland-Amerikanisches Kontrollgebeit-vom 10.11.1947, printed in Reinhard von und Hans Freiherr von Godin (commentary). *Rückerstattung feststellbarer Vermögensgegenstände in der amerikanischen und britischen Besatzungszone und in Berlin 1950*, p. 1. The AJC was behind an editorial entitled "An Act of Justice," which appeared in the *New York Times* of November 14, 1947, fending off criticism of the comprehensive restitution program in the American zone of occupation on the grounds it was a burden on the American taxpayer. See Goschler, 2005, p. 109.

The restitution laws enacted by the three Western occupying powers between 1947 and 1949 form the legal basis for the restitution of identifiable property confiscated from individuals between September 1935, when the Nuremberg Laws were promulgated, and May 8, 1945 (in the subsequent Federal restitution law enacted by Germany after 1953, this date was amended to January 30, 1933, the date of Hitler's accession to power). "Confiscated" is defined as property involuntarily taken away because of one's race, religion, nationality, worldview, or political opposition to National Socialism, whether by way of a legal transaction (indirectly confiscated) or an act of state (directly confiscated). Individual restitution encompassed primarily real estate and businesses that had been "aryanized," i.e., the ownership was transferred to the authorities or to non-Jews. If restitution in kind was impossible, one could alternatively claim the replacement value of the property or compensatory damages. Civil restitution courts adjudicated the restitution claims. In contested cases, the courts of appeal were the Supreme Restitution Courts on the level of the German Länder with an international staff of judges.

Individual restitution based on laws of the American, British and French zones came to a close in the 1960s after paying out an estimated DM 3.5 billion, of which about DM 300 million went as global payments to Jewish successor organizations.[14] While this sum referred to identifiable property, which often involved taking it from someone to restore it to its original owners, the largest part concerned the restitution of movable property, such as securities, precious metals, jewelry, and works of art, that the German Reich had plundered on its own territory

---

14. Walter Schwarz, Rückerstattung nach den Gesetzen der Alliierten Mächte (= Die Wiedergutmachung nationalsozialistischen Unrechts durch die Bundesrepublik Deutschland, ed by Bundesministerium für Finanzen in Zusammenarbeit mit Walter Schwarz, vol. 1) (Munich, 1974), p. 360, quoted in Goschler, 2005, p. 204.

or in occupied Europe and that were unrecoverable after the War. In these cases, the Allies held the German Reich, liable for full monetary compensation.

At this point, in the early 1950s, these were mostly virtual claims. In 1957, the Federal Republic of Germany, in its capacity as legal successor to the German Reich, adopted the Federal restitution law, the Bundesrückerstattungsgesetz (BRüG).[15] With this legislation, West Germany assumed monetary responsibility for the fiscal exploitation of Jews in the territory of the Reich and the plundering of Jewish property in occupied Europe under the BRüG, every party involved in the restitution process was required by law to cooperate in achieving its goals. Banks and insurance companies, for example, were charged with a complex set of rules obliging them to provide authorities with all the information they asked for pertaining to the comprehensive restitution that subsequently took place for bank accounts and confiscated or unsettled insurance policies.

This information requirement and the practical implications of the currency reform from the old Reichsmark to the new Deutsche Mark in 1948 precluded the possibility that any "dormant accounts" or unpaid insurance policies might somehow linger on. By the mid-1970s, when the 1948 currency reform was legally concluded, companies had to identify and surrender any remaining Reichsmark-denominated deposits and securities to the Federal Settlement Office.

German experts estimated that monetary obligations under the Federal restitution law would cost DM 5–7 billion, as opposed to an Allied prognosis of DM 1 billion.[16] In the end, the amount came to approximately DM 4 billion.

---

15. Everybody refers to the law as Federal Restitution Law. The actual title was more complicated: Federal Law on the Settlement of Restitutionary Monetary Obligations (BRüG), German Civil Code I, 1953, at 734.
16. Goschler, 2005, p. 149.

Compensation

As opposed to the restitution of property, which commenced in the Allied zones of occupation, compensation for personal damages really got underway only after the Federal Republic was established in May 1949. Since each of the Länder was in charge of implementing the compensation in that particular state, there were a variety of different provisions as it evolved from a mere social benefit into something far larger and more comprehensive. The model was still the Compensation Law promulgated in the American zone. The federal structure of the compensation legislation however set out different legal requirements for various categories of victims, while the Allies, who still reserved the right to oversee the *Wiedergutmachung* process, pressed for greater standardization as well as for the inclusion of about 230,000 displaced Jews and non-Jews who lived on West German territory.

Multilateral influences — 1952/1953

The evolution of national legislation on *Wiedergutmachung* was to a large measure shaped by three international agreements: the Transition Treaty and the Luxembourg Agreement, both of 1952, and the London Debt Agreement of 1953. They established the partial sovereignty of the Federal Republic of Germany (which only became total after the 2 + 4 treaty and German reunification in 1990) regulated its external debts and made *Wiedergutmachung* an integral part of Germany's post-War economic, political and financial landscape. These three international agreements also set the stage for the inclusion and exclusion of beneficiaries under priorities that did not focus so much on the reality of individual loss and damage as on the overarching political setting of the Cold War.

In the Transition Treaty of May 1952, the integration of West Germany into the Western world was made conditional on its meeting its obligation to maintain the Allied restitution and compensation regulations as applied in the U.S. Zone and to expand on them.[17] It stipulated two fundamental criteria of eligibility for *Wiedergutmachung*. First, the beneficiary had to be "someone who was persecuted because of race, religion, or political opposition to National Socialism." The second established the principle of territoriality, which meant that a claimant had to demonstrate a relation to German territory that was not defined by citizenship alone but alternatively also by residence during a certain time period.

The criterion of territoriality at first deliberately excluded foreign nationals, whose compensation was in theory left to reparations, which would be assessed under an eventual peace treaty. Actually, the London negotiations conducted between the Federal Republic of Germany and 22 creditor states on what to do about the German Reich's external obligations put a stop to whatever claims foreign nationals might make. In order to re-establish German credit, it was agreed that the servicing of commercial obligations should have priority over other claims. In effect, the London Debt Agreement of February 1953 deferred "consideration of claims, arising from the Second World War . . . until the final settlement of the problem of reparations," meaning until a definitive peace treaty was signed.

These regulations, which became known as "article 5, section 2," was to become the most far-reaching provision in the complex and overlapping field of reparations and *Wieder-*

---

17. Part III (restitution) and Part IV (compensation) of the Convention (with annex) on the Settlement of Matters Arising out of the War and the Occupation (so-called Transition Treaty) of May 26, 1952, as amended pursuant to Annex IV to the Protocol on the Termination of the Occupation Regime in the Federal Republic of Germany, signed on October 23, 1954, in Paris, in: German Civil Code II 1955, at 405–459.

gutmachung. The limitations it put on reparations enabled the Federal Republic to allocate resources to such costly other projects as Cold War rearmament or paying off external commercial obligations and postwar credits due the Allies. With the consent by the United States, these obligations took priority over compensation for Nazi persecution.

The distribution of the global payments was left to the recipient states, with the result that, in many cases, because of differing perceptions of who was a victim of German persecution, the money reached the originally intended target group only in part, if at all. In most cases, this did not reflect Bonn's original intention but rather the hierarchy of beneficiaries, where top priority was accorded to those who had actively resisted the German occupation.

A special case in the selective architecture of *Wiedergutmachung* is the 1952 Luxembourg Agreement between West Germany on the one hand, and the State of Israel and the Conference of Jewish Material Claims Against Germany (Claims Conference) on the other. The Claims Conference was founded in October 1951 as an umbrella association of 23 international Jewish organizations with the purpose of representing the Jewish Diaspora outside Israel in the negotiations over indemnification. Jewish reparation claims beyond the individual level were an emotion-laden issue, not only in Germany but also in Israel and the U.S. There was a fierce debate within the Jewish world that focused on the question whether, given the enormity of the crimes committed against the Jews during the war, any payments at all were acceptable, and if so, since it was Jewish existence as such that the Nazis had sought to eradicate, who should represent the collective Jewish claim.

There were many very real psychological barriers to any contact with Germany, and before official negotiations could start on neutral ground in Wassenaar, Netherlands, early in 1952, the first tentative contacts were conducted in total secrecy. Although the Allies, especially the U.S., steered clear of becoming directly involved, they did not conceal their sympathy for the Jewish claims and would from time to time remind the German side of that fact. In the end, the success of the undertaking rested heavily on the mutual personal respect and understanding that had been built up between Nahum Goldmann, President of the World Jewish Congress, and in that capacity, head of the Claims Conference as well, and Federal Chancellor Konrad Adenauer. More than most of his colleagues in his government, Adenauer was aware of the profound symbolic and political significance of such an agreement with Israel and the Claims Conference, and he saw it as advancing the moral and historical rehabilitation of Germany. For its part, the Jewish side maintained that there could never be total compensation for what all the Jewish people had suffered, nor could that guilt ever be expunged with money.

This fundamental dichotomy in perceptions of the nature and intention of *Wiedergutmachung* shaped the future development of the German restitution and compensation program, in which the Claims Conference came to play a central role. The Luxembourg agreement allocated the Jewish umbrella association a lump sum of DM 450 million to satisfy heirless property claims in those parts of Europe that had been under German occupation. It was earmarked for the benefit of Jewish victims who lived outside of Israel (Hague Protocol No. 2).[18] Far more significant as far as the future was concerned, however, was another protocol in the treaty (Hague Protocol No. 1) that gave the Claims Conference a political mandate to directly influence German legislation on restitution and compensation

---

18 . For the text, see the Luxembourg Agreement of September 10, 1952, German Civil Code II 1953, at pp. 94–97. For the Hague Protocol No 1, idem pp. 85–94.

and to make policy in this area. The Luxembourg Agreement also included a separate treaty with Israel, in which the Federal Republic pledged DM 3 billion to assist in the resettlement of about 500,000 victims of Nazi persecution in Israel. Both the Israel agreement and the political mandate for the Claims Conference to shape national compensation legislation were novelties in international law.[19]

The German compensation legislation: The LAG (1952), the BEG (1956) and the BRüG (1957)

Complying with its international obligations under the Transition Treaty (which for political reasons stemming from French opposition to German rearmament came into force only in May 1955), and the Hague Protocol No. 1 of the Luxembourg Agreement, Bonn promulgated a series of laws between 1953 and 1965 that lay down the rules for compensation payments and restitution on an expedited basis. The centerpiece was the Federal Compensation Law (*Bundesentschädigungsgesetz*—BEG), which was unanimously adopted by the Bundestag in June 1956.[20] According to its operative clause, a beneficiary was defined as "someone who was persecuted because of political opposition to National Socialism, race, religion, or worldview and, as a result, suffered damage to life, body, health, freedom, property, or to professional or economic advancement." (BEG §1, 1). Unlike the provisional law that preceded it (*Bundes-Ergänzungsgesetz*—BErgG 1953), the principle of territoriality referred now to the German Reich as its borders existed in 1937

---

19. The all in all DM 3.45 billion should be paid over 14 years, a third of which should be covered by the delivery of German goods, another third was foreseen for the purchase of crude oil. The amount corresponded to about 12 percent of the Federal Budget of 1953. *idem* p. 159.
20. Federal Law for Compensation of Victims of Nazi Persecution of June 29, 1956 (BEG, German Civil Code I, 562).

or to potential claimants who had taken up residence in West Germany by December 31, 1952 (before the time limit had been January 1, 1947). The BEG awarded lump sums as well as pensions and compensation for unsettled and/or confiscated insurance policies.

Its overall orientation was towards restoring the former social position of the claimant and not actual need. The basic principle was that the state should "pay to restore the legal situation which would have existed if the damaging event had not occurred."[21] Reduction in earning capacity was a decisive criterion in determining monthly pensions, for example. Moreover, the sums were linked to pensions being paid in West Germany, thus reflecting the gains of an increasingly thriving economy. Over time, these payments consumed the largest share of BEG outlays. In calculating pensions, compensation for loss of opportunity for professional advancement was usually assigned greater weight than physical disabilities. Most of the BEG payments went to surviving concentration camp inmates who showed damage to their health and to emigrants who claimed loss of opportunities for pro-fessional advancement.[22]

Additionally, a "diplomatic clause" explicitly disqualified potential claimants who lived in a country with which the Federal Republic had no diplomatic relations, i.e., the Eastern Bloc. No compensation money was to go to communist countries.[23]

Sections 127 to 133 of the BEG provided for compensation for endowment and annuity insurance policies with private insurance companies on which premiums were still being paid or which had been designated "paid-up."

---

21. Quoted in Gerald D. Feldman, *Allianz and the German Insurance Business, 1933–1945* (Cambridge, 2001), p. 529.
22. Goschler, 2005, pp. 254ff.
23. For a very complicated exception that allowed payments for displaced persons living in Eastern Europe see Hockerts, 2006, p. 39.

Covered were insurance contracts that had been terminated by individual order following enforced assignment or being pledged to the German Reich or where the insurer had remitted the surrender value directly to the German Reich. Also, covered were cases where termination had taken place because the fiscal authorities had attached or seized as security any rights arising out of the insurance contract. Moreover, the BEG provided for compensation for any transfer of assets to the Reich under Section 3 of the infamous 11th Regulation on the Law on German Citizenship. According to this rule, any Jewish-owned life insurance contracts which had not been taken away and terminated by administrative order by that time had been considered to have been transferred to the Reich and terminated by December 31, 1941. Finally, Section 56 of the BEG assigned compensation for loss of assets which had occurred, if, for instance, the rightful claimant was forced to terminate a life or annuity insurance contract prematurely to enable him to emigrate or to pay penalties. While the insurance companies were no longer liable for policies that had been directly or indirectly confiscated during the Nazi era (See Chapter VI), they did have an obligation to cooperate in finding the policies of claimants, and, above all, calculating what was legally due the beneficiary. As it worked out, it proved to be in the companies' interest to have as many of their former customers compensated as possible. (Section 182 of the BEG).

Statistics about how much insurance figured in the BEG compensation awards are not available. Official numbers give only the overall amount paid out under BEG, more than 46 billion euros by 2002, of which 80 percent went to beneficiaries abroad.

Even before the BEG was implemented, there were the compensation schemes in the zones of occupation, as already mentioned, and the Federal German Law on Equalization of

Burdens (*Lastenausgleichsgesetz*—LAG). This last-named came into effect as early as September 1952. Over the years, the LAG, complemented by a multitude of supplementary laws, developed into a comprehensive integration and compensation program that dealt with claims for insurance benefits by persons who were disqualified under the territorial restrictions enshrined in the BEG.

Under the LAG, persons eligible included Germans, persons of German ethnic origin and persons whom the National Socialists had compelled to leave their place of residence or who had suffered pecuniary losses in connection with events before and during World War II in areas outside the 1937 borders of the German Reich. Claimants were compensated for insurance policies that had not yet fallen due at the time the loss occurred with two-thirds of the premiums that had been paid in. In the case of insurance policies which had been prematurely terminated, the benefit depended on the nominal value of the matured claim.

Legally established conversion rates applied for losses in currencies other than Reichsmarks. The deadline for filing applications was December 31, 1969. Like the BEG, the LAG included a ban on paying benefits to applicants whose residence was in a country with which the Federal Republic had no diplomatic relations (see Brodesser, pp. 174 *et seq.*). All of these Federal German compensation laws included rules according to which any benefits otherwise received were deducted from the claim (see, for instance, Section 249 (2) of the LAG, Sect. 130 of the BEG).

A "diplomatic clause" applied to the restitution of property. Anyone, irrespective of nationality or citizenship, could make a claim against Germany for loss of movable property because of Nazi-persecution as long as it could be proved that the effects had in fact been physically transferred to the territory of West

Germany or to West Berlin. However, under the Federal restitution law, only those who lived in a Western country could actually receive payments. At the insistence of the Claims Conference, the legal basis for restitution claims had been considerably expanded beyond the stricter Allied rules to allow for a property claim merely on the presumption that it had been brought to the territory of West Germany or Berlin without having to indicate an exact location.[24] The internationally agreed cap of DM 1.5 billion (Transition Treaty) ceased to apply when the Federal Restitution Law was amended in 1964. Ultimately, around DM 4 billion were paid out under the German Federal Restitution Law.

It was again the Claims Conference which used its political mandate to keep pressing for material improvements, the prolongation of application deadlines and the expansion of the groups of beneficiaries to include Eastern European Jews. A so-called Special Fund that amended the BEG in 1965 and another Hardship Fund introduced in 1980 were designed to help victims who had emigrated from the Eastern Bloc to the West. They added amounts of DM 1.2 billion and DM 400 million respectively.

Further measures along these lines were enacted following the reunification of Germany in 1990 and the subsequent extension of the restitution and compensation program to the newly acceded Länder. Unlike the Federal Republic of Germany, the German Democratic Republic had had no restitution and compensation program of any consequence. Restitution, being an act of "reprivatization" was ruled out for ideological reasons. Personal compensation claims ("honoraria") were allowed under the rubric of "antifascist resistance."

---

24. § 5 BRüG

Under the new circumstances of a reunified Germany, the Claims Conference became the successor organization of heirless Jewish property in former East Germany as well. Moreover, it successfully negotiated regular monthly payments for needy Jewish victims from Eastern Europe living in the West, and, since 1998, those still residing in Eastern Europe (Article 2-Fund).[25]

The plight of Nazi victims from Eastern Europe had been a main concern of the Conference ever since the beginning of *Wiedergutmachung*. In its secret "relief-in-transition" program, which only recently became public, the Claims Conference had managed to circumvent the exclusion of Eastern Europe from the German program as far back as the 1950s, when the Cold War was at its peak. It covertly diverted some of the funds it received under the Luxembourg Agreement as well as global payments from major German companies intended to compensate Jewish concentration camp inmates who had been turned into slave laborers during the war.[26] All in all, compensation payments for Jewish emigrants from Eastern Europe stemming from different provisions and funds added up to an estimated DM 30 billion up to the end of the 1990s, though this figure does not appear anywhere in the official statistics, which derive only from the letter of the laws, such as the BEG and BRüG, or global agreements.[27]

After reunification the subject of compensation to victims of Nazi persecution continued to be on the agenda in the Federal

---

25. The Article-2-Fund refers to an amendment to the Unification treaty between the Federal Republic of Germany and the German Democratic Republic from September 1990. BGBl 1990 II, at 1239. About 92,500 pensions (as of 2002) were awarded, one fifth of them going eastwards. The estimated total amounts to DM 1.6 billion. Goschler, 2005, p 52.

26. Ronald Zweig, *German Reparations and the Jewish World. A History of the Claims Conference*, 2001, 2nd edition, pp. 132–135.

27. Hermann-Josef Brodesser, et al. (eds.), *Wiedergutmachung und Kriegsfolgenliquidation. Geschichte—Regelungen—Zahlungen* (Munich, 2000), p. 108.

Republic of Germany, and claims are still being addressed under the Law on Compensation for Property (*Vermögensgesetz*) and the Nazi Victims Compensation Law (NS-*Verfolgtenentschädigungsgesetz*).

These laws dealt with the restitution of assets taken by the Nazis between 1933 and 1945 in the territory of the former West Germany or the former German Democratic Republic. If someone filed a claim by the end of June 1993, he or she was also entitled to restitution for insurance policies that had been confiscated. The asset itself was not returned. Earlier compensation for pecuniary losses (according to Section 56 of the BEG) was deducted, but, under Section 127 *et seq.* of the BEG, previous compensation for insurance claims was not deducted. If no legitimate claims were forthcoming from Jewish beneficiaries or their heirs, the Claims Conference was considered to be the legal successor (see website of the JCC, "Summary of Major Holocaust Compensation Programs," and Neumann in ViZ, pp. 7 *et seq.*)

From the end of the 1960s, the issue of compensation for Nazi victims in Eastern Europe played an important part in the ongoing state-to-state negotiations on political detente and rapprochement. While Eastern European states were unable to obtain the kind of favorable "global agreements" that the Federal Republic had concluded with 11 Western states, there were some breakthroughs in direct compensation. The Federal Republic made funds available for victims of medical experiments (Yugoslavia 1961/63; Czechoslovakia 1969, Hungary 1971; Poland 1972), and some financial support for needy survivors was envisaged in the framework of agreements that were officially earmarked for broader economic purposes (Poland 1975).

The hour of "compensation diplomacy" towards the East came with the end of the East-West-confrontation and

Germany's reunification. As its counteroffer for the de facto waiving of reparations claims, Germany concluded bilateral agreements to compensate Nazi victims, first with Poland in 1991, and then, in 1993, with three successor states of the Soviet-Union, Russia, Ukraine, and Belarus. A total of DM 1.5 billion went to establishing foundations for "understanding and reconciliation" Additionally the three Baltic states, Estonia in 1995, Lithuania in 1996, and Latvia in 1998 each received DM 2 million, and a German-Czech Future Fund was set up in 1995 with DM 140 million from Germany.

From "compensation diplomacy" to "plaintiffs' diplomacy"

In a final, multilateral push to redress the longstanding asymmetry towards the East, German business became involved, partly as a result of the threat of class actions suits brought against individual companies for their part in the persecution and exploitation policy of the Nazi regime. That the companies' involvement in state crimes 60 years earlier can become a matter for litigation in American civil courts vividly reflects the pervasive consequences of the globalization of economy and law. The end of communist rule in Eastern Europe sparked a restitution movement that put a long ignored chapter of history on the international agenda. Problems left over from the Holocaust era—the disposition of nationalized Jewish property, compensation of forced laborers, stolen art or the role of neutral states in prolonging the war—were suddenly the stuff of newspaper headlines. Two years of negotiation between an array of public and private actors, governments, non-governmental organizations and business companies led to the establishment of the German Foundation "Remembrance, Responsibility and the Future" in August 2000. Its funding of DM 10 billion was pledged half by the German state and the other half by German business. The purpose was to compensate the people, mostly Eastern Europeans, who had been forced to work for the Nazi war machine as well as to make available additional funds for property losses, including whatever insurance policies that remained unpaid, and special groups of Nazi victims throughout Europe.[28] This Foundation was designed to close the book on *Wiedergutmachung*, but threats of new class actions still remain. On the basis of its market share, the German insurance industry's contribution of over DM 500 million was much greater than what it had been assessed.

The charts that follow do not reflect the political wars fought in domestic as well as international arenas to establish the principle of redressing Nazi crimes on a large scale, nor do they document the often frustrating mechanics of implementing the *Wiedergutmachung* program. They do summarize the payments made over the past 60 years to the different legal categories of beneficiaries. What can be said at this point is that despite all its structural shortcomings, practical difficulties, and its allegiance to the cold logic of geopolitics, *Wiedergutmachung* remains nevertheless an achievement of moral responsibility and historical consciousness. The definitive judgment, however, belongs to those whose lives were irrevocably scarred by Nazi persecution and who have at last received some acknowledgement for what they suffered.

---

28. For a detailed account, see Stuart Eizenstat, *Incomplete Justice* (New York, 2002), as well as Susanne-Sophia Spiliotis, *Moral Responsibility and Legal Closure. The Foundation Initiative of German Business* (New York, 2007), (German original, 2003).

Nominal payments made by the Federal Government up to 2006 under the German Restitution and Compensation Program (in millions of euros).[29]

BEG (Federal Compensation Law)	44,538
BRüG (Federal Restitution Law)	2,023
ERG (Compensation Pension Law)	722
NS-VEntschG (Nazi Victims Compensation Law)	1,221
Treaty with Israel	1,764
Global agreements (and related payments)	1,460
Miscellaneous services (civil servants; victims of medical experiments, etc.)	4,628
Payments of the Länder beyond the BEG	1,528
Hardship funds (federal without Länder)	2,784
"Remembrance, Responsibility and the Future" Foundation	2,556*
Total	63,224

*This represents the amount paid by the government. The same amount, plus about 50 million euros, was put up by German business as the share of its contribution to the Foundation.

It should be kept in mind that there is a distinction between the Foundation Initiative "Remembrance, Responsibility and the Future," which was German business's vehicle for raising the money, and the Foundation "Remembrance, Responsibility and the Future," which was the legal entity established in July 2000 and which amalgamated what business had raised with government funds.

---

29. Bundesministerium für Finanzen (ed.), *Entschädigung von NS-Unrecht. Regelungen zur Wiedergutmachung*, Ausgabe, 2003. p. 38.

Chapter III

Fertile Ground

Germany and Jews are inextricably linked by events that took place more than 70 years ago. For many among the dwindling community of survivors, all in their senior years, the Holocaust remains a deeply personal experience. It is tattooed on the arms of some and in the minds of all. Most can neither forget nor forgive.

For the survivors' family members, who were either not yet born when the last Jewish victim was murdered, or who were in the United States or other countries that were not infected by the Nazi plague, the memory is kept alive in many ways, from prayers at Sabbath services to agonizing accounts shared by those who lived to tell the tale. From time to time the embers of memory are fanned by new films, books, articles, and plays.

For many Jews the words "Never Again" evoke a personal response, ranging from academic curiosity to emotional pain. It is also the title of a landmark book by Abe Foxman, a Holocaust survivor who is head of the influential Jewish Anti-Defamation League. But while "Never Again" speaks of the future, the past lingers, waiting for closure.

The prevailing climate in America harbored deep-seated distrust of everything German. It was on this "fertile ground" that the seeds of litigation against European insurance companies began. They would be waged in the courts and across national borders. Some idea of the attitudes that informed public opinion are expressed in this quote from an English weekly newspaper, *John Bull*:

> Millions of Marks must still be left in Germany, just waiting to be wrested from the vanquished. We don't need to be afraid. Germany will be able to pay. We will take Germany's money from her and grow bigger and fatter ourselves in the process. So let's pursue our goal with renewed energy! Gold awaits the victor! Germany can pay us! Let's force her to.

The war was over. The Germans were soundly defeated, and cries for revenge and restitution were heard around the world. None were louder than those published in *John Bull*. But this was not 1945. It was 1918, and it is remarkable how similar the sentiments were after the curtain came down on Hitler's Third Reich.

While World War I reparations focused largely on territory, steel, coal, and agricultural products, the Nazis added a cruel new dimension to losses in World War II: genocide. Civilians had been killed in many wars through the ages, but none were specifically targeted for death in such incomprehensible numbers, and with such cruelty and efficiency. American troops liberating Nazi concentration camps were horrified at what they encountered and remained haunted by the memories for decades to come. And for the victims, the lingering, bitter aftertaste of degradation and stolen lives left them scarred by psychological trauma. Some tried to simply wipe the Holocaust chapter from their minds. For others, it engendered a resurgent Jewish pride and a determination that the events of those nightmare years would "Never Again" be allowed to happen.

In effect, murder and degradation played a major role, a half-century later, in energizing individual and group legal actions seeking reparations. Whether driven by a need for closure, monetary restitution, retribution, justice or greed (some Jews and non-Jews, survivors and non-survivors, considered reparations nothing but "blood money"), all would have to put up with the slow pace of legal proceedings and serious negotiations. Many survivors, having waited 50 years for this opportunity, convinced themselves and each other that they could wait a while longer. Many others succumbed to age, their hopes, and memories dying with them.

The German author, Heinrich Böll, summed up the survivor's dilemma this way: *The war will never be over as long as even one wound left by it still bleeds.*

Within months of Germany's surrender, the Allied forces instituted a program that sought to somehow alleviate some of the most egregious of Nazi excesses insofar as far as property was concerned. On assuming office in 1949, the first Chancellor of the newly-constituted German Federal Republic, Konrad Adenauer, stated publicly that the entire German nation bore responsibility for the Holocaust and urged that reparations be paid.

In the United States the postwar economy was booming and communism had replaced fascism as the most potent threat to democracy. While Americans dealt with the challenges of day-today life, the many Holocaust survivors who immigrated to the U.S. wrestled with their own demons. In a study that included interviews with hundreds of survivors who had filed restitution claims with the West German government, American psychologists William G. Niederland and Henry Krystal described what they called "The Survivor Syndrome." Its symptoms included:

> (1) fear of renewed persecution, repeated nightmares, and apprehension about being alone; (2) memory loss and confusion of the past with the present; (3) chronic depression; (4) self-isolation; (5) psychosomatic ailments, such as ulcers, headaches, respiratory problems, and heart conditions; (6) severe feelings of guilt over having survived when so many others had not; and (7) blocked maturational development that in severe cases took the forms of complete inertia, delusions, and paranoia.

They, and other researchers working independently in several countries, also found that these symptoms affected the development of the survivors' children, causing them to suffer chronic depression and obsessional traits. In their book, *Massive Psychic Trauma*, Niederland and Krystal reported that many survivors were so troubled that they were beyond the aid of psychotherapy and could never return to a normal life.

If the arts are often a reflection of a society's culture, they are also an influence on that culture. Although there were a number of Holocaust-related European films in the late 1940s and early 1950s, Americans were first exposed to the subject on a national level with the release in 1959 of *The Diary of Anne Frank*. It was not until an American-made, multi-part television docudrama, *The Holocaust*, was aired in 1978, that the stark realities of the Nazi era sank in. Some other noteworthy films of that genre included *Judgment at Nuremberg* (1961), and *Schindler's List* (1993).

Books also kept the memory of the Holocaust alive. Scholarly studies like Daniel Goldhagen's *Hitler's Willing Executioners*, Elie Wiesel's impressionistic *Night*, the comic book treatment of *Maus*, and exposés like *IBM and the Holocaust: The Strategic Alliance Between Nazi Germany and America's Most Powerful Corporation* were on bestseller lists. In the theatre there were *The Diary of Anne Frank*, *Cabaret*, Martin Sherman's *Bent*, and even Mel Brooks' satirical musical *The Producers*. Taken as a whole, history, and humanity, were, for many Americans, cast in a candid new light.

With the exception of two major points of agreement—the survival of Israel and the survival of the Jewish people—the Jewish-American "community" is virtually as diverse as the general population. Jews are rich and poor, powerful and disinterested, Orthodox and non-practicing. And in sentiment and conviction, it is neither a non sequitur nor an exaggeration to cite a bit of humor shared among Jewish-Americans: "Put two of us in a room and we'll come out with three different opinions."

The birth of the State of Israel in 1948 instilled pride and a renewed sense of security in Jews throughout the world. The realization that there was "at least one place" where they could go if anti-Semitism drove them from their own countries was a powerful one. To most Jews, anything that threatens Israel, threatens them. Paul Breines, in his 1990 book, *Tough Jews: Political Fantasies and the Moral Dilemma of American Jewry,* cites the popularity, following the 1967 War in the Middle East, of the so-called *Rambowitz* action novels (a takeoff on the macho Rambo character made popular by actor Sylvester Stallone in a series of films).

While the social background of this newer literature remains basically the same…its conceptual foundation has expanded to include Israel and Jewish power in addition to the Holocaust and its Jewish victims. … [T]he tough Jew of the new fiction should not be seen as a reversal or inversion of the Jew as "exemplary victim" but as a fusion of the old victim and the new avenger." The Rambowitz genre faded away in the 1990s, but the image and reality of the "strong" Jew who will not be pushed around remains.

In the 2004 syllabus for his course, "The Holocaust: An Anthropological Perspective," University of Colorado cultural anthropologist Paul Shankman observed:

Although these events seem far removed from our own experience, they are among the defining moments of our times. Even half a century later, the name Auschwitz still signifies the unthinkable, just as 9/11 does today. These events are reminders of where we have been and where we do not wish to return.

[In 1995], the 50th anniversary of the end of World War II was commemorated. The liberation of the Nazi concentration camps also received attention, but most experts thought that the Holocaust would recede from consciousness after the commemorations ended. However, it did not. Attendance at the Holocaust Memorial Museum in Washington, D.C. increased. There were new Academy Award-winning films and documentaries on the Holocaust. The discovery of secret Nazi gold in Switzerland and the recent payments to slave laborers of the Nazis have reminded the world of the legacy of the Holocaust… The Holocaust has not gone away and left us alone.

Individuals, survivor groups and Jewish membership organizations draw on the lessons of the U.S. Holocaust Memorial Museum in Washington and similar, smaller museums around the country to keep the Holocaust alive as a stark reminder of the depths to which mankind can sink, and as a vehicle through which new generations can learn.

In 2002–2003, a series of interviews with Jewish-American leaders and opinion makers probed their views on Germany, its people, language, industry, sincerity, and Holocaust legacy. From the very first interview, it became clear, as anticipated, that there truly is no single Jewish-American community view on Germany. There are, however, two areas about which there was no disagreement among project participants—the absolute need for Germany to strongly denounce and combat anti-Semitism at every opportunity and support Israel's right to exist, despite whatever external and internal pressures to the contrary may arise.

That said, all of the participants believed—to one extent or another—that Germany had taken decidedly positive steps in helping to rebuild its shattered relationship with the Jewish people. These steps were most often described with the word "correct" which, on its own, suggested actions that were synonymous with "proper," "appropriate," or "by the book". In short, "correct" seemed to provide a narrowly defined, dispassionate assessment.

Still, many of those same participants went beyond that definition to express their belief in the sincerity of the efforts, and cited examples to support that perception. Most notable on an individual level were the across-the-board words of praise for Germany's representatives in the U.S., including, but not limited to, embassy and consular staffs. The relationships that developed between many Jewish-American leaders and the non-Jewish Germans with whom they came in contact in the course of their professional activities seemed unquestionably to go beyond basic courtesy and to extend into respect, admiration, and friendship.

The project participants also shared similar positive sentiments regarding Germany's efforts to—and here, the difficulty in choosing the proper words is symbolic of the differing views within the Jewish-American community and within Germany—in some way "make amends" for the Holocaust. Those efforts have included apologies, monetary reparations, close ties with Israel, and multilayered efforts to reach out to the Jewish community, in particular in the United States.

> "For me," said David Harris, Executive Director of the American Jewish Committee, "as an American Jew, Germany has been almost a model of how to deal with the challenges of historical memory and unspeakable tragedy.... [It] has been a trailblazer in its dealings with its own past. No other countries have done what Germany has done in dealing with the Second World War. Japan has not done the sort of reckoning Germany has, nor has Austria. There is no playbook for how something like that is supposed to work, and for that reason I see Germany as being in the forefront."

On the other hand, a good example of the depth of Jewish-American sentiments where Germany is concerned was voiced by Muriel Segal, then president of the New York City chapter of the American Society of Travel Agents (ASTA). She has had close and ongoing ties with Germany and is quick to compliment the country for its efforts in dealing with "what was probably the worst public relations problem ever." She offered a more pragmatic view of the Jewish-American/German relationship:

The notion that the Germans are really not bad, the Germans are really not evil, the Germans really don't dislike the Jews; it was that damn Hitler. It is remarkable. To me, I deal with them and they are correct, and that's all I expect. I'm not interested in reading their minds. In fact, I'm very uninterested in knowing what they're thinking. It doesn't matter to me. They don't know what I'm thinking, either… I've been socialized to behave well in public. We don't have to love each other; we have to deal with each other, and we do.

But, she added, "For me to say everything is good, it's not." Referring to reparations paid to survivors and family members of victims: "[Germany has] been paying out bupkis [very little] as far as I am concerned."

Project participants expressed a belief that the first generation—those who survived the Holocaust or whose families were destroyed—has been too deeply scarred to be convinced that Germany has made a 180-degree turnabout since the end of the Hitler era. To that generation, said Harriet Mandel, at the time the director of Israel and International Affairs for the Jewish Community Relations Council of New York, "Germany is the country of the Nazis, the perpetrators, the evil-doers, and no matter what [it] can or would do, they will always bear the burden of guilt for killing six million Jews. Boycott German goods, not travel to Germany, just chill at the sound of the German language… It's a generational issue; it's a matter of a little more critical view of Germany on the part of the Jewish community overall; and… At many levels of society, there has been an acknowledgment and a recognition using the words 'guilt' and 'responsibility.' The generation now prefers the word "responsibility" for the crimes against humanity and, specifically, against the Jewish community…"

Rabbi Jo David, executive director of the Jewish Appleseed Foundation, said that "people who are of the survivor generation—they may not have been survivors themselves, but they are Americans who were adults during the war—tend to react very negatively to anything German... They are very stuck in the past."

Not all agree. "I think most Jews have an open mind about Germany," commented Kenneth J. Bialkin, former chairman of both the Anti-Defamation League and the Conference of Presidents of Major American Jewish Organizations "[They] have relatively positive feelings about the country while reserving their hatred and reservations about the country's past. It's how you look at someone who is part of a Mafia family: he may not be Mafia, but you know where he comes from and where he has been. A lot of us feel that official Germany has tried very hard to expiate its sins, and has spent tremendous amounts of money in restitution, in publicity, in popular issues, in open discussion and [in de-Nazification]." (Bialkin was later hired as lead counsel for the Italian insurance company Generali (Assicurazioni Generali SpA), and represented it in its class action lawsuits and in the International Commission on Holocaust Era Insurance Claims).

Regardless of the generation, the mere thought of Germany and Germans still stirs vaguely negative emotions among many Jewish-Americans. "There is a real underlying taboo," said Jacob Horowitz, editor of the *Boston Jewish Advocate*, a weekly newspaper with a circulation of 35,000. "People really feel a little unsettled with the idea of Germany. I don't want to call it a prejudice, but I do think it's a little bit of discomfort. There is a little bit of unease when the Jewish community sees things related to Germany. Whether it's cultural, or the language, I'm not sure."

There was also an element of exploiting an understandable Jewish antipathy against Germany for political gain. Insurance commissioners in a number of states began to mine the opportunities presented by revelations about Swiss bank accounts to pursue their own agendas. As far back as the spring of 1997, in the wake of revelations from the Swiss bank lawsuits, the office of Deborah Senn, the Insurance Commissioner in the State of Washington, tracked down resident Holocaust survivors and asked them if they had any recollection of insurance benefits that were never paid. Ms. Senn later organized a number of commissioners from other states to pursue the subject on a national level (See Chapter V, "The Accusation").

Another insurance commissioner, Chuck Quackenbush of California, took the Holocaust insurance issue as a personal crusade and vowed to pursue it to the end. "Insurance companies that sold policies prior to World War II are continuing to turn their backs on Holocaust victims and their families," he said in 1998. "Such unconscionable injustice can no longer be tolerated. For the thousands of Californians who may be affected, I will use the full scope and authority of my office to ensure that these companies, at long last, live up to their contractual, as well as moral, obligations."

He went on to say that there are potentially billions of dollars in unpaid insurance claims owed to Holocaust survivors and their heirs. California has a survivor population of upwards of 20,000, the second largest in the U.S., after New York. As elected officials, the commissioners appreciated the exposure they were receiving on an issue that, as far as they could see, had no down side. Nor were they the only ones. Members of Congress from states with large numbers of Jewish voters, like California, New York, and Florida, were all active in raising the issue in public forums. Sometimes they simply lost patience with what they saw as attempts by the European insurance companies to dodge the issue.

Those unsettling feelings of discomfort and unease—even distrust—resurfaced with the reports that German insurance companies were still sitting on huge sums of money that were owed to beneficiaries of policyholders killed in the Holocaust. As might be expected, those Jews who could "never forgive" Germany for the Holocaust were the least surprised. The fact that German insurance companies participated in restitution programs between 1950 and 1969 had done little to lessen their distrust.

Whether seeking reparations from the insurance companies was justifiable and worth the effort and expense was a question individuals as well as organizations had to confront in the late 1990s. More than 50 years after the war, survivors found themselves able to devote time to contemplating their Holocaust experiences. Actuarial tables and logic suggested that if they were to take any action, this was the moment. Many individuals in and out of political office chose to remain silent or temper their wording rather than risk being labeled "politically incorrect." While the need to not challenge the timing and propriety of the lawsuits or the reparations played no direct role in the launching of class action suits against the German and other European insurance companies, it can be argued that it cleared the road of potential obstacles.

Among American elected officials, there occasionally was a built-in prejudice against what were seen as German interests. A representative of the German Foundation Initiative, which emerged in early 1999 to address the many class action lawsuits pending against German industrial and financial companies, gave an example of encountering this kind of bias during a series of meetings he held in Washington in 2002. "While there were good sharp questions from most of the parties, we were generally treated with respect," he said. "The only time we felt we were not getting through and were treated disrespectfully was our conversation with Rep. Jan Schakowsky, from Skokie, Illinois, a suburb of Chicago with an active Jewish constituency. A Polish-American herself, she certainly must have heard from that constituency as well, since non-Jewish Poles were being compensated for the first time for forced labor under the Nazis.

"She arrived ten minutes late and left after ten minutes to go and vote.

She made it clear she really did not want to hear anything from us, that her mind was made up. Instead, she used the time to berate us for not doing anything these many years and telling us that the Foundation agreement "does not do very much anyway." She did not want to listen to how much restitution had been paid in the past, saying "that is not what my constituents tell me." We tried in vain to steer the conversation in a more positive direction.

After she left, her political advisor allowed us to show him some of the documents Ms. Schakowsky had not wanted to look at. I had a follow-up conversation with the advisor a week or so later. I asked him if there was something more he wanted that could help the Congresswoman and he told me no. We never heard from them again."

It is not enough to just talk about the prevailing anti-German attitudes of American Jews. Those attitudes are being reaffirmed in public again and again, especially in connection with insurance. Here are some of the testimonies of survivors and their heirs at a meeting of state insurance commissioners in September 1997.

The first was Rudy Rosenberg, a New Yorker who was then 67. In 1942, he and his family lived in Brussels, including his father Hillel, his mother, Frieda, and his sister. He came to America in 1949 and served three years in the U.S. Army during the Korean War. He told the conference:

I come here today to tell you how the Swiss insurance company Winterthur sold insurance policies to Jews in Belgium, knowing full well that we were going to be exterminated. I remember that one day in March or April of 1942, two men came to the house to sell us life insurance. They said they were from Winterthur, the Swiss insurance company, and that other Jews had given them our name. They said Winterthur was offering Jews a special deal. You only had to pay half the premium on signing and the balance on the anniversary of the policy a year later. They must have known at the time that nobody would be around a year later to pay the second half, and the policy would be cancelled. I was 12 at the time and, under the circumstances, thought it was very nice that someone was willing to insure us. It was only after the war that I understood how callous and greedy these men and the Winterthur company were.

I only learned about the policy after my father died in 1988, and I went to Brussels to close up his apartment. I found some documents which showed that there had been a policy. By then I was 58 years old and I had other things to do. But one thing is certain. Winterthur never tried to locate me or my sister or my mother before my father died.

Another witness was Margret Zentner, who was born in 1923 in the small town of Schluechtern, near Frankfurt. Her parents owned a wholesale and retail tobacco business, and were quite well off. They purchased an annuity policy for her with Allianz. It was for a dowry, to be paid either on her twenty-first birthday or on her wedding day. In 1933, the family fled to Czechoslovakia.

I married Fritz Zentner on October 24, 1941, in Prague. A month later, my husband and I were sent to

Theresienstadt. A year later, my parents arrived in the concentration camp. The Nazis confiscated all our possessions, including our insurance policies. Eventually, I was sent to Auschwitz where Dr. Josef Mengele inspected us regularly to separate the strong from the weak. I was healthy and survived, and so did my husband and my parents. All our other relatives were exterminated.

After the war, I went back to Schluechtern. It was there in 1947 and 1948 that I first tried to get Allianz to pay me the proceeds of my insurance policy. I even remembered the name of the agent who sold the policy to my family. But Allianz refused to pay. The company told me it had already paid out the proceeds to the SS. Outraged, I wrote to Allianz to complain, but never received a response. The fact is, Allianz took what my parents had provided for me and gave it to the Nazis.

Just last month [August 1997], I went to Germany to see what there is about the policy in the Holocaust victims' restitution files. When we got the files, we saw that as far back as 1957, Allianz lied about my policy. In 1957, the company told the German government that I canceled the policy in March 1942. That's a physical impossibility. I was an inmate in Theresienstadt from December 1941 on.

A third witness was Tibor Vidal, a 77-year-old man, born in Czechoslovakia and living in a New York City suburb:

My father was an insurance agent who worked for the Riunione Adriatica di Sicurtà, an Italian company [RAS, today owned by Allianz]. Like most insurance agents, my father bought a policy to provide for his wife and children. Then the government took away my father's license to sell insurance, and shortly afterwards, he was taken to Mauthausen and forced to work in the underground mines. No one comes out of the mines alive. My mother and my three sisters were taken to Auschwitz, where my mother was gassed. My sisters survived and were liberated at the end of the war. In all, 200 members of my family were killed during the Holocaust. Only six of us were left alive.

In the 1950s I returned to Italy and personally went to the RAS head office. I wasn't thinking about insurance policies then, but wanted some kind of acknowledgement my father's 20 years of service with the company. They said we cannot do anything: it's not our company any more. First government took it over, and later on the communists. I, as a young man then, believed everything. I just said goodbye and left. That was their final answer.

Marta Cornell was the fourth survivor to testify. She was the lead plaintiff in a landmark class action suit brought against a number of European insurance companies in New York earlier in 1997. Born in 1927 in a small town in Czechoslovakia, she now lives in New York City. Her father, Leopold Drucker, was a well-to-do physician. Marta, an elder sister and her mother and father shared the house with her maternal grandmother. Her story:

My father started buying insurance policies when my older sister was born in 1924, and kept it up until March 1939, when the Nazis occupied our country. We were evicted from the house and had to move in with another Jewish family. In 1942, we were all deported to Theresienstadt.

My father continued to work as a doctor, and I was assigned to work in the fields. In December 1943 my sister was sent to Auschwitz and then to Bergen-Belsen. She managed to survive the actual camps but then died of typhoid in 1945 shortly after being liberated by the Allies. In October 1944 my parents were sent on a transport to Auschwitz to be exterminated. The only family members who survived the Nazis were my 80-year-old grandmother and me. And although my grandmother survived physically, she never really left the camps. She was mentally mutilated for the rest of her life. After the war, my grandmother and I struggled to get by in Prague with no money and no income.

Then I found a piece of paper with my father's handwriting, and it seemed like it was the answer to our prayers. It was the details of insurance policies—the date of purchase, the policy number and how much each policy was worth. An insurance agent who tried to help me in 1945 told me that the policies had been purchased from Generali and RAS. One of the agents who sold my father the policies said I would get the policy proceeds. However, in the end, Generali and RAS refused to pay or even explain why.

In 1948, Czechoslovakia became a communist country. In 1964, I managed to immigrate to the United States. Shortly after I came to New York I again tried to get my inheritance money from Generali and RAS. Both companies turned me down. They said they didn't have to pay because of the "extraordinary circumstances," meaning the war. They said my father had failed to keep up the premiums, and that they had applied the accumulated cash value to cover the missed premiums, finally using up all the available monies and there was nothing left for me. Finally, they argued that the policies were nationalized when Czechoslovakia became a communist country in 1948 and they had lost all contact.

I contacted the lawyer Edward Fagan, and filed a class-action lawsuit on behalf of all Holocaust victims whose insurance policies were never paid by these companies. Last month I went to Munich to pursue my claim against RAS, now an Allianz subsidiary. In a brief meeting with a spokesperson, I was told that all the records related to my policies were destroyed 30 years ago, shortly after the companies had written me the excuses they were hiding behind rather than pay my claims. If Generali and RAS had paid the claims when I made them in 1945 I could have given my grandmother the psychiatric and medical help she needed. She would not have had to live her last few years in torment.

I needed those monies then, and I want them today. The insurance giants Generali and Allianz have become even greater and wealthier because they refused to pay out on policies like my father's policies that were bought and paid for. It was not only the Nazis who victimized innocent people. Europe's insurance giants benefited from the theft of assets, policy proceeds, and accumulated cash value from Holocaust victims.

The stories these survivors told had a profound impact on the insurance commissioners. They had suffered an outrageous humanitarian injustice and this was an area where the commissioners could actually do something. On the other hand, it was an opportunity to gain national exposure on an issue that did not seem to have a political downside. The conference established a task force that was charged with recommending how to get the insurance companies to meet their obligations. The establishment of the International Commission on Holocaust Era Insurance Claims (ICHEIC) was the logical next step.

In the end, the rest of the U.S. population, whether unaware of the lawsuits, supportive of them, disinterested, or choosing to be "politically correct," stepped back. It was not a subject that invited disinterested comment.

The "fertile ground" was ready to be seeded.

Chapter IV

The Jews and Insurance

In the search for unpaid Holocaust-era insurance policies, one of the more damaging allegations is that companies in Germany colluded with the Nazis to single out Jewish policy holders. For their part, the companies have maintained that they had no way of knowing which policies belonged to Jews, and insist there was no way to identify a client's religious affiliation from the information they collected when writing the policy.

It has also been a widely-held view that Jews were especially prone to take out insurance. According to Washington State Insurance Commissioner Deborah Senn, life insurance policies were favored assets among European Jews in the decades preceding World War II. In addition to affording protection against loss or injury to life and property, they saw it as a sound means of saving and investment, an issue of heightened concern to a vulnerable minority group. In her paper on the subject, she also says that because of their relatively high socioeconomic standing, Jews were more prone than the general population to purchase insurance. Jewish family breadwinners, she says, were more likely to be self-employed business owners and professionals, who purchased insurance directly from agents rather than through group or workplace plans. She cites what she calls "anecdotal evidence" that Jewish families tended to purchase larger-than-average policies.

On the other hand Glenn Pomeroy, Insurance Commissioner of North Dakota, in a report to the International Commission on Holocaust Era Insurance Claims (ICHEIC), said that there is no reliable material on Jews' insurance predilections. He pointed out that since insurance companies did not normally ask their customers about their ethnic or religious affiliation, any statement on the behavior of the Jewish population towards insurance, whether in terms of the number of policies per capita, or of average policy value, cannot rely on statistical information that predates the Holocaust.

According to the German census of 1933, just under half a million "Jews by belief," that is, persons who positively affirmed that they were Jewish, rather than being simply of Jewish extraction, were living in Germany. Many of them were impoverished refugees from Eastern Europe. When Jews sought to flee Germany during the 1930s, did insurers connive to put the policy surrender value into blocked accounts?[30] What emerges from the literature is a conflicting mixture of options.

---

30. A carefully researched study of this aspect is contained in Prof. Gerald D. Feldman's *Allianz and the German Insurance Business, 1933–1945*. In 1997, Allianz commissioned Prof. Feldman, an eminent historian who teaches at the University of California at Berkeley, to write a totally independent profile of the company's Nazi-era history and gave him unfettered access to its files. His book provides a wealth of information, and I freely acknowledge my debt to him.

There is no question that the regime was determined to seize whatever Jewish assets it could as an ideologically sound way of defraying the cost of Germany's massive rearmament. For the insurance companies, it was strictly a business consideration. They were understandably reluctant to lose customers in good standing, whether Jewish or non-Jewish. This meant canceling the policies, paying out the assets and foregoing future premiums. At the same time the Jews wanted to turn their assets into easily transported cash.

In his book, Prof. Feldman dismisses as false the assertion that German insurance companies refused to pay out what they owed to Jewish policyholders. He says that the real tragedy surrounding the insurance assets of Jews was that such a large proportion of the Jewish population was forced to cash in their policies to pay the extortionate taxes connected with their emigration. He maintains that the narrow focus on the search for what is a relatively small number of unpaid policies casts a veil over what they truly lost.

When this drastic method of despoiling Jewish insurance policyholders proved too slow and cumbersome for Hermann Goering's Four Year Economic Plan, he set up a foreign exchange investigatory bureau at the end of 1936 to expedite the confiscation of assets. The bureau was empowered to take control of all the assets belonging to anyone suspected of wanting to flee the country which, under the circumstances, meant mainly Jews. This was the administrative bridge to get into private accounts to which the legitimate owners would later be denied access. A decree issued in April 1938 that required Jews possessing assets of more than RM 5,000 to file a full statement of the contents of their accounts. This meant that the Jews themselves would have to provide the Nazis with a complete list of their insurance policies and their numbers. The head of the Four Year Plan was empowered "to take whatever measures are necessary to secure the mobilization of the assets in question for the benefit of the German economy."

According to the Eleventh Regulatory Decree issued under of the law of November 25, 1941, a Jew who is resident of a foreign country, for instance in a concentration camp in Poland, was automatically deprived of his German citizenship and his assets were seized by the state. Prior to 1941, the companies duly paid out the benefits as they fell due, directly to the state of course, or indirectly into blocked accounts. The policy proceeds did not remain with the companies as had been alleged by some of the plaintiffs' lawyers. The procedure for settling seized insurance contracts was laid down in circular R 53/42 of the Insurance Supervisory Authority (*Reichsaufsichtsamt*) of July 29, 1942. This circular informed insurance companies that endowment policies made over to the German Reich were considered cancelled as of December 1941, and that the surrender value should be turned over to the state. The companies were charged interest from January 1, 1942, until the day it was paid. The thirteenth decree under the law was published in the *Reichsbürgergesetz* of July 1, 1943. It laid down that the German Reich was heir to the assets of Jewish persons upon their death.

From the very beginning, the Nazi decrees posed serious problems for German insurers. One example was the Isar Life Insurance Company, which had been cobbled together in 1936, with the assistance of German insurers, after the Austrian insurance giant Phoenix collapsed due to financial mismanagement.

On November 17, 1938, a week after the infamous *Reichskristallnacht* pogrom ("The Night of Broken Glass"), Isar sent an urgent message to its German insurance company shareholders and their association seeking permission to refuse payouts to alarmed Jewish life insurance policyholders who wanted to cash in their policies at their current repurchase value and emigrate. It said that a large proportion of the Phoenix policies in its portfolio belonged to what it termed "non-Aryans," and they were rushing to get out of the country. Company directors said that demand for the surrender value of policies had increased so much in the last few days that the very existence of the company was threatened.

Company executives cited a new decree that had been issued after *Kristallnacht*, excluding Jews from the economic life of Germany and Austria, as the legal pretext that would enable Isar to convert the status of the policies to paid up, and thus avoid having to pay out cash. It also suggested that the ruling gave it the right to recalculate the value of paid-up policies to reduce their worth even further.

Feldman calls this "an unabashed effort to cheat Jewish policyholders" just when they desperately needed the cash to pay the *Reichsfluchtsteuer* (the emigration tax), as well as the actual costs of emigration. In an interesting move that ran counter to Nazi policy, the insurance supervisory authorities firmly opposed Isar's request. They said there were no existing legal regulations limiting the repurchase of policies owned by Jews and, consequently, Isar had to pay the owners. The company's repurchase expenses in 1938 were RM 6.41 million, compared to RM 2.43 the previous year.

From this perspective, the incident demonstrated that neither the leading insurance companies nor their regulatory authority, the Reich Supervisory Office for Insurance (Reichsaufsichtsamt fur das private Versicherungswesen), considered it legitimate or economically politic to deny payment on Jewish-owned policies. As the Isar story suggests, the pogrom was a central event in the run on insurance companies and, in some instances, it was causing problems to their bottom lines.

Reichskristallnacht was the "writing on the wall" for most Jews. It brought home with devastating impact that in the anti-Semitic climate that had spread over Germany since Hitler's accession to power, little was needed to provoke a major out-break of violence against the Jews. The pretext for the pogrom was a Jewish student living in France, Herschel Grynszpan, whose parents had been expelled from Germany to Poland. Seeking revenge, he assassinated a counselor at the German embassy in Paris. This touched off a wave of officially inspired excesses in which several hundred synagogues and 7,500 shops and businesses were destroyed, and at least 91 Jews were murdered.

The orgy of vandalism spread across the country. Another 30,000 Jews were rounded up and dragged away to concentration camps, if only for a brief but terrifying taste of what the future held in store.

The pogroms of 1938 were a quintessential example of how the Nazis cynically went about pillaging the Jews and then made them pay for the damage. What was called a *Judenaktion*, quite simply a pogrom, had been preying on Jewish-owned shops throughout the spring and summer. The depredations, which were mostly in Berlin, were carried out by Hitler Youth and SA militiamen, some of them in uniform. Most of the injured merchants had glass insurance, and the insurance companies were being saddled with the bill for replacing the glass.

Feldman quotes an executive with one of the largest insurance companies, Johannes Tiedke of Alte Leipziger, as arguing that the Jews were not really hurt by the rioting. It was the non-Jewish German public that in the final analysis had to foot the bill. He maintained that they were the real victims.

If the German Supreme Civil Court (*Reichsgericht*) could maintain that parties injured in an earlier pogrom, in April 1933, were victims of a "domestic disturbance" and were not entitled to compensation, by 1938 the actions were being officially characterized as an exercise of righteous civic virtue, and therefore the insurers should pay—however not to the victims but to the fiscal authorities. Obviously, neither the Jews nor the insurers were prepared to sue the Third Reich for damages resulting from officially sanctioned vandalism.

Much of the heat generated in the resurgence of interest in restitution for Nazi crimes against the Jews has dwelt on the concept of "blocked accounts." In effect, the Nazis sequestered Jewish assets and put them into accounts to which the Jews had restricted or no access. The thought that the Third Reich arbitrarily prevented Jews who were trying to flee Germany from drawing on whatever money they had, and even the insurance policies that they had cashed in, fed the righteous indignation that inspired the postwar campaign to right the injustices of the past.

The issue of blocked accounts was one of the most contentious topics in the negotiations leading up to the final agreement on compensating insurance policies from the Holocaust era. The negotiating parties, ICHEIC, the German Foundation and the German Insurance Association (GDV), were at odds over how to deal with a situation where a company could produce clear proof that payment had been made into a policyholder's bank account, but the designated beneficiary or heir could just as definitively say he had no access to that account and therefore no payment was received.

Normally, an insurance contract ends with the occurrence of an insured event, or, under certain circumstances, when the policy is terminated by either the policyholder or, under certain circumstances, by the insurance company. In the case of a life insurance policy, which, unlike a non-life insurance policy, accumulates assets based on the premiums that are paid in, the policyholder is free to cancel the insurance contract at any time, to "surrender" the policy. If the insurance contract had existed long enough for the premiums to have covered the insurance company's administrative expenses, the owner, on surrendering the policy, is also entitled to the interest as well as the accumulated capital. If it was surrendered before term, it means that not all the accumulated premiums fell short of the capital denominated in the policy, and its value is less than the sum insured. Sometimes, an owner will decide to convert the policy to paid-up status, leaving the surrender value with the company in order to retain the insurance coverage. Most policyholders who opt to surrender their policy want to take the cash, however. The insurance company has no say in the matter, and it is solely up to the policyholder to decide whether to convert the policy or to collect the surrender value.

There are many reasons why a policyholder might choose to end an insurance contract by way of surrender. Certainly, one of the most common reasons is to help the policyholder out of financial difficulties or if he can no longer afford to pay the premiums. In the prewar Nazi Germany, Jews were just anxious to get out. Another major reason to surrender a policy was when a policyholder moved to another location and wanted to terminate all his local business. In the 1930s, when electronic bank transfers were still unknown and bank accounts were far from universal, the surrender value was generally paid out in cash directly to the beneficiary or to the policyholder.

While a policyholder had to sign a receipt for the surrender value, the only record the companies usually kept was a mark on their internal files, simple name cards, which indicated that a surrender value had been paid and that the insurance contract was terminated. Consequently, most company documents from that period only indicate whether and when a policy was paid, but not to whom, nor do they say whether the payment was in cash, a money order or deposited into a bank.

As persecution spread, a majority of German Jews decided that they would be better off elsewhere, and money tied up in insurance assumed greater significance. In the census of 1925, 564,000 people were counted as Jews "by belief." By 1933, the figure was down to 499,000, of whom half said they were gainfully employed. More than 200,000 Jews emigrated over the next six years, and by May of 1939, barely 200,000 remained in Germany. Only 15 percent of them said they had a job.

Those who could afford to leave were generally active in business and the liberal professions, in the arts and sciences, and, for the most part, well integrated into German society. Once they had made the decision to pull up roots, like all emigrants they looked for ways to take as much of their possessions with them as possible. Not only did they try to sell all immovable assets, such as houses, cars or real estate, but they also tried to get some money out of their insurance policies. Unlike real estate, where the price depends on the market or personal situation of the seller or buyer, the surrender value of a policy is calculated solely on the basis of a fixed mathematical formula. It does not reflect economic or political circumstances.

Of course they still had to contend with a rigid administrative state bureaucracy intent on preventing a flight of capital. During the financial crises of the 1920s and even after World War II, most countries put up barriers to protect their currency, including a high tax on emigration. In Germany this tax, the *Reichsfluchtsteuer*, or "emigration tax," was introduced in July of 1918, while the First World War still going on. It was a universal, non-discriminatory measure designed to protect the German economy and applied to every emigrant, Jewish or non-Jewish. Until 1934, it was a 25 percent tax on whatever sums were transferred abroad. In August 1934, this was increased to 65 percent; to 81 percent in October 1936, to 90 percent in June 1938 and, in September 1939, to the confiscatory level of 96 percent. The original law provided that, on emigration, persons having taxable assets in excess of RM 200,000 had to turn over 25 percent to the state. In 1934, the law was amended to start at RM 50,000, and on April 26, 1938, the starting point was lowered still further to anything above RM 5,000.

Feldman says the lowering of the assets threshold, along with the inclusion of assets like Reich railroad bonds that had till then been exempt, was clearly aimed at the Jews. He quotes a Finance Ministry statement that says it was designed to force the Jews to make "a last contribution" to compensate for future taxes the state would lose because of their departure.

In order to secure payment of this emigration tax (as well as other state and local obligations), the authorities routinely blocked bank accounts owned by would-be emigrants, so-called *Auswanderer-Sperrkonten* or "emigration blocked accounts." All fees and taxes, including the *Reichsfluchtsteuer*, were deducted from these blocked accounts before the emigrant was allowed to leave the country. Prior to 1935–1936, however, the accounts were not completely blocked, and the account owner could draw out money for certain other specified expenses, including insurance premiums.

If emigrating Jews elected to collect the surrender value of their insurance policies, the payments, if not in cash, often went into such blocked accounts.

Because the company was acting on the instructions of the policyholder to pay the value of the policy into a designated bank account, it had no way of knowing whether the policyholder had indicated his intention of emigrating and that account was blocked. Once the insurance money was paid into the designated account by the policyholder, it became part of whatever was in the account that was being used to pay living expenses inside Germany prior to actual emigration, other debts, and, of course, the *Reichsfluchtsteuer*. If the money never reached the account holder, the insurance companies point out in their defense that it was the German state that had blocked access to the policyholder's bank account and subsequently diverted the money to its own use. It is the state, therefore, which is responsible and should pay.

This is an interpretation that the government of the Federal Republic of Germany has accepted. As the legal successor to the Third Reich, it put up half of the German Foundation's DM 10 billion, thus implying a final obligation on its part to see that these cases are settled as well, and blocked account claims have been included in the mix of issues involving compensation for insurance policies.

In the course of the difficult negotiations over lists of names, audits and setting a procedure for appeals, ICHEIC made it very clear that it wanted to include blocked account cases in the insurance compensation mix. It insisted that the companies not only had to prove that they had made a payment for each policy whose existence could be established, according to the agreed-upon relaxed standards of proof, but that they also show that each payment had gone to the correct beneficiary or his rightful heir. ICHEIC argued that a payment by a company was of no use to the beneficiary if he could not enjoy it, an argument that was regarded sympathetically by the Foundation as representative of the German state.

Since the Federal Republic had assumed responsibility to pay compensation for assets seized in blocked accounts, the German Foundation took the logical next step. It saw to it that holders of blocked accounts who had not received compensation for an insurance policy under the BEG be eligible under the agreement between ICHEIC, the Foundation and the GDV.

While the insurance companies agreed with the Foundation's intention in principle, they maintained that blocked account cases should be assigned to the Foundation's banking fund category and not be part of the compensation scheme for "unpaid" and "previously uncompensated" insurance policies. They argued that at the time, in the 1930s, they had done precisely what their Jewish policyholders had asked them to do, that is pay the surrender value of the policies into a designated bank account. From a strictly financial point of view, it was bad business. They point out that canceling the contract back then had meant that they had to relinquish the accumulated assets and waive future premiums.

During the negotiations, the Foundation expressed the fear that the funds allocated for bank account compensation would most likely be insufficient if blocked account cases were included. It pointed out that the number of surrendered and paid out policies that belonged to emigrating Jewish Germans accounted for a very large part of the companies portfolios of payments on surrendered German policies, and the money is presumed to have gone into blocked accounts. The Foundation maintained that only the insurance companies were in a position to determine whether a surrendered policy existed or not, even if they could not tell from the individual policy information in their archives what happened with the surrender value after it was paid out to the policyholder.

The three negotiating parties could only agree that persons who did not receive their insurance proceeds should be eligible for compensation. How such payments should be made and under what category of compensation remained very much in dispute during the long, drawn-out negotiations that eventually led to the Trilateral Agreement between ICHEIC, the Foundation and the GDV on October 16, 2002.

The solution eventually arrived at was suggested by the Foundation. It proposed that compensation for blocked account cases be paid out of the DM 350 million general humanitarian fund that was originally intended to be used at the discretion of

ICHEIC and its members for purposes not necessarily linked to insurance policy compensation. It pointed out to ICHEIC that this category of claimants would otherwise receive no compensation under the program to deal with unpaid insurance policies. In effect, companies had paid out the policies according to the policyholders' instructions and only subsequently were the proceeds confiscated by the Nazi regime through the instrument of blocked accounts.

Although ICHEIC, as the designated trustee of the humanitarian fund, eventually agreed to this suggestion, it said it did not have sufficient staff to handle the blocked account cases. Here, the GDV stepped forward in a gesture intended to show that the insurance industry as a whole would address the issue on purely humanitarian grounds, absolving the individual companies of responsibility for blocked account banking cases. Accordingly, the payment offer for a particular, identified policy would be sent out from the GDV "on behalf of the entire German insurance industry" and on "purely humanitarian grounds."

The last major issue that had to be resolved was the criteria of who was eligible for compensation. In the absence of any details about where the payments by the companies, 70 years ago, had gone, it was agreed that all cases where it could be clearly established that payment was made into a blocked bank account should be dealt with through the compensation process for insurance policies. However, because company documents did not distinguish between payments made in cash or deposited in a bank account, or whether the bank account was blocked or not, it was decided to deal with these cases according to more or less generalized assumptions.

For policies issued in Germany, it was agreed that if payment was made to a bank account between 1933 and the end of 1937, and there was evidence according to the "relaxed standards of proof" that the policyholder had already emigrated or that he or she was trying to emigrate or had been arrested or deported, that his or her bank account "is deemed to have been blocked." For the period from the start of 1938 through the end of 1939, when anti-Jewish measures became progressively more severe, every payment into a bank account, no matter what the stated intentions of the Jewish policyholder or beneficiary, was assumed to have been made into a blocked account.

According to the agreement, when an insurance company determined that the proceeds of a policy were deemed to have been paid into a blocked bank account, the company informed the GDV, which in turn notified the claimant, with a copy to ICHEIC, that, although the claim concerned a policy that had been properly paid by the insurance company, the policyholder was entitled to a humanitarian payment of the same amount as if the policy had remained unpaid. The claimant also enjoyed the same right of an appeal if he or she found the offer unsatisfactory. The compensation amount was not drawn from ICHEIC's "claims" pool but from the general humanitarian fund. This little bit of legal legerdemain underscored the fact that the policy had been paid off by the insurance company, but that the beneficiary did not receive the surrender value because his or her bank account had been sequestered by the Nazi regime in power.

Over the years, the GDV received 2,624 claim forms from ICHEIC that the companies determined were eligible "blocked account cases." Each such form could contain the names of as many as 40 persons and evidence of several different policies. Careful research of these 2,624 forms turned up 2,888 eligible beneficiaries who received compensation on 3,861 policies. As with the non-blocked account cases, a claimant occasionally received compensation for more than one policy or the compensation for one policy had to be divided among several heirs. The total sum paid out to blocked account beneficiaries came to

US$28.15 million, an average of US$10,727 per claim, which came out, on average, to $9,759 per beneficiary.

Chapter V

The "Accusation"

Seeking compensation for the atrocities perpetrated by the Nazis became a cause célèbre in the mid-1990s. Attention was first drawn by the Swiss bank affair, and while that was being settled, lawyers sought out clients who could claim they were owed money on insurance policies that either they or their parents had taken out prior to World War II. The process was catalyzed by the end of the Cold War, which released a flood of documentation from behind the Iron Curtain.

During the period that led to the creation of the International Commission on Holocaust Era Insurance Claims (ICHEIC) and the first year of its operation, one of the more outspoken proponents of forcing European insurance companies to pay was the Insurance Commissioner of the State of Washington, Deborah Senn. A widely-quoted paper she published in April 1999, "Private Insurers and Unpaid Holocaust-era Insurance Claims," set out to demolish the insurance companies' claim that nationalization of their assets by the communist authorities after the war ended relieved them of all liability for policyholders in those countries. She focused on the situation of the large concentrations of Jews in these lands.

For a comment on her allegations, I canvassed several German insurance company executives, including Gert Schlösser, a special advisor to Victoria, which had the largest prewar insurance portfolio of any German company in Eastern Europe. It was their contention that in building up her case against the insurance companies, and especially those domiciled in Germany, Ms. Senn had focused almost exclusively on events that occurred in Central and Eastern European states immediately after the war, ignoring what happened in West Germany itself. They point out that the German Federal Republic launched a comprehensive compensation process in the 1950s that also covered German insurance policies written prior to and during the Second World War. As a result of the evidence that was unearthed during years of research into restitution claims, they maintain that the vast majority of hitherto unsettled policies written by German companies were compensated long before Senn got involved.

Reference was made to the "Law on Equalization of Burdens" (Lastenausgleichsgesetz or LAG), which came into effect as early as September 1952. It said that persons eligible for restitution had to be German citizens (including Jews who, after the war, were entitled to reclaim the citizenship that the Nazis had deprived them of) or persons of German ethnic origin that the National Socialists had driven from their homes or who had suffered pecuniary losses in areas outside the 1937 borders of the Reich (principally, Germans expelled from Poland and Czechoslovakia after the war). From 1956 on, the Federal

Compensation Law (*Bundesentschädigungsgesetz*) or BEG, had paid compensation for endowment and annuity policies issued by private insurance companies on which premiums were still being paid or which had been designated "paid-up." These included insurance contracts that had been terminated by the individual after being pledged to the German Reich or where the insurer had remitted the surrender value directly to the Government. Also, covered were cases where termination had taken place because the fiscal authorities had attached or seized as security any rights arising out of the insurance contract.

Under the LAG, claimants were compensated for insurance policies on which two-thirds of the premiums had been paid in but which had not yet fallen due at the time they were seized. Insurers doing business in countries inside and outside the 1937 borders had to provide the authorities with all the information they had about former insurance contracts. Like the BEG, however, the LAG did not accept applications from a resident of a country with which West Germany did not have diplomatic relations. Policies confiscated outside Germany's 1937 borders were assumed to have been repatriated to the Reich and were therefore eligible for compensation.

The German insurance executives stated that much of what Deborah Senn complained about, i.e., the fact that East Europeans had no redress when it came to Holocaust-era insurance claims, was partly resolved through efforts of the U.S. State Department and ICHEIC Chairman Lawrence Eagleburger. They had made a point of bringing East European countries into the ICHEIC process, establishing the principle that life insurance contracts concluded with German-owned companies or independent foreign branches qualified for compensation. To the extent that claims would have qualified under the BEG laws, the payments were distributed from the German Foundation's Claims Fund. Under a compromise necessitated by the need to maintain parity with payments made under the BEG, the higher compensation that ICHEIC demanded under certain circumstances, the "top-up" amount, was allocated from the Humanitarian Fund. This distinction was maintained in the offer letters that went out to claimants, indicating on the one hand the BEG-calculated or minimum payment and on the other the actual compensation amount.

Then of course there were claims against subsidiaries of German companies in Eastern Europe, some of which were no longer in business. Here, too, the compensation came from the Humanitarian Fund that had been earmarked by the German Foundation to see that all claimants got some recognition of the obligations owed them. Since the Communist governments which assumed power in Eastern Europe after the war seized all the subsidiaries of foreign-owned insurance companies and transferred them to their own state-owned firms, the German insurance executives said that these new companies were responsible for compensating the policies that the nationalized foreign companies had issued.

Prior to the end of World War II, with few exceptions, life insurance written by German-owned companies was confined to the territory of the Reich. According to the Financial Supervisory Authority of the Third Reich (the *Reichsaufsichtsamt*) only 1.37 percent of the premium income of German life insurance companies came from business outside of Germany, including reinsurance. The biggest foreign portfolio was held by Victoria, which that year accounted for 80 percent of what the German life insurance companies did abroad. The reason for the relative lack of interest in expanding abroad was strictly a business decision. After World War I, an ever-growing number of countries issued insurance supervisory laws that favored domestic insurance companies. At the same time, changing currency regulations reduced the value of Reichsmark deposits abroad. The insurance portfolio of an independent branch in a foreign country had to cover the expenses of acquiring new business as well as establishing the required premium reserves. Added to this, the need to cover the risk premium and agents' commissions, the break-even point would be reached in about year twelve of a policy, and profits only started accruing in the final years. A company's interest was (and still is) to ensure that contracts reach the full term. Owing to the long-term character of the life insurance business and the amount of investment in foreign exchange that was required, setting up an operation abroad was already difficult under normal circumstances. It became even more difficult with the foreign exchange controls imposed by the Third Reich, though this did not affect the conduct of existing insurance business abroad.

For example, every independent foreign branch of Victoria was licensed to operate in a particular country, and the manager was responsible for seeing that the branch complied with supervisory laws and regulations of that particular country. Insurance contracts were written locally and the policies issued locally. The premiums were paid to the independent branch, which also disbursed benefits. The general insurance conditions that form part of every contract designated the country where the foreign branch was located as the legal place of payment, usually in the city in which the branch had its headquarters. Every independent branch had to prepare its own balance sheet and submit it to the respective national insurance supervisory authority, which naturally also oversaw where the branch invested its actuarial reserves.

Liability for individual insurance contracts in the portfolio of a licensed foreign branch of a German insurer rested solely with the respective branch.

Contrary to Ms. Senn's theories about the "financial transactions of German life insurers," the mother company was not involved. The dynamics of the life insurance business, which depend on the development of actuarial reserves, do not allow for diversion of invested funds, which seems argue against allegations that, even under wartime conditions, German life insurers were able to repatriate money from their independent foreign branches. But most important, contrary to what Ms. Senn had to say about "Insurance Systems Abroad," no German insurers were licensed in the prewar years to do business in Poland or the Baltic states of Lithuania, Latvia, and Estonia.

The large number of "potential Jewish policyholders with unsettled policies" was the center piece of her paper. Giving an idea of the dimensions of what she was talking about, she said "a regime of confiscation, looting, and benefit denial was perpetrated on hundreds of thousands, and perhaps millions of Jewish and other policyholders in Europe." She was presumably referring to Poland, which had just over 3½ million Jews when war broke out. All but 700,000 perished in the Holocaust.

According to a description of the European insurance business in *Neumann's Zeitschrift für Versicherungswesen*, Poland was the least developed insurance market in East Central Europe. Premium income of public and private insurance companies came to 133 million zlotys in 1937 (a zloty at the time was worth about half a Reichsmark). About 60 percent of it was in fire risk insurance. Life insurance accounted for only 21 percent, working out to about three zlotys a year per capita.

Although the number of life insurance policies increased from approximately 192,000 in 1934 to about 261,000 in 1937 in a population of 35 million, the average sum insured declined from 3700 zlotys in 1934 to 2400 in 1937. Despite the increase in the number of policies, the overall sum insured declined from 709 million zlotys to 634 million.

Poland of the 1930s was characterized by sharp contrasts between the social strata. A small, relatively well-to-do upper class coexisted with the great masses of farmers and blue collar workers. There was practically no broad middle class. The consequences this had on the economic and cultural life of the country also had an impact on the insurance industry. People attached importance to insurance only in Warsaw, the capital, and in those territories which had been German provinces before the Treaty of Versailles.

The market share of all foreign life insurance companies active in Poland, none of them German, was about one-third of the total premium income. In the late 1930s, the largest by far were Italian companies, Assicurazioni Generali, with 14,000 contracts, and RAS (Riunione Adriatica di Sicurtà), with 9,600. These figures of course represent policies issued to the total population, Jews and non-Jews. Bearing mind that Jews accounted for less than ten percent of the total population, it would appear that Ms. Senn was overreaching herself in her estimates of what could be owed.

Allegations about unpaid policies issued to Jews in Ukraine were also made by a prominent Holocaust-era investigator, Adrienne Scholz, in an article published in the respected *New England Journal of International and Comparative Law* in January 2003. She characterized the practice this way:

> Often used as a form of retirement planning amongst Jews in even the poorest areas, insurance salesmen would go door-to-door collecting weekly premium payments. Jewish insurance consumers in the pre-war period ranged from successful attorneys, bankers, and doctors in Germany to the impoverished peasantry of the Ukrainian shtetls (hamlets).

While the Soviet Union did have more than three million Jews, mostly in Russia and Ukraine, all private business, including insurance of course, came to a halt after the Bolshevik

Revolution in 1917. Under the circumstances, talk of Jews in Ukrainian shtetls lining up to buy life insurance policies for retirement planning is sheer fantasy.

After their blitzkrieg victory in Poland in September of 1939, the Germans moved quickly to bring a measure of normalcy to the newly acquired territories. One of the first moves was to issue a series of regulations aimed at "avoiding an insurance crisis, preserving the accumulated capital values for the insured, and bringing order to the insurance system as quickly as possible." The regulations were territory-related, some affecting regions which were simply annexed to the Third Reich and others that applied to areas which were under military occupation. What they had in common was they all ordered the transfer of the insurance portfolios of Polish and English companies operating in prewar Polish territories, in trust, either to German companies or to companies of "non-enemy" countries. This meant that the trustee companies assumed the obligations as well as the assets. The portfolios were not integrated into their German portfolio, but maintained separately. With respect to life insurance, however, a contract guaranty was only granted to persons who were officially recognized as ethnic Germans as defined by the Nuremberg laws. Policyholders or beneficiaries had to register with the trustee German insurance company by October 31, 1940, and pay all outstanding premiums "without another reminder."

According to Hitler's decree of October 12, 1939, Polish territories that had not been annexed fell under the authority of the *Generalgouvernement*, now the government of Poland. It authorized Polish insurance companies and companies of non-enemy foreign countries that had permits to operate prior to the war to continue to function. However, their activities were limited to the territory of the *Generalgouvernement*, which remained separated from the Reich, with its own police, currency (the zloty continued to exist but was devalued) and customs regulations. The office of Custodian of the General Government was put in charge of administering the seized property of the former Polish state (which, according to the Germans, no longer existed) and of private Polish and Jewish property.

In the period between the two world wars, Czechoslovakia, with a population of 15 million, was one of the most highly industrialized countries in Central and south Eastern Europe. Seventy percent of the industrial production of the former Austro-Hungarian Empire had been concentrated in what became the Czechoslovak Republic although it contained only 26 percent of the population.

After the collapse of the Austro-Hungarian Empire's "common market," the fledgling state had to export at least 30 percent of its industrial production for its economy to survive. Czechoslovakia eventually ranked among the top ten member states of the League of Nations in manufacturing output per capita, and was one of the seven biggest weapon suppliers in the world.

Its insurance industry prospered. The largest life insurance carrier was the Czechoslovakian company, Slavia, followed by three foreign firms: Victoria, Generali, and RAS, whose combined premiums in fact exceeded Slavia's in the mid-1930s. However, as a result of a concerted effort by the Czechoslovakian government to promote national companies at their expense, the foreigners' market share was halved, between 1930 and 1935, from 40 percent to 20 percent. Victoria had a presence in Czechoslovakia that went back to before World War I. By 1933, more than 40 years after it first began to do business in what was then part of the Austro-Hungarian Empire, its independent branch in Prague had a portfolio of nearly 40,000 Jewish and non-Jewish contracts, more than it had in any other country outside of Germany. In 1924, the Czechoslovakian

Ministry of Interior promulgated a regulation barring insurance companies from issuing policies denominated in anything but Czechoslovakian currency. This was amended in 1933 to include gold-based policies as well. Subsequent legislation in 1934 mandated that reserve funds had to be maintained separately from the rest of the companies' property. Licensed branches of foreign companies were permitted to operate under certain stipulations:

    • the branch manger had to be approved by the supervisory authority in the Ministry of Interior;

    • the branch management all had to be residents of Czechoslovakia and at least two were required to be citizens who knew the language of the country;

    • reserves on contracts written in Czechoslovakia had to be maintained in Czech government securities unless an exception was approved by the supervisory authority;

    • foreign insurance companies had to report on the entire scope of their business abroad in Czechoslovakian currency, and, separately, on whatever business they had in Czechoslovakia.

Reserves accumulated by the branch office of a foreign insurance company could not be transferred to another country without the express permission of the supervisory authority. Foreign branch offices also had to establish separate security funds as a protection against bankruptcy for all their insurance business, life as well as accident and property damage insurance.

After the Munich pact of September 30, 1938, Czechoslovakia had to cede the Sudetenland to the German Reich. Two weeks later, the Reichsmark was introduced as legal tender in the province, and the city of Reichenberg was decreed its administrative capital. In November a broad swath of territory in southern

Slovakia and the southwestern part of Carpatho-Ukraine was turned over to Hungary. The entry of German troops into Prague on March 15, 1939, marked the definitive break-up of all that remained of Czechoslovakia. The territories of Bohemia and Moravia were declared German Protectorates on the following day.

The Germans also had an economic agenda for the new territories. While the main goal was the seizure of the gold and hard currency reserves of Czechoslovakia's central bank, the insurance industry was also a target. All insurance business in the largely German-populated Sudetenland was transferred from Czechoslovak companies to German, Austrian, Italian, or Swiss firms, effective June 30, 1939. The Nazi administration decreed that all insurance contracts written in the former Czechoslovakia prior to October 10, 1938, had to be assigned to insurance companies doing business in the Protectorate. This included policies issued in Slovakia and in the parts of the country annexed by Poland and Hungary.

Shortly after Munich, the vast majority of the Jewish population of the Sudetenland (about 27,000 in 1930) fled to the territory still remaining under Czechoslovak control. For those who did not, it is reasonable to assume that the fate of their possessions, including their insurance policies, was no different than the confiscation that befell the Jews of Germany and Austria. In the Protectorate, which did not become part of the German economic area, the koruna continued to be the legal tender, and the 1934 Czech insurance supervisory law remained in force. More than 400 insurance companies were licensed to conduct business in the Protectorate, and by the end of 1939, they had a combined portfolio of 2,345,225 life insurance contracts. Victoria's share was a tiny 0.42 percent (9,896 contracts) issued to Jews and non-Jews by its independent branch in Prague. In the Sudetenland, on the other hand, by the end of

1939, Victoria's branch office in Reichenberg had a portfolio of nearly 21,000 life insurance contracts. While the policies themselves had to be converted into Reichsmarks, they were nevertheless maintained separately from Victoria's German portfolio.

The first insurance regulation aimed directly at Jews was introduced in the Protectorate only a few weeks after the occupation began in the autumn of 1938. Then, in April 1939, the Ministry of Interior issued a circular entitled, "Regulation of insurance of non-Aryan policyholders." It stipulated that Jews, as defined by the Nuremberg laws, could only receive insurance benefits in blocked accounts in a select group of banks. Measures soon followed that obliged Czech insurance companies to obtain from every client a statement attesting to his/her Aryan antecedents. The circular stated that Jewish clients could cash in policies for more than kc 5,000 only with special permission from the Ministry of Interior and the National Bank. The Czech insurance association issued a detailed guide on how the "Jewish laws" were to be applied, including those relating to "Aryan and non-Aryan couples." By law, Jews could only withdraw up to kc 3,000 a month from their bank accounts from which they also had to pay the premiums on their private insurance policies. If the premiums exceeded kc 750, they could apply for a higher monthly limit. In June 1939, the *Reichsprotektor* of Bohemia and Moravia decreed that Jewish property had to be registered by July 31st and put under the control of the Protectorate regime.

On September 2, 1941, the Germans established an office to administer property they had confiscated. Gestapo headquarters in Prague reported in July 1942 that kc 54.4 million worth of surrendered policies and benefits which had fallen due in the meantime had been confiscated from insurance companies in the

Protectorate. There was no indication of the number of contracts involved or the names of the policyholders.

At the beginning of the Protectorate era, the authorities still viewed emigration as the most practical solution to the "Jewish question." It had two purposes. For one, it got rid of the Jews. For another, German banks and factories derived much of their financing from the systematic expropriation of Jewish emigrant property. At a meeting of representatives of German banks, the German Ministry of Economy, the Gestapo, and *Sicherheitsdienst* (SD), it was agreed that Jews would be permitted to emigrate only if they left their property in the care of a German bank. Jews seeking an emigration permit also had to deposit their personal insurance policies in an authorized bank, but if they had insufficient other means, they could use their insurance policies to pay the exorbitant emigration tax. According to a report of the Prague Jewish community in 1942, 25,977 Jews left the Protectorate between March 15, 1939, and November 30, 1942.

The Center for Jewish Emigration (*Zentralstelle für jüdische Auswanderung*), together with the Gestapo, was responsible for the confiscation of assets of Jews deported to concentration camps and to ghettos. People ordered to register for transport had to declare all their property, including private belongings such as clothing, furniture, food coupons and, of course, insurance policies, and give the Jewish Emigration Center a power of attorney to administer the property. The Pomeroy Report, a study commissioned by ICHEIC of prewar of Jewish insurance holdings, derived much of its information about the situation of Jews in the former Czechoslovakia from the asset declarations, including insurance policies, that the Jewish population had had to submit to the Gestapo. Taking into account the proportion of the Jewish population of Czechoslovakia that perished (it cites the figure of 67 percent, i.e., about 150,000 people), the report estimated that the proportion of unpaid policies was in the very high category (50 percent to 80 percent), and cited anecdotal evidence that Jews made up a large segment of the clientele served by foreign carriers. After the war, research uncovered 4,192 policyholders in the Czech Republic and 8,198 in Slovakia.

With the definitive defeat of the *Wehrmacht* in the beginning of May 1945, the Czech government-in-exile lost no time in reasserting its authority and decreeing the end of German economic occupation. One of the first actions by President Eduard Beneš was to place German insurance companies and their branches under the "national administration." Decrees issued in June ordered the non-compensatory confiscation and expropriation of all German property. A decree issued in October 1945 required that insurance contracts which had been concluded with companies operating in the territory of the Czech Republic be registered with the authorities by the next month. Otherwise, they reverted to the Czech state with effect from November 16, 1945. A subsequent decree provided for the nationalization of all private insurance associations. Only state-owned companies were allowed to conduct insurance business on a commercial basis.

On October 25, Eduard Beneš convened a mass rally Wenceslas Square in Prague to celebrate what he had achieved. More than 400 insurance companies, 14 commercial banks, 600 savings banks and 3,000 industrial companies had been transferred to state ownership with the stroke of a pen. And this was even before the Communists assumed power! In the course of nationalizing private insurers, the government established several monopolies. One was *Erste Tschechoslowakische Versicherungsanstalt* and the other Slovan, and these two took over the insurance business of all foreign companies, including Victoria's.

What happened in Czechoslovakia was replicated by the postwar regimes in Bulgaria, Hungary, and Romania, whether already Communist or not yet. One of the first moves was to nationalize all private business, including insurance. The entire insurance business was left in the hands of only one or a handful of interrelated state insurance companies. German insurance executives point out, however, that the nationalization process did not necessarily represent a contractual loss for the policyholders. It simply meant that the carrier with whom the policyholder had concluded the contract was no longer a private entity, but was now owned and controlled by the state, which in turn was legally liable for the insurance obligations. That the state expressed no interest in carrying out the contract was a different matter.

As we saw above, insurance contracts which had been concluded with companies operating in the territory of the Czech Republic had to be registered by November 15, 1945, or be forfeit to the State. If policyholders failed to meet the deadline, it was the State that had now taken over the value of the contract and could decide how to deal with the obligation that remained. Of course not every policyholder was able to register his policy, in which case it remained in the portfolio of an insurer, either as a benefit that had come due or as a paid-up policy backed by locally available assets.

Many insurance policies were cancelled or reduced in value for nonpayment of premiums when the owners were deported to other countries and/or killed. However, according to German insurance executives, it would be incorrect to assert, as does Ms. Senn does, that "once the policies' values were lost to their owners, the carriers saw themselves as released from having to maintain part or all of the reserves to back the policies." They insist that the reserves were maintained as part of the collective actuarial process, and that they were subsequently nationalized by a post-World War II communist government.

Systematic expropriation of insurance policies came into force in the Third Reich and its officially annexed territories, in Austria and in the protectorate of Bohemia and Slovakia, but not in other countries, as Senn alleges. Since it was the government of the day that seized the insurance policies, this would seem to refute Senn's basic argument that government seizures of insurance assets did not alter a company's obligation to pay out benefits on a death or property loss that occurred earlier at the hands of the Nazis. An insurance company can only be made responsible for what remained as a contractual obligation in its portfolio.

Further on, Ms. Senn had argued that the pre-World War II private insurance market in Europe was dominated by multi-national companies that routinely moved assets and premium income across national boundaries, either to their headquarters in Germany and Italy, or out of Europe altogether. She says that movement of funds from German and Italian-owned branches in Nazi-conquered territories into their home countries continued as the Axis powers overran Europe, and she maintains that those assets were never subjected to nationalization. She attributes most of her information to contemporary Allied military intelligence documents and trade publications that contended that German and Italian insurers reaped enormous financial benefits from the consolidation of all lines of insurance business in the conquered lands.

The document that Senn refers to has been identified as a classified report put out by the Allies' Board of Economic Warfare entitled "Axis Penetration of European Insurance." It was issued on June 15, 1943, and the country reports, *inter alia*, provide information on the insurance situation in Austria, the Baltic states of Estonia, Latvia and Lithuania, Bulgaria, Czechoslovakia, France (including Alsace-Lorraine), Greece, Hungary, the Benelux countries, Poland (both the *Generalgouvernement* and the annexed territories) and Romania. On closer examination, however, there is nothing in the report to back up Senn's statement that "German and Italian-owned insurance company branches transferred funds from the Nazi-conquered territories back to their home countries," or that these assets were never subjected to nationalization.

For the German executives, this classified report does not really support the thrust of Senn's argument about the "companies' abilities to move funds around freely." Even during the war, they say, the strictly regulated insurance business, together with the existing currency restrictions, made even a relatively restricted flow of capital between different states and markets impossible. As noted earlier, cross border insurance business was quite rare, and even in those cases where a German company was allowed to take over a significant share of a foreign insurance company, the portfolios of the two companies had to be kept strictly separate, each in its own country, under the supervision of the respective national supervisory authority. In order to avoid possible exchange losses, everything had to be denominated in the same local currency—whether premiums, insurance benefits or accumulated policy reserves. This principle also applied to insurance contracts issued and managed by independent foreign subsidiaries of private German insurance companies. And another requirement was that the place of payment and place of jurisdiction had to be located in the same country in which the insurance was written.

They also question Senn's assertion that many of the policies sold to Holocaust victims were touted as being redeemable anywhere in the world, which she interpreted as a key selling point to pre-World War II purchasers who feared political upheavals in their home countries. She saw this as "unequivocal proof" that the insurers were prepared to pay claims with assets located outside the Eastern and Central European countries where they were sold. Here the German insurance people emphasize that the stiff regulations the companies labored under absolutely required that premiums, insurance benefits and accumulated reserves had to be denominated in the currency of the country in which the policy was issued. They say that an obligation based on what Senn calls a "redeemable clause" could not possibly have been assumed by an insurance company. The executives believe Senn may have been confused by the existence of the so-called "world policy," that actually was an addendum to life insurance policies in common use from the beginning of the twentieth century. This addendum confirmed that if the policyholder chose to live abroad anywhere in the world, the life insurance contract remained in force. It was the policyholder's responsibility, however, to see that premiums were paid locally during his absence.

Ms. Senn also singled out re-insurance companies. She charged that prominent Axis re-insurers received a portion of premium income from carriers in occupied Europe during World War II, and that money was never nationalized after the war and has never been accounted for. The insurance executives point out that only a small portion of a policy for which reserves had to be accumulated was allocated to the re-insurer's account, while the accumulated reserves themselves remained with the primary insurer. In order to avoid currency exchange problems, the re-insurer's premium was normally paid into its bank account in the country where the primary insurer did business. The instrument of re-insurance, they add, was not intended to shift assets from the primary insurer, but to insure against economic risks. Contrary to the impression that Senn conveyed, re-insurers were not the parent companies of the primary insurers.

The Central and Eastern European companies that were nationalized were not really new enterprises. Regardless of the losses they suffered from wartime destruction, their assets, i.e. factories, buildings, client-databases or insurance portfolios that were subject to nationalization, were what they had prior to and during the war, irrespective of the postwar value. The German insurance executives argue that in those Eastern European countries where the regime seized individual insurance policies, claims for compensation cannot be laid at the doorstep of the West European company with whom the original contract was made. The obligation rightly belongs with the government that conducted the arbitrary confiscation. Since East European governments were in no hurry to acknowledge these obligations, the claimants have sued the West European companies that wrote the original policies. The German insurance executives suggest that the choice of whom to sue was motivated by the reputed "deep pockets" of the West European companies.

Summing up her case, Senn said the bottom line is that policyholders and their heirs were never paid, and she held the insurers still contractually obligated to honor claims relating to these policies, regardless of postwar Communist government nationalizations. Since the expropriation of insurance assets occurred after World War II, she maintains it is not connected to events that occurred during and before the war—specifically the deaths and property losses of Holocaust victims. Her paper then alleges that not only did these assets remain with the companies, free and clear after nationalization, but that they are justiciable in the U.S. Here, she cites a ruling called the "Bernstein Exception," which, according to her, permits U.S. courts to ignore state confiscations and to order property restored to victims if the executive branch of government gives them specific authorization to do so. (This was a case involving a suit against a Dutch company, N.V. Nederlandsche-Amerikaansche, relating to a claim that the Nazi-ordered confiscation of a Jew's (Bernstein's) property was not entitled to the protection of the Act of State doctrine. The State Department sent a letter to the court affirming this, and advising the court "that the Act of State doctrine need not be applied to a class of cases involving Nazi confiscations.")

Under this interpretation, the former Washington State Insurance Commissioner held that the companies that sold insurance to Holocaust victims were legally vulnerable. They are among the largest in the world today, she says, and operate directly or through subsidiaries in the United States that are subject to American regulation. She said that one large firm, Allianz, headquartered in Munich, collects in excess of $6 billion in U.S. premiums through its well-known subsidiaries in North America. Another, the Italian company Generali, earns over $600 million a year from premiums collected in the U.S., and from other, non-insurance, American investments.

German legal experts note that the so called "Bernstein Exception" never became a binding precedent, but remains exactly as Ms. Senn described it, "a politically motivated exception" which would not be applicable if directed against U.S. entities. They then cite another decision in American Insurance Association v. Garamendi, in which the U.S. Supreme Court on June 23, 2003 held that U.S. jurisprudence does not generally apply worldwide, "not even in the insurance business."

At bottom, the German executives were suspicious of what they believe were Senn's true intentions, i.e., to identify European insurance companies that have the means to pay claimants. They complain that making private West European insurance companies pay "because they can afford it," rather than presenting the bill to the state-owned companies in Eastern Europe is just not fair. It means putting those companies in a position where they would have to agree to pay claims they maintain are not their obligation solely out of fear of getting caught up in endless litigation that would have destroyed their cherished reputations, regardless of the underlying soundness of the arguments in their defense.

Chapter VI

The International Commission on Holocaust Era Insurance Claims

The search for unpaid insurance policies taken out by Holocaust victims seventy and even eighty years earlier proved a very tall order in the 1990s. It had not been just any seventy years. There had been a world war in the interim, as well as violent economic upheavals that at one point, in 1924, wiped out the value of almost all life insurance policies held in Germany, and again in the Great Depression in the 1930s.

The German insurance companies called upon to do the searching had suffered near total devastation in the war. Some of the largest insurance concerns were literally bombed out, their main archives destroyed. They knew they had insurance policies outstanding but no idea of how many. Insurance companies in other countries were not much better off. Those that had written prewar policies in Eastern Europe saw their businesses and assets nationalized. The prospect of trying to set the record straight after all those years was not promising.

At the time premiums were still collected manually in those years, and the bulk of the records could be reconstructed from documents in branch office distribution centers. Since the German companies had been obliged under the Nazis to maintain a high proportion of their collateral in what were now worthless government bonds, they were for all practical purposes bankrupt after the war and could not pay beneficiaries when a policy fell due. The West German government took it upon itself to back the companies up with what was called an "equalization fund." Essentially, this was a line of credit that matched the companies' liabilities only to the extent that someone lodged a claim. If the liability did not materialize, if no one lodged a claim, the subsidized credit went back to the Government, plus interest. A prewar policy that was not paid did not represent cash in the company's coffers; it was simply an obligation on the books with insufficient collateral to cover it.

The equalization fund was designed primarily to assist the insurance companies in the immediate postwar period and at the same time ensure that beneficiaries did not suffer from the degradation of company assets. In this respect, the Government stood in for the now worthless Nazi government bonds. Its principle aim was to help with policies where the actual policyholder showed up and asked for payment. In addition, there was a program originally set up by the victorious Allied forces to recompense anyone who had personally been despoiled by the Nazi regime, or, if he was no longer living, his heirs. It was later continued by West Germany as restitution and compensation "to those who had been robbed, persecuted, physically exploited, and murdered under the National Socialist regime." It was wistfully called *Wiedergutmachung*, or "making good again."

The program, which was instituted in 1954, had a cutoff date. Parties who thought they had a claim were encouraged to apply for restitution before the end of 1969 (See "German Reparations," Chapter II). According to one source, 4.5 million applications were filed, most of them by Jews. Among other assets, they cited extant insurance policies. If their claims were substantiated, they were paid whatever the policy came to, including adjustments for interest.

Germany breathed a collective sigh of relief that at least this particular chapter rooted in its Nazi past had been closed. But had it really?

The collapse of the Communist bloc in the 1990s cleared the way for claims against the once-Communist governments to disgorge the looted art, communal property and other assets that had been denied before the end of the Cold War. It also opened up access to long inaccessible archives and their accounts of how entire populations were despoiled of their possessions. Along with other categories of assets, the public perception was that there still were many thousands of insurance policies that had never been cashed-in that belonged to people who had vanished along with their entire families.

Added to that was the assumption that German Jews, as a class, were particularly prone to take out insurance policies, and for larger amounts than the general population. After all, more than 40 percent of the Jews listed in the German population census of 1933 were recorded as being self-employed, i.e., doctors, lawyers, factory owners and shopkeepers. According to the report of an ICHEIC Task Force, 15 percent of the lawyers (3,030 persons) and 10 percent of the doctors (5,557) in Germany were Jewish, although the 500,000 Jews accounted for only 0.8 percent of the population. Basing itself on an admittedly small sample of policies, the report gave a wide range of estimates of what the actual figure for insurance ownership was, from four times the national average in Hungary, to three times in Austria to 1.81 times in Germany. This last estimate was subsequently questioned on the grounds that it did not lend sufficient weight to the large numbers of indigent Jewish refugees from Eastern Europe who were living in Germany at the time and presumably did not invest in insurance. The two authors of the task force report were Glenn Pomeroy, a former state insurance commissioner, and Philippe Ferras, an executive of the AXA insurance company.

It should be kept in mind that, because of the pressure to turn their property into liquid assets prior to emigrating in the years prior to 1939, few identifiably Jewish policy owners remained in the companies' portfolios. The Jewish population of Germany in those last years before the war consisted mostly of children and the elderly, who were certainly not taking out new policies. Most observers agree that the Jewish share of the over-all portfolio at the end of the war was insignificant.

In the absence of any hard evidence to the contrary, the perception nevertheless continued to grow that untold billions were locked up in Jewish owned-insurance policies that European companies owed on but would not pay. An ardent proponent of this view was Adrienne Scholz, a lawyer specializing in Holocaust law. Writing in the respected *New England Journal of International and Comparative Law* in January 2003, she spoke about "the decades' long struggle of hundreds of thousands of Holocaust survivors and the heirs of victims" who fought, without success, to claim insurance assets that were rightfully theirs. She quotes industry analysts who estimate the total unpaid claims owed to Jewish policyholders at between one and four billion dollars. The World Jewish Congress, she says, puts the figure at $2.5 billion.

Ms. Scholz goes on to talk about the first insurance class action suit, filed in the U.S. District Court in New York in 1997 against the Italian company Assicurazioni Generali and several other European firms. The plaintiffs' attorneys thought that the class they represented would eventually encompass 10,000 claimants seeking an average of $75,000 apiece (i.e., $750 million) from this case alone. The suit sought compensatory damages in excess of $1 billion plus interest and punitive damages.

State insurance commissioners, led by Deborah Senn, the Commissioner from the State of Washington, jumped on the bandwagon and began demanding that major insurance companies search through their files and identify policies that had not been paid out. State insurance commissioners often attempt to play up the importance of the actions they take as a way of burnishing their image when they seek election to higher political office. In this case, the sheer size of the numbers being bandied about promised the kind of publicity they sought.

They also wielded a potent club. Without a license from the state commissioner, an insurance company could not do business in the state, and the commissioners could threaten European firms with the loss of their licenses if they did not comply.

In April of 1999, Ms. Senn's office put out a lengthy, highly legalistic brief that sought to rebut the insurance companies' position that nationalization of their assets in the East European countries that became Communist after the war actually absolved them of the need to honor policies written prior to the war. As stated in the preamble to the brief, the report

explains why post-World War II government seizures of insurance assets do not alter a policyholder's (or their heirs') right to collect proceeds due them from insurers as the result of a death or property loss that occurred earlier at the hands of the Nazis. Victims of the Holocaust and their heirs have long been denied payment of their insurance claims by companies asserting that the assets backing the policies were nationalized by the post-war Communist governments of Central and Eastern Europe.

Essentially, the paper maintained that the multi-national companies that dominated the pre-World War II private insurance market in Europe routinely moved assets and premium income across national boundaries to their headquarters in Germany and Italy and that these assets were never subjected to nationalization by the post-World War II Communist governments. (A detailed account of Ms. Senn's arguments and a rebuttal by some of the companies' experts are contained in Chapter V, "The Accusation.")

For large international carriers like Allianz, AXA, Generali, and Zurich, this attitude on the part of a leading state insurance commissioner represented a serious threat to their brands and their substantial investments in the United States. While it was the multi-billion dollar lawsuits that provided the headlines, the insurance commissioners posed a more immediate threat, and the companies were looking for some kind of framework that would hold the commissioners at bay. International Jewish organizations, emboldened by the success of the Swiss bank settlement, came up with the idea of an international commission that would make the insurance companies cough up what they supposedly owed. The Conference on Jewish Material Claims Against Germany, *aka* the Claims Conference, and the World Jewish Congress felt uneasy with the confrontational behavior of the lawyers in the class actions suits, and feared that even if the suits were successful, little of that money would go to the generic humanitarian causes their organizations promoted. They also resented the institutional competition posed by the state insurance commissioners. It was this convergence of what were essentially conflicting interests that led to the establishment of the International Commission on Holocaust Era Insurance Claims (ICHEIC) in August 1998 as a private association set up under Swiss law.

Six European companies who were faced with class action lawsuits and actions by state insurance commissioners signed on to ICHEIC's Memorandum of Understanding (MOU) in the hope that the "safe haven" it promised would stand up in court. ICHEIC also appeared to be the kind of institution that would provide a quicker and less expensive resolution of the issues. While fiercely competitive in every other area, the companies were united on one point: they did not want to engage in long, drawn-out court cases, from which only the plaintiffs' lawyers would benefit, or that would expose them to legislative and regulatory sanctions in any number of individual states that they would later have to fight through the U.S. court system.

A conference to discuss what should be done about recovering assets lost in the Holocaust, not confined to insurance, was held in Washington in December 1998, a few months after ICHEIC was founded. Among the participants were state insurance commissioners, the six European insurance companies, plaintiffs' attorneys, and representatives of international Jewish organizations, including the State of Israel. There was no attempt to hammer out a master solution, but the differing perceptions of what needed to be done was clearly understood. The parties were divided over an estimate of what the price tag would be, with "billions" being used as the starting point. On the question of insurance, agreement was reached on only one point: that they would cooperate with ICHEIC in seeking out legitimate policyholders.

The International Commission on Holocaust Era Insurance Claims began to take shape, with a London claims office and an administrative base in Washington. A distinguished former U.S.

Secretary of State, Lawrence Eagleburger, was installed as Chairman. The Commission was to be funded with an initial $50 million put up by the six corporate founding members: Allianz, the French company AXA, the Italian Assicurazioni Generali and the Swiss companies Winterthur, Zürich, and Basler. (Basler subsequently sold off its American interests and withdrew from ICHEIC). The founding firms were later joined by the Dutch Insurance Association. The Memorandum of Understanding (MOU) committed them to cooperate fully in paying off their companies' extant policies and providing funds for "humanitarian purposes." In return they were promised "legal peace" and a "safe haven" in return.

According to Chairman Eagleburger, ICHEIC was "the first organization ever to offer Holocaust survivors and their heirs an avenue other than litigation to pursue a claim against an insurance company at no cost." Together with the MOU companies, it assumed the responsibility of redressing contractual obligations on 70- and 80-year-old policies on which the statute of limitations had long expired but for which the overriding moral responsibility remained. This was particularly true in the former Eastern Bloc countries, where fair individual compensation had never been an option.

Deborah Senn, who led the insurance commissioners' group at the conference, says she first became aware of the Holocaust insurance issue from an article she read in a trade magazine in early 1997 about the class action suit filed in New York. In an informal survey of the several hundred Holocaust survivors living in Washington State, she says she found that up to a third of the respondents had a clear recollection of insurance coverage that was never paid out to them before or after the war. Some even had policy records and numbers but said they had never been able to file claims with the companies.

She contacted several of her colleagues in other states and they put together a paper that they read to an assembly of the National Association of Insurance Commissioners (NAIC) during the fall of 1997 in Washington, D.C. The NAIC named her to head a working group on the Holocaust claims issue, and she held hearings around the United States in the spring of 1998 to identify similar problems in other states. Later that year, NAIC replaced the working group with a task force in order to establish an international commission to resolve the claims, similar to the commission that was then working on the Swiss banking claims, the prototype of ICHEIC. This was the same group that attended the Washington conference in December.

A report commissioned by ICHEIC (the Pomeroy and Ferras report) cited an extensive study done by the German supervisory authority for insurance of a sample of two thirds of the policies still in German company files. After subtracting those that had been voluntarily surrendered by the policyholder before the war, those that had been borrowed against, and those for which restitution payment had been made after the war, the supervisory authority concluded that the individually "unpaid," Jewish-owned policies in the German market stood, at the most, at 15.5 percent. The report noted that this figure was hotly disputed by the Jewish organizations, which put it at between 40 and 50 percent. In the end, the state insurance commissioners' own task force came down on both sides of the issue, and settled on a range of between 15.5 percent to 40 percent of the value attributed to Jewish-owned insurance assets as still being unpaid.

In 1998, Allianz became the first German insurance company to commission an independent audit of its prewar files. Speaking to the Washington conference on Holocaust assets, Herbert Hansmeyer, of the Allianz Board of Management, said "the auditors from the international accounting firm of Arthur Andersen faced a daunting task, more than one point four million individual paper files on policies issued between 1920 and 1945." This figure contained an unknown number of policies issued to Jews. "[It found that] the vast majority of policies had in fact been previously paid out at the request of individual policyholders. Some 70 percent of the files audited involved cases in which the policy had been cancelled prematurely and been cashed in. Again, almost all were cancelled by the policyholder. They may have done so in a desperate effort to alleviate increasing financial burdens from unjust levies and taxes, or to facilitate emigration. They did so in order to escape no uncertain peril to their lives." He said that the research also showed that around 70 percent of the remaining Jewish contracts were later compensated under the German government's restitution program.

And here Hansmeyer went to the crux of the problem. "The question remains, whether despite earlier payments and comprehensive compensation programs, is it still possible that some policies remained unsettled? The answer is yes, but only a small number of cases where the beneficiary could not be located.

Did the companies keep the money, as was the case with the dormant Swiss bank accounts? The answer is no, they did not. After the war, all German insurance companies were technically bankrupt." They were kept alive through a system of "on-demand" government subsidies to pay off claims, the so-called equalization fund.

When the DM 10 billion German Foundation "Remembrance, Responsibility, and Future" that was to compensate people who had suffered at the hands of the Third Reich came into being in July of 2000, it also covered any possible obligations of the German insurance companies still outstanding. The insurance sector had contributed over DM 500 million to the Foundation through the German Insurance Association (*Gesamtverband der Deutschen Versicherungswirtschaft*), or GDV, considerably more than its assigned share of the DM 10 billion at which the Foundation was capitalized. In a joint statement in July of 2000 by the governments of the United States, Israel and Germany and endorsed by the Jewish organizations and class action lawyers, the Foundation set aside DM 200 million to cover insurance claims and expenses, with whatever was left over to go into a humanitarian fund, initially set at DM 350 million. All in all, DM 550 million was allocated to insurance.

An executive agreement between the governments of the U.S. and Germany stipulated that the Foundation should be "the exclusive remedy and forum for the resolution of all claims that have been or may be asserted against German companies arising from the National Socialist era and World War II." It was this agreement that integrated all German insurance companies into the ICHEIC process, whether or not they had signed the Memorandum of Understanding in 1998. It also contains a U.S. commitment to "assist in achieving an all-embracing and enduring legal peace for German companies."

At first ICHEIC was at first unhappy with the role that Foundation money was to play in settling validated claims. The issue came up in 2000, when the GDV sought to represent its members in the grand settlement envisaged in the Foundation Law adopted by the Bundestag. ICHEIC Chairman Eagleburger strenuously objected. He held that the GDV companies, with the exception of Allianz, had till then stood on the sidelines and not been party to all the obligations undertaken by those companies that had signed the MOU. To show his determination, he flatly refused to cooperate with the GDV, holding up the transfer of 75,000 claims that ICHEIC claimed it already had in hand that were supposed to go to German insurance companies for processing (in fact, in the end it produced a little over 19,000) and insisted on receiving all the money the Foundation had allocated to insurance claims in advance.

Eagleburger's position dismayed the insurance companies, who by now were eager to wind up the process. From their point of view, they felt the funding was now in place, and the processing of claims was being disrupted by what was essentially a bureaucratic bottleneck. The Chairman, they felt, was simply holding up the works over what he saw as a challenge to his authority. Despite the advanced age of the claimants, ICHEIC was refusing to turn over any of the claims that had reached its offices over the previous nearly two years.

Interestingly enough, this view was endorsed by Ambassador J. D. Bindenagel, the State Department liaison to ICHEIC. In a reply in February 2002 to one of the state insurance commissioners, he wrote: "I understand that ICHEIC has held back from processing thousands of claims directed at non-ICHEIC German insurance companies during the talks over the role of the Foundation money and the GDV, which have already dragged on for more than 20 months. Withholding claims cannot be in the interest of claimants, nor can it be in ICHEIC's interest in the service of justice to those claimants."

He then referred to testimony he had given three months earlier to a Congressional committee where he said: "It is distressing that the insurance negotiations have not yet been completed... Holocaust survivors and their families deserve at least some measure of justice that has been too long denied, and only through bringing all aspects of the "Remembrance, Responsibility and the Future" Foundation into full operation can this be achieved."

While the GDV felt that the DM 550 million that the Foundation had set aside for payment of insurance-related claims against German companies and for humanitarian purposes would be more than adequate for the relatively small number of anticipated legitimate claimants, it still had to resolve a number of problems. The most difficult one was the question of proof. How could you in all fairness demand of Holocaust survivors (or their heirs) that they produce documentary evidence of the existence of an insurance policy issued before the policyholder was shipped off to a concentration camp? At the same time, many insurance companies, whose all-important archives had suffered substantial damage during the war or else had been disposed of after the legal requirements for retaining them had expired, were called upon to research these claims to make sure that Foundation funds went only to legitimate claimants.

Since a large number of former policyholders perished in Nazi extermination camps or died a natural death in the more than 60 years since the end of the war, the vast majority of claims for compensation came from heirs who frequently had only the foggiest recollection of what insurance policy their parents or relatives may have owned, or if they were in fact insured. These direct descendants and other heirs could only provide a hearsay recollection of an insurance policy, that is, if an insurance policy was ever mentioned in their hearing at all.

They rarely knew the name of the issuing company, or whether the policy had been cashed in before emigration (which was still possible prior to 1939), or if any compensation had ever been paid through the German government's restitution program in the 1950s and 1960s. In many cases, they entered a claim only because they assumed that their dead relatives were likely to have purchased insurance. Most such claims were merely inquiries "to whom it may concern."

Other ICHEIC demands included audits on how the companies maintained their archives, processed claims and whether they have published lists of names of potential claimants, something that insurance commissioners in several U.S. states had already pressed for. The GDV opposed both demands as being outside the provisions of the German-American Intergovernmental Agreement as well as the Foundation Law itself. The negotiations for an audit of what the companies were doing and for an elaborate appeals process dragged on for another year and a half. It was only in October 2002 that ICHEIC finally signed an agreement with the German Foundation and the GDV on the processing and payment of Holocaust-era insurance claims against German companies, including German MOU companies, and agreed to a formula for evaluating what was due. The Foundation transferred to ICHEIC the full DM 550 million provided under the German law, and ICHEIC passed on to the GDV a first installment of what in the end turned out to be just over 19,000 claims it had collected that referred to German companies and the German market. Despite all the bumps on the road, ICHEIC could finally begin working.

While the actual processing could now start, it was not a propitious beginning. The issue of Holocaust-era insurance was very much in the public eye, and the picture of these elderly Holocaust victims being made to wait while bureaucrats procrastinated over turf issues was obviously unacceptable. The German insurance companies were accused of deliberately going slow in the sure knowledge that if the process only took long enough, there would be no claimants left. By the summer of 2002, however, it became clear to American state insurance commissioners and various Jewish organizations that it was ICHEIC itself that had been holding up the works out of what appeared to be deeply ingrained suspicions that the German companies would not do what they had promised to do.

Some of the problems associated with ICHEIC, and there were problems, arose from the very different perceptions of its founding partners. The state insurance commissioners regarded it as a vehicle to get the insurance companies to open up their entire portfolios to American regulatory scrutiny, force them to identify the Jewish policyholders and pay up—or else. Initially, they saw no reason to include the companies as active participants. The State of Israel, home to the largest concentration of survivors in the world, felt called upon to seek justice for its citizens wherever it could. The Jewish organizations, principally the World Jewish Congress and the Claims Conference, were fresh from their success with the billion dollar-plus settlement agreed to by the Swiss banks and had expectations of winning at least that much from the insurance companies, if not more.

The non-German signatories of the MOU thought that the International Commission would afford them the protection they needed for what they regarded as their relatively minor involvement. They allowed that while a few policies might still be unpaid, the number did not justify the magnitude of the threats posed to their businesses in the United States. German companies say they were initially caught off guard by all the furor. It had been their general understanding that the West German restitution program had taken care of all the loose ends left by the war. It was inevitable that these often contrary interests would occasionally disrupt the functioning of the International Commission.

Eventually, the quest for justice would require the cooperation of three major entities: ICHEIC, the DM 10 billion "Foundation for Remembrance, Responsibility, and Future," and the German insurance association. That cooperation did not come easily. ICHEIC saw itself as the prosecutor appearing on behalf of the injured parties, with the insurance companies in the dock. The relationship between them would prove to be a rocky one, exacerbated by the understandable prejudices of the plaintiffs and the natural disinclination of insurance companies to pay out claims they felt were not one hundred percent legitimate.

The choice of former U.S. Secretary of State Lawrence Eagleburger to be chairman of ICHEIC was an interesting one. A burly, "no-nonsense" retired career diplomat, at 68 he was considered arrogant by many and somewhat self-absorbed by others. His self-esteem could only have been reinforced when he was hailed as "Lawrence of Macedonia" after leading relief efforts following the 1993 earthquake in the Macedonian city of Skopje, and as "The Grand Playmaker" in the summer 2003 edition of *The International Economy* magazine. However, there was little question that he possessed the experience and the skills in international negotiations, management, strategy and economics that the position called for. He quickly discovered that it was not a bed of roses. On more than one occasion, a frustrated Eagleburger would compare the "antagonism" he encountered in negotiations between the companies and the Jewish organizations to what he had experienced in his dealings with the Soviet Union, the North Koreans, and the North Vietnamese. Those negotiations were tough, he said, "but I've never seen any that are worse than this."

In late May 2000, the GDV's CEO, Dr. Jörg Freiherr Frank von Fürstenwerth, and its President, Dr. Bernd Michaels, wrote Eagleburger that the GDV would be able to "ensure that its member companies, when answering enquiries, act according to principles which are in line with the standards of proof and valuation guidelines drafted within the ICHEIC.... We assume that our members will grant access to their files in an unbureaucratic way in the interest of mutual trust." In exchange, they said, payments made by German insurance companies to the Foundation Initiative would constitute "the final contribution" of the industry, and the companies would be fully protected against any future "legal and administrative measures directed against them."

Eagleburger and von Fürstenwerth had honed and mastered their respective negotiating skills, as they demonstrated numerous times during the ensuing days, months, and years. They each could be courteous, respectful, and diplomatic, while deftly re-shaping to their own liking the other's stance on any given point. At the same time, the two men also showed themselves quite capable of conveying a point without using any of the accepted niceties. At first, it seemed that they were both personally determined to work together to make the process succeed.

It would not be too long, however, before cordial and collegial words in e-mails and faxes would be punctuated by recriminations, finger-pointing, and excuses that transformed a relatively straightforward—albeit complex—arrangement into one of Byzantine intricacy.

From the outset, Eagleburger assumed that the insurance companies were not to be trusted and, even after the Tripartite Agreement among ICHEIC, the Foundation and the GDV, he explicitly insisted that participating German companies adopt ICHEIC's rules on "Admissibility of Evidence and Relaxed Standard of Proof." They have to "…commit themselves to complying with the procedures, guidelines and standards established by ICHEIC" rather than just acting "according to principles which are in line with ICHEIC's guidelines, he wrote.

He also proposed that the affected companies become full members of ICHEIC, with all the obligations that entailed. It was a proposal made with little leverage. Ever since ICHEIC had been established, he had been unable to convince any German companies (aside, of course, from Allianz, which was a founding member) to join the Commission. Also of concern on both sides of the Atlantic were the scope of the audits, the mechanics of the appeals process, and payment procedures.

In July, 2000, an Executive Agreement was signed between the governments of the United States and Germany and a month later the German Foundation "Remembrance, Responsibility and Future" was established based on a subsequent German law. As expected, ICHEIC was charged with "establish[ing] a just process to collect and facilitate the signatory companies' processing of insurance claims from the Holocaust period," and the GDV was designated as the representative of the German insurance industry. The Foundation was to serve as the "bank" through which reparation funds would be deposited and allocated. Within a short time, however, the optimism shared by the participants that they were well on the way to building a functioning claims-processing system along the very general parameters that had been laid down in the American-German Executive Agreement (see Article 1 (4)) and the German Foundation Law had faded away. While the Foundation had already begun carrying out its mandate to compensate slave and forced laborers and was taking applications for other crimes, it would be two years before the seemingly endless negotiations were concluded and ICHEIC began sending claims forms to the GDV for processing.

The Foundation was supposed to be the repository of the money set aside to settle valid claims against German insurance companies. But, as von Fürstenwerth reminded Eagleburger, direct reimbursement to claimants by the Foundation was prohibited by German law. Instead, von Fürstenwerth suggested, why not have ICHEIC begin passing on claims it had already received to the GDV? The GDV would facilitate settlements, he said, and then arrange for transfer of the funds from the Foundation pool and see to it that validated claimants received their awards. Eagleburger, however, would have no part of it.

Driven by his reflexive distrust of the German insurance companies, he declared that no transfer of money would take place until agreement was "reached on the outstanding issues of audits and publication of lists." It was a key sticking point that would only be settled nearly two years later.

By late March, 2001 the niceties of diplomatic communication had given way to expressions of frustration. Eagleburger conveyed his disappointment that despite his "hope and expectation…" many issues" had not been settled between ICHEIC and the GDV. In a clearly implied reproach, he informed von Fürstenwerth that ICHEIC would "…now attempt to resolve those matters directly with the Foundation."

The marriage between the Foundation and ICHEIC was such an unlikely pairing that initially it had some people worried. The man that German Chancellor Gerhard Schröder assigned to oversee the establishment of the Foundation, Otto Graf Lambsdorff, foresaw a problem over differing conceptions of what was at stake. Speaking about the negotiations between ICHEIC and the Foundation to a conference of American lawyers in Berlin in June of 2001, he stated that "they proved to be an especially arduous task to combine expectations linked to Mr. Eagleburger's ICHEIC with the Foundation. At the time, we were reasonably sure that open insurance policies written by German insurance companies and not paid or compensated after the war do not exceed DM 30 million, while the machinery set up by ICHEIC consumes a multiple of that amount with monstrous expenses still under negotiation."

The amount eventually came to a good bit more than DM 30 million. The GDV and German insurance companies paid out $102 million to validated claimants—$63 million for "real" claims on "unpaid and previously uncompensated policies" and $39.1 million as humanitarian payments. The latter covered the difference between what was owed on a policy and the minimum payment that was established by ICHEIC at the start of the process as well as compensation for "blocked accounts. But even that sum was far, far exceeded by what it cost the companies to validate the claims.)

Undoubtedly, for the three partners, ICHEIC, the Foundation and the GDV, money was definitely an issue. For its first years, ICHEIC had been underwritten from a pool funded by its member insurance companies. The amount they agreed upon, $80 million, seemed adequate at the time to cover the Commission's expenses. In early 2000, however, Eagleburger reported that he had reassessed his budget. In a memo to the companies, he wrote: "[Your] offer of $80 million is not enough on the most stringent of assumptions. We will need, at a minimum, $100 million from now to the end of the life of ICHEIC. That figure, plus what has been spent over the past year, leads me, inexorably, to a figure of $150 million."

Questions were also raised about what appeared to be ICHEIC's extravagance. Records showed that while most claim settlements made up to that point had been for amounts less than $10,000, Commission members were running up sizeable expense account bills. In 1999 alone, Neil Sher, then chief of staff of the Washington headquarters, was reimbursed for $136,653 for his first- or business-class trips to and inside Europe. Sizeable travel expenses were also incurred by state insurance regulators and members of Jewish organizations who served as ICHEIC observers. The ICHEIC leadership strongly defended the expenses. Geoffrey Fitchew, the Commission's vice chairman, was quoted as saying: "I don't think any of those who travel to these meetings regard it as some kind of holiday, because I can assure you, it is not."

In addition, Commission records revealed that although Eastgate Services, a British IT service provider, had been paid $17.6 million simply to put claims in a form so that they could be sent to the insurance companies, it routinely failed to meet deadlines. Thousands of claims lay untouched as the firm and the Commission argued about contractual and procedural issues. Pat Webber, a claims manager at the Commission's London office, criticized what she termed "inappropriate pricing" by Eastgate. After resigning from ICHEIC in the fall of 2001, she wrote a detailed memo to Eagleburger warning that "The process may very soon collapse without producing the results envisaged."

The expanding budget begged the question: was it more important to try to get as many valid claims paid out as possible, even though the administrative procedures had not been fully processed? In theory and according to the mission they had been given, every effort was to be made to have as many victims as possible file claims and get them processed completely. But there was not a bottomless barrel of funds available to satisfy proven claims.

Trouble was also brewing on another front. In a letter dated May 1, 2001, Washington State Insurance Commissioner Mike Kreidler, who succeeded Deborah Senn (regarding her role, see Chapter V, "The Accusation") that year, expressed "disappointment" that "many of the European companies" had not complied with his state's requirement that they provide his office with the names of European citizens who owned policies in effect between 1933 and 1945. Consequently, Kreidler wrote, he had posted on his department's website the names of those companies' American affiliates licensed to do business in the State. Perhaps, he added, the affiliates would "use their influence to get their parent companies to release the names of their Holocaust-era policyholders."

Kreidler's closing was rather blunt, stopping just short of directly criticizing Eagleburger's leadership:

> The introduction of Holocaust-era insurance legislation in several additional states [California and Florida] suggests a

growing loss of confidence that the ICHEIC process will be successful. I am concerned that further delays in the publication of policyholder names and the implementation of a fair appeals process will only exacerbate this crisis of confidence.

The letter stung Eagleburger so much so that the next day, he wrote a memorandum to "ICHEIC Commissioners, Alternates and Observers" explaining that he had, in the past, intervened with legislatures and courts on behalf of the companies, urging that they be given "safe harbor" because he "believed that the companies were, in fact, cooperating fully. I no longer hold that view." In fact, he said, he did not have any confidence that the companies were taking his concerns seriously, especially regarding money and adherence to his decisions. "My questions could have been answered with simple 'yes' or 'no' responses," he wrote. "Instead, I was treated to lectures and wandering disquisitions on my many errors of omission and commission. In short, I did not receive answers that I consider to be responsive to my questions. And I have long since learned that ambiguity in the ICHEIC context is a sure and certain precursor of conflict and charges of bad faith at a later date."

Kreidler was not alone in complaining about what had been achieved. In the fall of 2001, Eagleburger was called to testify before the House Government Reform Committee. The session was, at best, contentious. Rep. Henry A. Waxman, the committee's senior Democrat, was becoming increasingly concerned that the three-year-old commission was in disarray and, worse still, that of the $50 million it was on record as having spent, $40 million (80 percent) had gone for operating expenses while only $10 million (20 percent) had been awarded to claimants. As Waxman explained at the start of the hearings, his interest in the commission's work was made more poignant by requests for help he received from constituents who were either Holocaust survivors, the children of victims or deceased survivors. He said they told him that instead of receiving guidance and assistance in their individual efforts to settle their insurance claims, they were being ignored and treated disrespectfully.

The underlying animosity between Eagleburger and Waxman surfaced during one brief exchange between the two men. When Waxman asked Eagleburger about allegations of ICHEIC mismanagement and misallocation of funds, Eagleburger's answer was concise and blunt: "Frankly," he said, "that's none of your business."

In a later report to the House Committee on Government Reform in September 2003, Eagleburger gave a breakdown of the DM 550 million insurance portion of the German law establishing the Foundation. Aside from the DM 200 million for the payment of valid insurance claims involving German companies and DM 350 million for humanitarian purposes, up to $30 million from the claims fund was set aside for ICHEIC operating expenses. In the event that the DM 200 million should prove insufficient to pay all valid claims, the Foundation would provide up to a further DM 100 million to make up the shortfall.

Just what constituted the House Committee's business was one thing; what had been happening under Eagleburger's watch before—and while—he sparred with the GDV was another. In July 2002, a leading U.S. newspaper, the *Baltimore Sun*, published contents of internal commission records, many of which the paper said were stamped "Confidential." They painted a picture of disarray. The records showed that in late 1998, Eagleburger permitted Barbara Laumann, his personal business manager, to retain Triton Systems Corp., a firm in which she was a vice president, to oversee the commission's financial and business affairs. Triton had been paid "at least $1.5 million" by ICHEIC.

Karin Muenzel, an internal auditor sent over by the Swiss insurance company Winterthur, an ICHEIC member, told the *Sun* that Triton's "...accounting accuracy and efficiency of reporting..." raised very serious questions. Laumann's expertise does not seem "to be adequate to the job at hand" and the same held true for other staff members. Muenzel also pointed a stern finger directly at Eagleburger and other ICHEIC senior staff members, criticizing them for withholding financial information needed for her audit.

Eagleburger gave the article little credence and counter-attacked. He accused Muenzel of submitting an audit report that "misleads, insults and prevaricates." It did not, he said, take into consideration the need for additional outside expertise (beyond that supplied by Triton) that was necessary as the full scope of the Commission's work became clear. "When ICHEIC began," he said, "none of us had any idea that it would become the complicated nightmare that we now live with daily."

The challenges were, indeed, daunting. Six decades had passed. Not only had survivors died and national borders shifted, but insurance companies had been nationalized, changed ownership, or simply gone out of business. Many claimants were unable to produce any kind of documentation to support their claims.

According to Eagleburger and other ICHEIC staff members, delays and problems were directly attributable to the effort to meet the commission's mandate with little, if any, precedent or strategy on which to call. "It took us a year just to work out how we were going to do it," Philip Francis, chief of staff of the Commission's London office, explained. Bobby Brown, an official of the Jewish Agency for Israel, representing the State of Israel on the Commission, said ICHEIC "wasn't reinventing the wheel; it was inventing the wheel."

Intense criticism of the commission's work came not only from many of its members but from political supporters in the U.S. and Europe as well. In January 2002, Otto Graf Lambsdorff, Chancellor Schröder's special representative on Holocaust compensation, wrote to the U.S. State Department to say that the relationship of German insurers and the commission was "so entangled at this moment that they cannot make progress without our help." Even more pointedly, he accused ICHEIC of "a flagrant violation of the victims' interests" when it refused to forward claims to German insurance companies until "technical wrangles" were resolved. This referred to Eagleburger's demand that the entire DM 550 million that the Foundation had earmarked for insurance payouts be transferred to ICHEIC in advance as well as his insistence that GDV and its member companies publish complete lists of their policyholders from 1920s through the 1930s and accept ICHEIC procedures for conducting audits.

For their part, the insurance companies expressed concern that the commission would institute an open-ended processing system costing them additional millions in overhead, without a specific cutoff date. In an attempt to set parameters, the companies announced that they would not publish complete lists of Holocaust-era policies and would insist that there be limits set to ICHEIC's operating costs. To no one's surprise, the position was not greeted favorably by Jewish groups and insurance regulators in the U.S. who considered it a smokescreen that would allow the companies to use technical loopholes to avoid making payments.

So intense had the criticism of ICHEIC become that Eagleburger—then being paid $360,000 to serve as ICHEIC chairman, but saying that he was losing between $200,000 and $600,000 in income from speaking engagements or service on boards of directors that he no longer had no time for—unexpectedly resigned as chairman. Expressing frustration with the in-fighting, he walked out of a top-level meeting in January 2002, only to withdraw his resignation the next day.

Despite all the bumps on the road, the partnership with ICHEIC did eventually work out. On October 16, 2002, the Foundation, ICHEIC, and GDV came to terms on what became known as the Tripartite Agreement. The Foundation saw its way clear to send a check to meet Eagleburger's demands. ICHEIC could finally begin forwarding claims against German insurance companies to the GDV. By the summer of 2004, Eagleburger and von Fürstenwerth had shifted their focus. Could they adhere to agreed-upon deadlines for each step in the long claim-to-disposition process? If not, should they extend the established deadlines to make sure that all claims were processed thoroughly? The answer to the first question was No; to the second, Yes. Eagleburger lobbied for a new and final target date of December 31, 2005. Von Fürstenwerth replied that "the contrary interests of the various other parties involved" had to be taken into account, meaning the claimants. "Although your staff had informed us at the end of August that very few new claims would be sent to us," he wrote, "we have received another 1,488 completely new inquiries… The intended closing date will be hard to meet, if a substantial number of new claims are introduced into the process."

Several months later, in April 2005, the problem had not gone away. Instead of 1,488 new claims passed on from ICHEIC to GDV, there was a further batch of 8,800 others. This "discovery," von Fürstenwerth wrote, "puts us all in a difficult position." GDV, he wrote, needed a guarantee from Eagleburger that "there are no more outstanding claims…" As it was, he said, these claims might not be processed completely until September 2006.

So frustrated had Eagleburger become, that he ended an August 2005 letter with a humorous, perhaps sardonic, string of clichés: "Ever onward; there must be light at the end of the tunnel; this, too, shall pass; I know not what others may do, but as for me, give me liberty or give me death. These are all phrases I repeat every morning as I turn to my ICHEIC work." Within a month, any hint of humor had disappeared completely.

In a relatively scathing letter, von Fürstenwerth said that despite Eagleburger assuming "full responsibility" for the tardy claims, "this failure continues to this day. In the meantime, it is our impression that this is accompanied by almost total break-down in how claims are processed in the ICHEIC office in London." Von Fürstenwerth added that there were as many as 2,000 claims that GDV had still not received. Then, in the harshest wording that had ever been used in their dialogues, he exclaimed: "This is simply unacceptable!" After adding further concerns, he ended with, "The German Insurance Association or its member companies will not take any responsibility for the ineptitude of the ICHEIC process."

Eagleburger responded within hours and in kind: "I was shocked by your most recent message," he wrote, and then added that he would check out the allegations and get back to von Fürstenwerth in a conference call. His letter ended: "To say that I am upset with your message would be an understatement. I am, obviously, concerned at your use of the word 'ineptitude,' since, as Chairman of ICHEIC I must take that accusation personally." Then, recalling a comparison he had used before, he concluded: "Frankly, with the exception of an occasional conversation with Soviet, North Korean, and North Vietnamese officials, I haven't been talked to like this for many years."

As 2005 wound to a close, von Fürstenwerth sought to patch up his relationship with Eagleburger, writing: "It has never been my purpose to attack yourself [*sic*] and it has never been my purpose to blame you for mistakes that occurred in London. My feeling is that you were not properly informed about the practical problems... I deeply share your regret how the situation between the ICHEIC Insurance and the GDV has deteriorated, but in the closing months we must find a way to come together and complete the process in a respectable and mutually agreeable manner."

Eagleburger adopted the same tone in his response: "Your recent letter has lifted a great weight from my shoulders. I was afraid you and I would be at cross purposes... that the professional and personal relationship that you and I had built over the past years was in jeopardy. Your very kind letter removed all of those fears."

The relationship had been repaired. The two could—and would—continue to work together. They would have to. The December 31, 2005, deadline had been pushed back once more. As they entered 2006, ICHEIC and GDV were again partners.

Over the years, the Chairman said ICHEIC had concluded arrangements with several other partner organizations from countries other than Germany.

One was through the SJOA Foundation in the Netherlands, which signed onto the MOU in May 2000 on behalf of insurance companies in the Netherlands, putting up $7.5 million. They all undertook to follow ICHEIC guidelines in evaluating claims against Dutch companies.

In the summer of 2000, ICHEIC and representatives of the World Jewish Restitution Organization (WJRO) signed a separate agreement with ICHEIC member Generali (Assicurazioni Generali SpA). Under the agreement, Generali committed $100 million to settle insurance claims from policyholders, most of them Jews from Eastern Europe. Prior to a 2007 settlement of the last major class action suit against Generali, it had paid out about $135 million in Holocaust-era insurance claims, mostly through ICHEIC, including claims from Israel, France, Austria, Belgium, and Greece that it paid off independently. Under the 2007 settlement reached in New York Federal District Court, it agreed to pay an additional $35 million.

The deal that Generali reached with ICHEIC and the WJRO in 2000 had established a separate, Israel-based entity in order to pay off claims, "The Foundation in Memory of the Generali Insured in Eastern and Central Europe Who Perished in the Holocaust" ("GTF"). Technically, Generali itself was no longer involved in the handling of claims, and this specific task was left to the Generali Foundation, which undertook to employ ICHEIC standards of proof in processing all valid Holocaust-era insurance claims against Generali and its subsidiaries that ICHEIC may pass on to it. Excepted were claims against subsidiaries in Germany and the Netherlands, which were processed in accordance with other agreements. Generali's German subsidiaries, *Aachener und Münchener Versicherungsgesellschaft* and *Volksfürsorge*, as members of the GDV, were covered under the Trilateral Agreement.

The initial $100 million pledged to ICHEIC for compensation was in addition to funds Generali already had committed to ICHEIC under the MOU. Generali also undertook to make public the names of policyholders who had never been paid and who may have perished in the Holocaust. This promise was carried out only in part, and ICHEIC subsequently became disillusioned with the way the Generali Foundation was processing claims assigned to it. Beginning in 2005, all claims were referred directly to the company's head office in Trieste.

That's where the situation stood in March 2007 when New York District Court Judge George Daniels issued an order approving the settlement in a class action suit brought by disappointed Generali claimants. The judge told them that "the settlement is not perfect, but it may their only real opportunity for any monetary recovery." It extended the deadline for filing new claims against Generali until August 2008 to allow plaintiffs an opportunity to examine the recently opened archives at the International Red Cross's Tracing Service at Bad Arolsen. Generali said it had received 3,300 more claims just while the court case was pending, and a lawyer for the plaintiffs, Robert Swift, estimated that they would cost the company an additional $10 million.

Acknowledged to be the fourth largest insurance conglomerate in Europe, Generali paid out more to Holocaust victims than any other single European insurance company.

In April 2003, three of the ICHEIC member companies, the Swiss Winterthur and Zurich and the French, AXA (collectively referred to as "AWZ"), established a separate fund to cover their non-German portfolios. The AWZ Agreement added $17.5 million to the funds available to ICHEIC for claims payments and humanitarian initiatives.

In July 2003 ICHEIC reached an agreement with the Indemnification Commission of the Belgian Jewish Community (the "Buysse Commission"). It stipulated that all ICHEIC claims that name a Belgian company, including claims on MOU companies and any unnamed claims stating Belgium as the country of issue, are to be examined and, if valid, paid by the Buysse Commission.

Through the Austrian General Settlement Fund for Victims of National Socialism ("GSF") established in early 2001, the Austrian Government and Austrian companies together provided $210 million for various categories of restitution, $25 million of which was earmarked specifically for insurance. Under an operational agreement with ICHEIC similar to the one concluded with Belgium, ICHEIC was supposed to pass on to the GSF those claims that named an Austrian insurance company or indicate Austria as the place where the policy was issued.

In France, under an arrangement with the Commission for Victims of Anti-Semitic Legislation in Force during the Occupation ("CIVS"), individuals could submit claims to designated Jewish organizations which, with assistance from ICHEIC, would work to try to match claims with French insurance companies' policyholder lists or payments into blocked accounts. If a match was found, and the claim was valid, the company in question paid on the claim.

As its first order of business in 1998, ICHEIC had launched a global outreach program aimed at informing everyone who might have an insurance claim of the possibility of seeing it paid. The $10 million campaign included newspaper ads in a number of languages, with emphasis, of course, on Jewish papers, telling people how they could file a claim, as well as informing them of toll-free phone numbers in different countries where callers could have their questions answered in nine languages. Many respondents simply expressed interest in learning further details, and Chairman Eagleburger has admitted that the response in terms of number and value of the claims fell short of what had been anticipated. Only about 15,000 respondents could identify a relative that they thought had a policy and some could even give the name of the company, but by and large, the publicity did not yield a large number of claims, and most of the calls were just requests for information.

In addition to its initial advertising, ICHEIC tried to get the insurance companies to provide lists of policyholders in the hope that name recognition would jog people's interest. In the beginning, the companies flatly refused to comply, citing national laws governing privacy. They also feared that claims lawyers would mine the lists for potential clients. The Jewish organizations in ICHEIC were nevertheless particularly insistent on this point.

There was also an added complication. ICHEIC and GDV had agreed that closure would be the final goal of the multi-year project. Reaching that goal was another matter, and, over time, Eagleburger and von Fürstenwerth seemed out of synch. Eagleburger was not shy about stating his position. He asked the companies to release the names of all policyholders from the Holocaust era. It would speed up the process, he argued. Left unsaid was his concern that some companies, in an effort to limit the perception of their culpability and the size of their "contribution" to the reparations pool, would deliberately omit the names of non-claiming policyholders. And, not unexpectedly, ICHEIC-member companies also resisted the idea of publishing lists, arguing that such a release would place an additional tax on their budgets and resources, and would create an open-ended process with no specific cut-off date. They argued that it would mean that full closure might never be achieved. Taken at face value, each position had its merits. In the end, neither party got exactly what it wanted.

The publication of lists of potential German Jewish policyholders became a key element of the October 2002 agreement among ICHEIC, the GDV and the German Foundation.. First, the parties worked to compile a list of Jewish residents from German federal and state archives. No such list existed, and it was only thanks to the German insurance compensation process that the project got off the ground. In the course of this effort, ICHEIC has compiled what Eagleburger called the most comprehensive lists of pre-Holocaust Jews in Germany and Italy. While admittedly not the Commission's primary goal, he cited this in his Congressional testimony as a welcome byproduct that stands as a lasting tribute to the memory of those who suffered under Nazi persecution.

Given the ravages of war, the passage of more than sixty years as well as the destruction of documents in the ordinary course of business, he said the list in and of itself is a remarkable achievement.

This list was then matched against German companies' digital archives of policyholders. In a note of caution, however, Eagleburger noted that although ICHEIC made this extensive list public on its website, only a small number of the policies remained unpaid. He stressed that just because a name appears on the website, it did not necessarily follow that the heir or beneficiary was entitled to any payment. Many of the policies had been compensated previously through restitution programs or by the companies directly. "Why have we chosen to include such policies?" he asked rhetorically. "First, in the interest of time, ICHEIC elected to publish all the names to enable potential beneficiaries to come forth before investigating the details of the policy. Had we insisted on researching the fate of each and every one of these policies, we would never have been able to publish any lists. Rather than delay the process further and risk the loss of what living memory remains, ICHEIC chose to publish and run the risk of raising greater expectations than we can hope to meet."

He said the combined lists of 519,009 policyholder names became available to ICHEIC thanks to the research conducted by its member companies and its own extensive research in independent archives in several European countries. The privacy concerns which had prevented the companies from publishing the names of policyholders from the prewar period were eased in 2003, when the German Bundestag adopted an amendment to the Archives Law that would permit wider access to the personal records of victims of Nazi persecution.

For the German market, BaFin, the German financial supervisory authority, handed over to ICHEIC 363,000 names, and they were duly posted on the Commission's website. The list was generated by taking the names of the 499,000 "Jews by belief" as they were called in the 1933 census and seeing if they appear among the more than nine million life insurance policies sold to the general public in Germany before World War II and which were now available in electronic format.

This matching process entailed entering the names of known Jews and policyholders and then trying to find matches. There were all sorts of variables.

There were different spellings of the same name, mistakes made in transcribing information from frayed, crumbling paper records, dates of birth were sometimes missing or garbled. A 40-page report describing the methodology gave an example of how one woman, whose married name was Strauss, was listed under six aliases, all variations of her very common Jewish name of Hannah. Hanchen, Hana, Hanah, Hani, Hane and Iohana Strauss all shared the same birth date, the third of February 1904. The computer then had to figure out which, if any, also appeared among the policyholders whose names were provided by BaFin and the member companies of the GDV. What if there was no perfect match? The statisticians who conducted the search devised a system in which they assigned a number to indicate the degree of correspondence. A perfect scored for all six categories of correspondence would be zero. For example, if the last names were spelled identically, the card would get a zero. If merely close, it would get a one. If only similar, it would be awarded a two.

Birthdates, when known, were particularly significant.

Eagleburger on more than one occasion has said that ICHEIC was created as a means of addressing the gaps and shortfalls of the German restitution program of the 1950s, 1960s, and 1970s. Under the agreement between ICHEIC, the GDV and the Foundation, claims which had been compensated under the restitution program were not eligible, although it was agreed that the companies "would not search too diligently" for earlier restitution. As he saw it, after the restitution program concluded its acceptance of new claims in 1969, a deadline that was then extended till the mid-1990s, ICHEIC was the first organization to offer Holocaust victims and their heirs an avenue to pursue claims against an insurance company other than litigation, and one that was at no cost. It was intended to give them an opportunity to submit claims for the first time, and here the emphasis is on "first time." It also applied to markets outside of Germany, addressing people who had not qualified for Germany's restitution program.

In the end, over 100,000 claims forms were filed with ICHEIC. More than 40,000 were immediately eliminated as being outside its jurisdictional scope, i.e., they dealt with bank accounts, slave labor compensation, etc. The remaining 60,000 were passed on to the insurance companies. For the German market, a total of 19,421 were referred to the GDV.

It was one thing to get everyone on board the ICHEIC train. It was quite another to carry out its mission. Insurance companies are totally dependent on their filing systems. That was as true 70 years ago, when everything was filed in manila folders and stashed away on shelves, as it is today, when most of the information is stored on computer disks. While many of the companies in Germany managed to reconstruct their liabilities from available secondary sources, gaps remained. What does an insurance company do when its files are discarded in the normal course of business or irrevocably lost because of acts of war? Here, the German government stepped in; if a claim was lodged that the company considered legitimate, the equalization funds kicked in to see that the beneficiary was paid.

As was to be expected, the condition of the archives varied considerably from one company to another. In order for the operation to be credible, the companies had to establish standards and benchmarks to ensure that claims could be handled fairly and expeditiously. Five standards were agreed upon and had to be verified by independent audits. They were:

- A company "family tree" that would lay out all the mergers and portfolio transfers during the period under review;
- Securing and organizing relevant archives;
- Collating company records of policies in force between 1920 and 1945;
- Entering them in an accessible database;
- Designing a "work flow" pattern to deal with incoming inquiries.

There was considerable discussion among U.S. regulators and representatives of the Jewish partner organizations partners whether the reports by independent auditors indicated sufficient compliance. In the end, ICHEIC gave them a stamp of approval, after another set of "peer-review audits" conducted by auditors selected by the ICHEIC administration.

With all the goodwill in the world, the process of searching for unpaid insurance policies became a bureaucratic nightmare. There are no generally accepted formats. Databases did not talk to each other. The prewar insurance contracts were all in paper files. A claim received by ICHEIC had to run a gantlet of tests before it could reach the finish line and qualify for payment or denial.

A claim that named a particular German insurance company was first sent to the German Insurance Association, the GDV, which passed it on to the Central Archive of the Bundesentstschadigungsgestz (the BEG) to see whether anyone by that name had ever received compensation back in the 1950s or 1960s, and if so, in which West German state (there were 11 of them). According to the rules of ICHEIC, a policy for which compensation had already been paid was no longer eligible for further payment. If it was established that compensation had been paid on the policy, the state archive notified the GDV, which informed the company. It was the company that then denied the claim.

If there was no evidence that compensation for insurance was ever paid, the state archive informed the GDV, which notified the company, which then, employing ICHEIC's relaxed standards of proof, had to establish whether a policy in fact had existed and whether it remained unpaid. If it indeed determined that it had never been paid, the company calculated the compensation it should offer the claimant based on a scale agreed between ICHEIC, the Foundation, and the GDV.

The GDV's final analysis of processed claims found that, given the limited research options agreed to between ICHEIC, the Foundation, and the GDV, prior compensation could be traced in around 35 percent of the policies for which claims were lodged with ICHEIC. The analysis attributed the statistical difference to inconsistencies between what claimants for BEG restitution had said and what their children and grandchildren reported when they filed again for compensation 40 to 50 years later through the ICHEIC program.

One of the principal difficulties in determining the facts is that BEG files are alphabetized only under the name and date of birth of the person who submitted the claim for compensation during the proceedings in the 1950s, 1960s and 1970s, i.e., 30 to 50 years prior to the submission of the ICHEIC claims, not the name of the policyholder. Claims submitted through ICHEIC of course refer to the policyholder by name. Also, by the turn of the millennium, claimants often did not remember the birthdates of their grandparents or the exact names of other relatives.

Let's say the claim was not paid off under restitution. It went back to the company which checked, to the extent it could, if it had been surrendered or if premiums were paid. Assuming that it was truly an unpaid policy in good standing, the company made an offer, which the claimant could accept or file an appeal. If the claim from ICHEIC did not name a specific company or was not sure, the GDV sent it to the 67 of its member companies who were in business then, and each one was expected to search its archives for a match to one of the up to 30 persons the claimant may have named as the policyholder. If none was found, the claim was referred back to ICHEIC. Legally, life insurance contracts have to be archived for only 10 years after they were paid out or otherwise terminated. Someone who lodged a claim for a policy today may find that the company has no record of it because the beneficiaries had received some compensation from the BEG, and the record of the policy was removed from the company archives. Since the BEG compensation was based on information provided by the companies in the 1950s and 1960s, for some companies, this correspondence is the only record they may have about the policy.

BEG's files have been collecting dust since the restitution program formally wound up in the 1980s, although restitution payments are still being made for pensions and other long-term obligations. A suggestion at the time to computerize the files was dismissed as too expensive for all the good it would do. The files are stacked in crumbling, brown manila envelopes, and the understaffed federal and 11 state offices understandably do not move very fast.

However, once a claim was found to be eligible for compensation under the agreed guidelines, an interesting element entered the picture. The money that the company mentioned in its offer did not come out of its own pocket but was drawn from the DM 550 million already transferred from the companies via the German Foundation to ICHEIC. The companies themselves were no longer individually liable for the payouts and therefore, in the case of Holocaust-era claims, were no longer in an adversarial position towards the policyholders.

I visited the Cologne headquarters of AXA-Colonia and of Victoria in Düsseldorf to see how the process worked. Colonia is today the German subsidiary of the French company AXA, while Victoria is a German company which did a great deal of its pre-World War II business in the countries of Central and Eastern Europe. What I found particularly interesting were signs that a culture has built up in the claims settling process of leaning over backwards to see that applicants get what is due them. After all the ugly public haggling that preceded the establishment of the German Foundation, it was interesting to see that the high moral tone that had been set by German industry when it was trying to raise money for the Foundation seems to have taken root among the dozens of clerks assigned to verifying the thousands of claims that each company got to check. It was they who had to piece together the evidence from the actual frayed remnants of 70-year-old documents inscribed in gothic script, and, on the basis of what they found, decide whether to make an offer of payment. The young Germans doing the work seemed to revel in the opportunity of being on the right side of history.

The AXA people gave me a typical file plucked at random from the stack that had gone through the process. It was more than an inch thick. The claim filed with ICHEIC was signed by Lore Hirsch from a little town in New Jersey. She was asking about an insurance policy taken out by her father, Paul N. Stern, for the benefit of his wife, Amelie. Paul Stern was born in Frankfurt/Main on September 17, 1889, and Amelie six years later, also in Frankfurt/Main, where Ms. Hirsch was born in 1921.

In the application she filed in July 2000, Ms. Hirsch did not know who had issued the policy or its number, how much it was for and in which currency it was denominated, how much the premiums were nor when it was issued. She believed that the premiums were paid until her father fled Germany to Brussels in 1935, and then, one step ahead of the German army, to Vichy France in 1940. The Gestapo got onto him, and he spent some time in the St. Cyprien concentration camp before being released under house arrest. Somehow, the three got visas to the United States from the American Consulate in Toulouse and bribed their way though Spain to Lisbon, where they boarded a ship to New York.

Although both her parents managed to get to the United States in 1940, before America entered the war, Ms. Hirsch answered yes to the question on the ICHEIC questionnaire if they had been victims of the Holocaust. Among other beneficiaries, she listed a brother, Kurt Stern, who lived in New York City.

AXA's files survived the war fairly well. Dr. Udo Bertermann of AXA said the company had several kilometers of shelves with paper files arranged in numerical order going back more than 80 years. While they did not have the contracts themselves, they did find two name cards and a file relating to Paul Stern in the archives of Colonia's predecessor company, North Star Life Insurance (Nordstern Lebensversicherung). The cards gave the policyholder's name, date of birth and the numbers of two policies. One was for RM 25,000 taken out in 1916. And here the hyper inflation of the mid-1920s entered the picture. In a convoluted exercise to preserve the value of the policies, all outstanding contracts were legally revalued and reissued in 1924. Mr. Stern's policy, the second number listed, was now worth 688 new Reichsmarks, payable on his death or on February 14, 1975. The policy was converted to paid up status after Mr. Stern fled Germany in 1935.

In the letter to Ms. Hirsch, the company said that based on available documents "we assume that the benefits of the policy were never paid out." The "available documentation," in this case provided by the BEG authorities, was more than 150 pages of correspondence recording efforts to determine whether anything had ever been borrowed from the policy or whether Mr. Stern or his heirs had ever received any money under the restitution program. Well, it turned out that Mr. Stern and his wife in fact had. In 1954, they had filed separately for restitution for loss of possessions, loss of earning power and deprivation of liberty. Altogether, they received over DM 50,000, and Mrs. Stern, a DM 335 monthly pension. Originally, they both had applied too late, and her pension was approved only in 1961, six years after he had died.)

This painstaking search of the BEG archives took the better part of a year. While it makes for fascinating reading, none of the voluminous, back and forth correspondence between Colonia and the various restitution offices indicated any restitution for insurance, and Colonia went on to the final step in the process, the involved calculations to determine how much the policy was worth today. This entailed establishing what it would have been worth in 1969, when the BEG program was still in operation. The offer sent out to Mrs. Hirsch had to take into account the currency reform of 1948, when 10 Reichsmarks was now worth one deutschemark, then multiply that figure by eight to bring the value up to the year 2000, and then add the interest that accrued until the offer was sent out. The letter to Ms. Hirsch said she was entitled to 664 euros (about $820).

However, another consideration had to be factored in. After all the explanations, the company letter said that all that was unimportant, since under the agreement between the German Foundation, ICHEIC and the GDV, payment on any policy to a Holocaust survivor is set at a minimum of $4000.

That's the amount offered to Ms. Hirsch and her brother Kurt, which they accepted. In a power of attorney, Kurt Stern assigned his share to his sister, and the GDV sent her a check for $4000. The 664 euros were deducted from Foundation Claims Fund and the difference to top it up to $4000 came from the Humanitarian Fund. Of course, the distinction between the two sums made no difference to Ms. Hirsch, of course, but for the insurance companies it was important to show that the amount owed on unsettled claims was low, while at the same time, the Jewish organizations had an interest in keeping outlays from the Humanitarian Fund down to a minimum. Whatever remained of the Humanitarian Fund was supposed to revert to them to use at their own discretion.

This was one of the searches that ended in what passes for success in the business of tracking down policyholders. Dr. Bertermann showed me statistics that made Ms. Hirsch's case appear as something of a rarity. Prior to December 2006, ICHEIC had passed on more than 33,800 named and unnamed claims to AXA-Germany, and the company had tried to match up all of them. After applying the relaxed standards of proof in favor of the claimant, 1,531 claimants were sent letters offering a settlement.

Victoria, founded in Berlin in 1853 as Allgemeine Eisen-bahn-Versicherungsgesellschaft, is the grande dame of German insurance companies. Its archives of insurance contracts were totally destroyed by the Allied bombing of Berlin in February 1945. All that survived were a number of large ledgers, 30 by 14 inches, with entries that listed policy numbers, where and when they were written and for how much. One thing was missing. The ledgers did not name the policyholders.

These ledgers, added to information from secondary sources, were the main sources of information on insurance policies written in the prewar period. By sheer chance, in the late 1980s,

40 boxes of correspondence dealing with postwar activities materialized from some forgotten corner of a storeroom. Downloading the material into an electronic data base, researchers found references to 26,000 former policyholders and the beneficiaries. A further study turned up information about more than 1,200 restitution proceedings in the framework of the BEG and other German restitution or compensation procedures after 1945. Another resource was the *Vermögensverzeichnisse*, the property and asset declaration that every Austrian Jew had to make in 1938 and which is stored today in the Austrian State archive in Vienna.

To this must be added the data that Victoria was able to obtain from ICHEIC following the research it conducted in various archives all over Europe. All told, Victoria's database now contains the names of 110,000 owners of prewar life insurance policies, though it cannot ascertain which were owned by Jews.

After observing the sheer mountain of paperwork involved in verifying insurance claims from more than half-a-century ago, I asked if anyone had any idea of how cumbersome, time consuming and expensive the process was going to be when they acquiesced in the ICHEIC process? One official from Allianz said much of it derived from the companies' need to assert their innocence. He said the companies constantly had to prove beyond the shadow of a doubt that they had not expropriated the policyholders' cash, and that they were not still sitting on the money. "They were prepared to go through 20 or 30 separate steps to prove that the case had been settled properly, even if it cost ten times what it would have cost to simply pay what was being asked. German, Italian, French, Belgian, Dutch companies take particular exception to the accusation that they intentionally defrauded, and they will go a long way to prove their case," he added.

"On the other side," he goes on, "you have an ICHEIC that says it has to install every kind of control and oversight to make sure the companies are not cheating. There are audits, verification procedures and monitoring committees that review every decision of every German company." ICHEIC member companies were subjected to the Commission's own rigorous audit procedures, while ten of GDV's members were audited by BaFin, the German government's regulatory agency, overseen by two Israeli auditors representing ICHEIC. "Basically," the official said, "ICHEIC does not trust the insurance companies, or for that matter, any of the big five international auditing companies. It says that they are in any case on the companies' payrolls and insisted that its own auditors review the original audit to see that it was done properly."

On top of that, there were the appeals panels. Every offer sent to a claimant contained the standard line that if he or she was dissatisfied with the offer, it could be appealed, at no cost, to either the ICHEIC Tribunal for cases involving companies that are signatories to the MOU, or to the Appeals Panel, which dealt with claims submitted under the Trilateral Agreement, meaning that they involved GDV member companies. As it worked out, the only member of ICHEIC which was not covered in some way under the Trilateral Agreement was Generali, and the Tribunal dealt principally with appeals against Generali. For reasons of economy, the Tribunal and the Panel were located in ICHEIC's London office.

The Appeals Panel consisted of three judges selected by the Foundation and ICHEIC. According to the guidelines, "every Panel member shall be and remain impartial and independent of the parties in each appeal to which he or she is appointed." They were chosen for their "impartiality, availability, expertise, and language skills." Another consideration was "the attendant costs associated with the nomination." This later became an issue, when some of the members of ICHEIC complained about the slow pace of the appeals decisions and the healthy salaries the judges were drawing for what was turning out to be very part-time work.

At the beginning, there was disagreement over the makeup of an Appeals Panel. The GDV recommended that one panelist be appointed by the Foundation, one by a German Jewish organization, and one by an international Jewish organization. ICHEIC agreed on the Foundation appointment, but wanted to select the other two panelists itself, arguing that "the key requirements are the experience, integrity and independence of the panelists, and not that they should represent particular constituencies."

After the full Panel had handed down a body of judgments that could serve as reliable precedents, it was empowered to transfer cases to a single member of the Panel or to a pool of arbiters that had been selected. Although a claimant could request an oral hearing, very few were prepared to undertake the trip to London, and decisions were generally based on written submissions. From the time of submission to the final decision could take as long as six months.

The Tribunal and the Panel published quarterly reports summing up what they had done. As with all the papers connected with the insurance claims process, the actual names of the persons involved are not divulged, and the reports dealt only in statistics. As they were published on the ICHEIC website, they were listed under an arbitrary number, with anything that might identify the claimant or the company involved redacted out.

The Tribunal heard 1,257 appeals and allowed 281 in which the company was found to have erred in calculating the payment due. Awards in excess of what the company had offered came to almost $5 million. Another 880 appeals were dismissed and 96 were withdrawn before a verdict was handed down, usually because the company had revised its offer. The Panel, which dealt solely with German companies, heard 952 appeals and allowed 103, just over 10 percent, awarding claimants an additional $1.25 million. It dismissed 771 appeals, and 80 were withdrawn before a verdict.

In its comment summing up the process, ICHEIC made a point of emphasizing how conscientiously the companies had followed the payment guidelines, as shown by the small size of the awards, just over $6 million, when compared to the overall total of $306 million that was dispensed.

Chapter VII

Conclusion

After years of struggling to achieve a just solution to a vexing issue, what was the real outcome of the process to close the books on Holocaust-era insurance policies? Did ICHEIC succeed in its basic mission of providing some measure of restitution to people who had been scarred by the atrocity of the Holocaust? Given the enormity of what had happened, the answer is a qualified yes.

It certainly had an inauspicious beginning. In the wake of the Swiss banking scandal, the insurance companies were singled out as the next target in a high-profile witch hunt seeking billions of dollars from European firms tarred with the Nazi brush. ICHEIC was established in an effort to obtain the cooperation of the insurance companies in tracking down unpaid policies without resorting to the courts and at no cost to the claimant. In return, the companies were promised a "safe haven" from class action lawsuits and threats of regulatory sanctions. After a difficult start, threats and legal and legislative maneuvers, it succeeded in achieving thousands of amicable settlements between companies and claimants and generally getting the issue of Holocaust-era insurance off the front pages.

Dealings with companies whose prewar clientele lived in Western Europe went the smoothest. Not surprisingly, much of the attention was focused on ICHEIC's partnership arrangement with the German Insurance Association (the GDV) and the German Foundation "Remembrance, Responsibility, and Future."

Separate arrangements covered Swiss, French, Dutch, Belgian and Austrian companies. Problems still remained, however, with firms that had sold life insurance primarily in Eastern Europe, notably the Italian insurance conglomerate, Generali (Assicurazioni Generali SpA).

One of ICHEIC's founding organizations, the American National Association of Insurance Commissioners (NAIC), wrote a glowing account of what had been accomplished. In a report summing up the nine-year operation, Diane Koken, former insurance commissioner of the State of Pennsylvania, wrote that she was "particularly gratified by the results of ICHEIC's archival investigations and matching processes." She said they had led to awards on thousands of Holocaust-era insurance policies which would otherwise never have been identified. Prior to the establishment of ICHEIC, the NAIC had been one of the most outspoken critics of the European insurance companies and initially had wanted to exclude them from membership on the commission. (See Chapter V, "The Accusation").

As the Holocaust-era insurance compensation process wound down, charts published by ICHEIC and the GDV tell the story of what was achieved in quantitative terms. What they do not reflect are the hundreds of thousands of hours of painstaking research that went into compiling these numbers or the efforts of hundreds of dedicated clerks in Germany who took on the search as their contribution to the country's collective atonement for Nazi crimes, complementing the previous compensation programs of the 1950s, 1960s, and 1970s. They also say little about the recipients themselves, aside from the impersonal statistical reports of where so many thousands live today, where they were born, their sex and their age bracket.

From the beginning of 2003 to the end of 2006, compensation claims for the German market, meaning policies issued to persons living inside the boundaries of the Third Reich as they existed in 1937, were forwarded by ICHEIC to the GDV for processing. This entailed a cumbersome and complicated search through crumbling paper files and rolls of microfiche, trying to discover from the restitution archives whether a policy had ever existed and whether compensation had ever been paid for a policy in the Federal Republic's restitution programs.

As far as the GDV was concerned, the nearly 20,0000 claims identified by ICHEIC referred either to a specific German insurance company, so-called Named Claims, or Unnamed Claims, which included a reference to Germany in its 1937 borders but did not name a particular company. The 16,200 Unnamed Claims were of course the most difficult to track down. They had to be circulated to all 67 GDV member companies who had insurance portfolios prior to 1945 with the request that they search their archives for any hint of a "contractual relationship" between the persons named by the claimant and the company. Each possible match was reported to GDV, and it then became a Named Claim. By the end of the process, the German companies had checked their records for more than 86,000 names of potential policyholders. Of these, 15,800 were from the 3200 named claims and 70,400 from the 16,200 Unnamed Claims. All in all, 11,400 policies were compensated, over 3800 of them blocked account cases. The average compensation payment for each policy was just under $9000. Of the 92,000 eligible claims ICHEIC received, two thirds, or more then 60,000, fell into the unnamed category.

For policies issued in Germany, eligible claims from survivors received a minimum payment of 4000, regardless of the amount of the original policy. All other eligible claimants received at least $3000. For policies issued in Eastern Europe, if the claim was less than $100, the minimum payment was set at $500; if above $100, the minimum payment was $2000 for survivors and $1000 for heirs. In a few rare cases, persons who submitted claims on more than one policy received benefits of more than a million dollars.

ICHEIC and all its members—the U.S. insurance regulators, the Jewish organizations, the State of Israel, the GDV and the European insurance companies maintain that the settlements are fair and reasonable.

ICHEIC also instituted an appeals procedure based in London for cases involving GDV companies. Its mandate was to review, again at no cost, the documents filed by a claimant regarding a company's decision. In the end, fewer than 1,000 appeals were filed, with over 100 awards rendered in favor of the claimant, totaling $1.24 million. Only 11 percent of the appeals reversed a company decision. A similar system dealt with appeals against offers made by other ICHEIC member companies. It heard 1,257 appeals and allowed 281 in which the company was found to have erred in calculating the payment due. Awards in excess of what the company had offered came to almost $5 million.

Summing up what it had accomplished during the nine years of its existence, ICHEIC reported that the total compensation amount offered was over $306 million. The money went to more than 48,000 Holocaust survivors and their heirs. In addition $170 million was committed to a variety of humanitarian programs that would benefit survivors worldwide

Speaking at the Commission's concluding meeting in Washington in March 2007, Chairman Lawrence Eagleburger declared that, "while no amount of compensation can redress the suffering inflicted by the Holocaust; I believe that ICHEIC has achieved its goal of bringing a small measure of justice to those who have been denied it for so long."

GDV's CEO, Dr. Jörg Freiherr Frank von Fürstenwerth, struck a similar note. "It was a long process to get here today, and we had all hoped to complete it much sooner. As we come to the end of ICHEIC, we can only hope we have finally addressed all unresolved Holocaust-era insurance policies."

This spirit of achievement was also reflected in a joint declaration by ICHEIC, the German Foundation and the GDV acknowledging the successful completion of the agreement they had signed in October 2002. It affirmed that:

> • "ICHEIC's comprehensive process regarding compensation of individually unpaid or confiscated and previously uncompensated insurance policies from the Holocaust-era issued by German insurance companies has been successfully and properly completed,
> • "Based on the GDV's attestation, German insurance companies have fulfilled all their obligations established by the agreement and are deserving of an all-embracing and enduring legal, regulatory, legislative, and administrative peace, and,
> • "In recognition of the above, the remaining funds originally allocated for the compensation of claims may now

and henceforth be used by ICHEIC at its discretion for generic humanitarian purposes."

It was inevitable that ICHEIC would be left with cash on hand. If, at the outset, there were concerns that claims would add up to far more than the money set aside, as claims processing went on, it became increasingly clear that millions of dollars would be left over. Chairman Eagleburger estimated there would be between $10.6 million and $14 million in the till when ICHEIC formally closed down in March 2007. After canvassing all the members of ICHEIC, he came up with a formula for distributing the residual funds that he hoped would satisfy both those who thought it should all go to assisting needy survivors, and those who wanted a share to go towards Jewish organizational and educational activities.

After confessing that no clear consensus had emerged from his informal poll, he said he would follow the pattern of how the Jewish world over the years has generally allocated funds reclaimed from Holocaust-related assets. This meant, he said, that 80 percent would go to the Claims Conference for the care of survivors, and 20 percent would be divided equally between Yad Vashem and Jewish Agency Holocaust-related education programs. ICHEIC would retain oversight over how the money was spent. In addition, he said, $6 million was earmarked as a contingency fund if more valid claims turn up. He believed that much of this money as well will probably become available for distribution.

The sense of accomplishment expressed by ICHEIC and other parties involved was not universally shared. A bill was introduced in the U.S. Congress after the formal conclusion of the compensation process that would turn the clock back to the time when billions of dollars were believed to be locked up in uncompensated Holocaust-era insurance. A Florida Congresswoman, Ileana Ros-Lehtinen, said her bill would give what she calls "forgotten [Holocaust] survivors" the right to sue insurance companies in U.S. federal courts. She and her supporters maintain that despite the efforts of "international bureaucrats," presumably a reference to the ICHEIC leadership and staff, thousands of survivors have actually been prevented from receiving insurance benefits that are their due. Her "Holocaust Insurance Accountability Act of 2007" maintains that "Holocaust-era insurance companies continue to withhold names of owners and beneficiaries of thousands of insurance policies sold to Jewish customers (before) World War II." She estimates the 2006 value of unpaid insurance policies "at between $17 billion and $200 billion."

Ros-Lehtinen based her case in part on the fact that the vast Nazi-era archives at Bad Arolsen, Germany, have been closed to researchers for the past 60 years. The International Tracing Service of the Red Cross, which maintains oversight over the papers, announced in June 2007 that the archive would finally be opened to scholars, albeit with some limitations.

ICHEIC had earlier dismissed the Bad Arolsen archives as largely irrelevant to its own quest for records bearing on Holocaust-era insurance policies. It said that while the 50 million file cards have information on more than 17 million victims of the Nazis, they "do not assist with determining policy details other than health insurance or social security information, categories of claims that are not eligible under the ICHEIC process."

Shortly after Congresswoman Ros-Lehtinen's initiative became public, a one-time ICHEIC appeals arbitrator alleged that a "phantom rule" applied by other ICHEIC arbitrators resulted in the denial of an astounding 84 percent of all claims filed. The former ICHEIC official and New York State insurance superintendent, Albert L. Lewis, called for a reopening of these cases. Using the approach advocated by Ros-Lehtinen, he urged that survivors and heirs be able to press claims in the courts, and suggested that the National Association of Insurance Commissioners become involved. Lewis said that under the alleged "phantom rule," in the absence of an actual policy, the burden of proof rested on the claimant. He said this is certainly not according to the "relaxed standards of proof" that ICHEIC boasted about.

ICHEIC, which has praised the appeals process for its dedicated approach, dismissed the allegation as totally unfounded.

Despite nearly a decade of close cooperation with ICHEIC, the German insurance companies do not rule out the possibility that additional claims against them may yet surface elsewhere. To deal with such a contingency, the GDV has issued a statement that should the need arise, their offices would be open to potential claimants for the filing of all documents. Claims deemed to be justified would be paid by the companies themselves, an not from German Foundation funds.

Chapter VIII

Epilogue

The statistics put out about the numbers of people who received compensation for Holocaust-era insurance policies are impressive. They tell the story in terms of quantities, of numbers, amounts, where so many thousands live today, where they were born, their sex and their age bracket. The question they do not answer is, how did the claimants accept the outcome, and whether they were satisfied with the compensation they received after so many years of waiting and of uncertain expectations? Here are the stories of a few of them.

Henry David Mendelson's experience with the ICHEIC process was typical of most of the claims for Holocaust-era insurance compensation. That he was still around to undertake it was remarkable. He had been born in Germany in 1929 and managed to get out with his little sister, in one of the kindertransporten to Great Britain in 1938. Their parents remained behind.

Then, just three days before war broke out, the parents, who had valid visas to the United States in their pockets and sensing that time was running out, boarded a train from Hamburg to the Netherlands, where they caught the last ferry to England before hostilities interrupted the channel service. They each carried a suitcase. The rest of their worldly goods were left on the dock in Hamburg, waiting to be shipped to the U.S.

Eventually, all four ended up in Australia, where Mendelson built a business and had a family of his own. One day, his brother-in-law, who receives a pension from Austria, spotted a restitution notice on the Internet that talked about lapsed insurance policies in the names of parents or grandparents. It was from the International Commission on Holocaust Era Insurance Claims.

Mendelson wrote away for an application form. He found he could supply very little of the information the 13 pages asked for, just the stark details of where and when his mother's father, Siegfried Samuel Cohnreich, was born in the northern German province of Pomerania on January 12, 1867—and, thanks to Nazi punctiliousness, where and when he died. He remembered the grandfather well as an amiable, cigar smoking general practitioner who made his house calls riding a motor bike through the streets of the little Silesian town of Görlitz (later in East Germany). When it came to the kind of insurance policy his grandfather may have had, how large it was or who had issued it, what the premium was and if it had been paid, he could only say that he did not know.

What he could state was that Siegfried Cohnreich was barred from practicing medicine in Görlitz in 1938 and had to move to Berlin, where he eked out a living treating Jewish patients in the privacy of his apartment. On December 15, 1942, he and his wife (numbers 0134490 and 013491, respectively) were deported to Theresienstadt, the "model" concentration camp that the Nazis had built to delude the world into believing that the Jews did not really have it so bad. Ironically, here he was permitted to practice medicine. Mendelson says this might have spared him from being deported to the death camps earlier. The camp recorded his death (again, the number tattooed on his arm) on August 26, 1943.

Mendelson filed the claims form in November 2003. As a matter of course, ICHEIC passed it on to the GDV, which sent it as a so call "Unnamed Claim" to the 67 of its members who had been in business since 1925. It was not until May 2006 that the GDV could send him a letter confirming that a policy in his father's name had in fact been taken out in 1928. Searching its archives, AXA Life Insurance found the record of a group insurance contract between a predecessor company, Deutsche Ärzteversicherung AG (DÄV), and Ärztekammer Schlesien (the Silesian Medical Association). Dr. Siegfried Cohnreich was on the list of policy holders.

But the story does not end there. AXA also noted that the contract for Dr. Cohnreich was terminated on September 30, 1938, and the surrender value of RM 302 was paid to the Silesian Medical Association. This professional association was the legal contract partner of the insurance company and as such designated as recipient of the benefits. For its part the association was expected to distribute the benefits to its members, such as Dr. Cohnreich. The insurance company itself, which had effected the payment to the association, had no way of knowing whether it had ever paid out money to Dr. Cohnreich.

Here the letter refers to the agreement between ICHEIC, the GDV and the German Foundation that stipulates that any payment made between 1938 and the end of 1939 is deemed to have been made into a blocked account. It goes on to say that

Mendelson is entitled to a humanitarian payment of the same amount as if the policy had remained unpaid. The check sent to him and his sister, Marion Beecher, was for $9,375.

Mendelson acknowledged the check with a note on behalf of himself and his sister expressing their "appreciation for the time and dedication that has gone into researching this claim and to thank everyone for the attention to detail that made it possible."

***

Another case is that of Gabriele Hammerstein, who comes across as a very tough lady. She has a commanding presence and an alertness that belies her age of 84. Her parents, both successful psychiatrists, ran a sanatorium and outpatient clinic for the mentally ill in the medieval city of Schwerin, in the northern region of East Germany.

She comes by her self-confidence naturally. She tells the story that when the Nazis seized her parents' treatment center in 1935, her father, Dr. Erich Rosenhain, undaunted, went to court and forced the authorities to hand the properties back. It was a pyrrhic victory however. Apprehensive about growing Nazi extremism and anti-Semitism, the family understood that it was time to leave Germany and fled to the United States shortly after the court ruling.

After World War II, Schwerin became part of East Germany, and Ms. Hammerstein's efforts to find out what happened to the insurance policies she knew her father had taken were put on hold. Ever since the Berlin Wall came down, however, she frequently traveled to Germany, busy trying to get the facts.

Both Dr. Erich Rosenhain and his wife Gertrude were insured under a group policy between the Silesian Medical Association, of which they were members from when they lived in Breslau and Bad Landeck from 1921 to 1932, and DÄV. DÄV was subsequently taken over by AXA Life. As members of the German Medical Association, they also had group policies with Leipziger Verband.

Ms. Hammerstein received an offer of 12,124 euros for their policies with the Silesian Medical Association and another $8,000 for the German Medical Association policies. She accepted on her own behalf and on behalf of the four children of a sister who died several years ago.

She was volubly grateful for the assistance the GDV had given in getting the insurance money. "All I can really say about them is that they were wonderful."

In the course of a lengthy interview, she also spoke of her childhood home, which she said had been in one wing of the building that housed the sanatorium, surrounded by a vast park. The whole complex was once the palace of the Grand Duke of Mecklenburg. After the fall of the Berlin Wall, she lodged a claim to get it back. And here she encountered a peculiar situation. Standing in the way of recovering her property was not the German bureaucracy, but the Conference on Jewish Material Claims Against Germany. She said that the Government awarded her the property in 1992, but that the Claims Conference, citing a Nazi record that said Dr. Rosenhain had "sold" it to the Gestapo and that she no longer owned it asserted its own claim in 1995—and won. She finally got it back in 1999, but only after a long court battle.

Ms. Hammerstein pursued a career in opera and never married. I asked why she is not known by her father's name, but rather by her mother's maiden name. She says that when the family came to the United States, her mother's cousin, the popular composer for the musical stage, Oscar Hammerstein III ("Oklahoma," "Carousel," "South Pacific," "The King and I," and "The Sound of Music") told her that no one in America had ever heard of her father, but for a singer, the name Hammerstein was, as he put it, "money in the bank."

***

Some of the people who received compensation checks were prepared to talk about their experiences. Some had second thoughts about it. Renee Rubinstein, who had agreed at first to be interviewed, changed her mind. It was too painful, she said.

Ms. Rubinstein, nee Renate Gerichter, had first come across her father's name in a list of German policyholders on the ICHEIC website in June 2003. All it said was Isidor Gerichter, Berlin, Germany. She filed an application for compensation for a life insurance policy of which she had no direct knowledge. She answered the questions about the policy number, the currency in which it was denominated, the sum, the date of issue and when it would mature, with a simple "unknown." What she could say with certainty was that her father was born August 13, 1883, in Kempen, Poland, which at the time was part of Prussia, and that he left Germany with his family in June 1938. She was 12 at the time.

She sent a photograph of an upscale dress shop at number 233 on Berlin's fashionable Kurfürstendamm, together with the application form. A large sign that extended above the entrance and the show window said Gerichter & Co. She also enclosed her father's death certificate. Both her parents passed away in Florida, her mother in 1984 and her father in 1969. Since her only sister died in 1989, Ms. Rubinstein is the only surviving heir.

Under the agreement among ICHEIC, the GDV, and the German Foundation, her application was duly sent out to all GDV members. Allianz Life did find an entry for Isidor Gerichter in its central archives, but noted that this was merely evidence that Mr. Gerichter had applied to buy two policies, in 1928 and in 1930, rather than the fact that he had actually purchased them or that they were even issued by the company.

Nevertheless, Allianz wrote that, in order to avoid any unequal treatment with claimants whose contracts could be found, the company assumed they were issued in this case as well.

Allianz then stated it had negative documentary proof that the policies had to have been settled, and referred to the company register for 1941, which does not include Isidor Gerichter's policies, numbers F 246 836, F 240 832.

Since the agreement with ICHEIC stipulates that any payment made between 1938 and the end of 1939 is deemed to have been made into a blocked account, Ms. Rubinstein was entitled to a humanitarian payment of the same amount as if the policies had remained unpaid (see Chapter IV). However, since the amount for which Mr. Gerichter was insured is not known, Allianz, also as per the agreement, took the size of the average insurance policy in Germany during the Hitler era and calculated how much it should be worth in today's currency. The sum the company came up with was 1,251 euros for each policy which, it noted, was below the agreed upon minimum payment for survivors. Its offer of $4,000 for each policy was accepted by Ms. Rubinstein.

Her thank you letter to the GDV said it all. "Both your letter and the one sent by Allianz gave us a good explanation as to the process you had to engage in. I want to thank you sincerely... and stress my appreciation for the very thorough manner in which both you and Frau Frederike Sell from Allianz have handled this case."

Interestingly, all three cases had their origin in the former East Germany (Görlitz, Schwerin, Berlin) which had not introduced the kind of comprehensive restitution program in the 1950s, 1960s, and 1970s that West Germany had implemented (see Chapter II). They are a good example of the success of the program undertaken by the German Foundation and the GDV in the framework of ICHEIC in closing the last existing gap in the German restitution process: compensating people who had been deemed ineligible because they had lived in countries like Czechoslovakia, Hungary or Romania that later became Communist.

Glossary

American-German Executive Agreement

The agreement between the Federal Republic of Germany and the United States of July 2000 designating the Foundation "Remembrance, Responsibility and the Future" as the exclusive remedy for all claims asserted against German companies arising from the National Socialist era and World War II.

Anti-Defamation League

The Anti-Defamation League (ADL) is a Jewish advocacy group founded in the United States 1913 by B'nai B'rith whose stated aim is "to stop, by appeals to reason and conscience and, if necessary, by appeals to law, the defamation of the Jewish people. Its ultimate purpose is to secure justice and fair treatment to all citizens alike and to put an end forever to unjust and unfair discrimination against and ridicule of any sect or body of citizens." It is based in New York City. The ADL fights anti-Semitism and all forms of bigotry, defends democratic ideals and protects civil rights for all. (For further information, click on www.adl.org)

Appeals Panel (of ICHEIC)

The arbitration body established under the Trilateral Agreement concluded between ICHEIC, the German Foundation and the GDV on October 16, 2002. The three Panel Members were the supreme independent and impartial decision-making body for ruling on appeals against a decision made by a German company handling an insurance claim. The Panel's London office closed at the end of the ICHEIC process in March 2007.

Appeals Tribunal (of ICHEIC)

The ICHEIC Appeals Tribunal considered appeals of decisions by ICHEIC member companies from before and German MOU company decisions dated before October 16, 2002 (see Appeals Panel, *supra*). The Tribunal provided claimants with an opportunity to lodge an appeal at no cost against decisions on named company claims or matched unnamed company claims.

Asset declarations (*See Vermögensverzeichnis*)

Audits

In order to establish the credibility of internal investigations conducted by the European insurance companies, ICHEIC maintained a comprehensive audit process to make sure that claims were handled in accordance with guidelines laid down by the Commission. While the MOU companies were fully audited by independent audit firms and supervised by ICHEIC's Audit Mandate Support Group, ten German companies, selected by ICHEIC as representative of the German market, underwent audits by the German federal agency for the supervision of financial services (BaFin). The BaFin audits were closely monitored by ICHEIC specialists in coordination with the Jewish organizations.

Austria

On the eve of the March 1938 *Anschluss* between Austria and Nazi Germany, there were 185,000 confessional Jews in Austria, almost all living in Vienna. Full-fledged deportations began on October 15, 1941. Altogether, 65,000 Austrian Jews died in the ghettos and concentration camps of Eastern Europe.

Austrian General Settlement Fund for Victims of National Socialism ("GSF")

The GSF was established in 2001 to compensate persons who were persecuted by the National Socialist regime on political grounds or because of their religion, nationality, sexual orientation or physical or mental condition. Eligible were persons who personally suffered as a result of events that occurred on the territory of the present-day Republic of Austria or their heirs. The GSF also applied to confiscated insurance policies. (For more information, see www.en.nationalfonds.org)

Auswanderer-Sperrkonten (*See* Blocked Accounts)

AWZ Agreement

This agreement from October 2002 covered the operations of German companies in foreign markets and the operations of non-German based MOU signatories in the German market. The French and Swiss MOU signatories, i.e., AXA, Winterthur and Zurich, came to a separate agreement with ICHEIC in May 2003 to pay $25 million to satisfy claims and share the expenses of the Commission's humanitarian endeavors.

BaFin (*Bundesanstalt für Finanzdienstleistungsaufsicht*)

The Federal Financial Supervisory Authority *(Bundesanstalt für Finanzdienstleistungsaufsicht*—known as BaFin for short) was established in 2002 to oversee banking and financial service providers, including insurance and securities trading. Its goal is to ensure the proper functioning, stability and integrity of the German financial system. As regards insurance, it is the successor agency to BAV (*Bundesaufsichtsamt für das Versicherungswesen*), the federal insurance supervisory agency that was established after World War II.

Blocked Accounts (*Auswanderer-Sperrkonten*)

The so-called emigration blocked accounts chiefly affected Jews who wanted to emigrate. Anyone who applied to emigrate and transfer money to another country had to first move all his money into a blocked account in a bank licensed to deal in foreign currency. Payments out of blocked accounts were regulated by the exchange control authority and allowed mainly for subsistence costs and taxes. Special permission was granted for investments in the German Reich and for the payment of insurance premiums. However, any insurance proceeds had to be paid into the blocked account. The 11th Regulatory Decree on the Law of German Citizenship of 1941 deprived all Jews living abroad of their German citizenship and seized all their assets, including blocked accounts.

BEG (*Bundesentschädigungsgesetz*)

The centerpiece of the German *Wiedergutmachung* program (see below) was unanimously adopted by the Bundestag in 1956. It provided for compensation for the loss of life or freedom, impairment of health, professional damage and loss of property, including confiscated insurance policies. Recipients were victims of religious, political or racial persecution living in Israel, the United States or Western Europe. Residents of Central and Eastern Europe and the Soviet Union were specifically excluded.

Claims Resolution Tribunal

The CRT was initially established in 1997 to arbitrate claims to 5,570 dormant accounts in Swiss banks that were made public prior to the completion of the report of the Independent Committee of Eminent Persons (Volcker Committee). The actual claims resolution process rested on a decision reached on a Holocaust victims class action suit in the U.S. District Court for the Eastern District of New York and subsequent appeal court rulings upholding it. The settlement agreement provided for a payment of $1.25 billion to settle claims by members of five represented classes: depositors, looted assets, refugees, and two slave labor classes. Relying on results of a three year examination of Swiss bank accounts by the Volcker Committee, up to $800 million was set aside for the depositor class. (For further information, see: www.crt-ii.org)

Conference on Jewish Material Claims Against Germany (Claims Conference)

The Claims Conference was set up in 1951 to secure compensation and restitution for survivors of the Holocaust. Composed of 23 Jewish organizations with headquarters in New York, it was recognized by Germany as the legal successor of heirless Jewish property. (For further information, see: www.claimscon.org)

Czechoslovakia

After Hitler's rise to power in Germany in 1933, many German Jews fled to Czechoslovakia, to be joined by more refugees after the German entry into Austria and the Sudeten region in 1938. By 1945, the Germans and their collaborators had murdered almost all of the approximately 263,000 Jews who resided on the territory of Czechoslovakia in 1938.

Eleventh Regulatory Decree under the German Citizenship Law

The decree, dated November 25, 1941, completed the seizure of all Jewish assets. Jews became denaturalized as soon they were deported from Germany (Section 27), and Section 3 stipulated that assets of deported Jews were the property of the Nazi government. (*See Reichsbürgergesetz*)

Equalization fund

The Fund, the *Währungsumstellungsgesetz* (1948) and the *Rentenaufbesserungsgesetz* (1951) was established at the Bundesbank to keep financial institutions, including the insurance industry, from going bankrupt after the government bonds of the Third Reich that they had had to invest in became worthless. For more information see *Deutsche Bundesbank—Monthly Report*, November 1995, page 55 *et seq.*

Federal Compensation Law (*See* BEG or *Bundesentschädigungsgesetz*)

Federal Restitution Law (*See* BRüG or *Bundesrückerstattungsgesetz*)

Foundation Claims Fund

The fund set up under the Trilateral Agreement of October 16, 2002, when DM200 million were transferred to ICHEIC for payment of claims and a portion of ICHEIC's operating expenses. According to the Agreement, the fund was to pay half of ICHEIC's operating expenses and to pre-fund German insurance companies for claims that were paid by them under the Agreement. The $26.9 million left over at the end of the claims process on March 20, 2007, was to go for humanitarian purposes at ICHEIC's discretion.

Foundation Law

The Law establishing the Foundation "Remembrance, Responsibility and the Future" was enacted in August 2000. The purpose was to provide financial compensation to former slave and forced laborers and certain other victims of National Socialist injustices, among them holders of not yet otherwise compensated unpaid or confiscated insurance policies. In June 2007, the Foundation concluded payment of 4.37 billion euros to more than 1.66 million people in almost 100 countries. About 78.5

million euros went to holders of previously uncompensated insurance policies.

GDV (*Gesamtverband der Deutschen Versicherungswirtschaft*)

The Berlin-based German Insurance Association, *Gesamtverband der Deutschen Versicherungswirtschaft,* or GDV, is the umbrella organization of German insurance companies.

Generalgouvernement

After they invaded Poland in September 1939, the Germans split the country into three parts: the western territories were annexed to the Third Reich; the eastern territories were occupied by the Soviet Union; and the central part was administered Krakow and known as the *Generalgouvernement.* This sector had a separate police, currency, foreign exchange and customs border.

German Foundation Initiative (*Stiftungsinitiative*)

In February 1999, German industry embarked on a program to compensate former forced laborers and others who suffered particular hardships at the hands of the Nazi regime. This effort became known as the German Foundation Initiative and eventually led to the creation of the joint government and industry Foundation "Remembrance, Responsibility and the Future." The German Foundation Initiative contributed DM 5 billion to the Foundation and the government DM 5 billion. (For further information, see www.stiftungsinitiative.de)

German mark (symbol DM)

West German currency that replaced the Reichsmark of the Third Reich on June 20, 1948.

Hague Protocols

Hague Protocol No. 1 was designed to amend existing German legislation dealing with individual compensation and restitution of persons who had suffered under the Nazis. It was drawn up by representatives of the West German Government and the Conference on Jewish Material Claims Against Germany and signed in the context of the landmark agreement between Germany and Israel of September 1952 (*see* Luxembourg Agreement). Under Hague Protocol No. 2, Germany undertook to pay DM 450 million to the Claims Conference as compensation for heirless claims, the money to be used to assist survivors and for other humanitarian purposes.

Humanitarian Fund

A sum of DM 350 million that was settled on ICHEIC by the German Foundation in October 2002 under the terms of the Trilateral Agreement between the GDV, the Foundation and ICHEIC. It was to be used for payment of claims against insurance companies that no longer exist; claims for proceeds that had been deposited in blocked accounts; to make up the difference between the value calculated according to the BEG method and the minimum payment set out in the Trilateral Agreement; to assist needy victims of the Holocaust and for other related humanitarian and educational purposes; and, at the discretion of ICHEIC, for the payment of costs related to administration of the funds.

Hungary

With the arrival of refugees from other parts of Europe, by 1941 Hungary's total Jewish population was just over 825,000, more than half of them living in Budapest. The first 40,000 Jews were deported by the Hungarian authorities in 1941, but it was only after German troops occupied the country in March of 1944 that mass deportations to the death camps began. Between May 5th and June 7th, about 300,000 Hungarian Jews from outside Budapest were deported. By July the total had reached more than 500,000 persons. About 200,000 Hungarian Jews survived.

International Commission on Holocaust Era Insurance Claims (ICHEIC)

ICHEIC was established in August 1998 following negotiations among European insurance companies, U.S. insurance regulators, and representatives of international Jewish and survivor organizations and the State of Israel. Working together with 75 European insurance companies throughout Europe, ICHEIC resolved more than 90,000 claims. Through the Commission's work, a total of $306 million was awarded to more than 48,000 Holocaust survivors and their heirs. ICHEIC also committed more than $169 million in additional funding for humanitarian programs, such as social welfare benefits for Holocaust survivors worldwide. (For further information, see: www.icheic.org)

Jewish Agency

The Jewish Agency for Palestine was established by the World Zionist Organization at the 16th Zionist Congress in 1929, and was recognized by the League of Nations Mandate for Palestine (1922) as the official representative of the Jewish community in Palestine. Since the establishment of the State of Israel, its main mission is to promote immigration to Israel and ensure the immigrants' successful integration into society. (For further information, see: www.jewishagency.org)

Jewish Restitution Successor Organization

The Jewish Restitution Successor Organization (JSRO) with its seat in New York was established by the Allies after the war in the American Zone of Occupation. Its brief was to see that any property which had been owned by Jews but who had not survived the World War II did not revert to the state or remain in the hands of usurpers.

Jewish Trust Corporation

The Jewish Trust Corporation (JTO) was established by the Allies immediately after the war in the British Zone of Occupation, and a French section began operating in 1952. The JTO performed the same functions in the French and British Zones as the JSRO in the American Zone.

Kristallnacht

Also known as Crystal Night, *Reichskristallnacht*, the "Night of Broken Glass," was a pogrom against Jews throughout Germany and in parts of Austria from November 9 to 11, 1938. The assassination of a German diplomat by a German-Polish Jew in Paris served as the pretext for the genocide that was to come. Four hundred Jews were killed in the rampage, more than 7,000 Jewish-owned shops and department stores were damaged or ransacked, and over 1500 synagogues and many Jewish homes were vandalized. Moreover, insurance policies all contained clauses that excluded damage resulting from either riot, civil unrest, or looting, and no compensation was paid.

LAG (*Lastenausgleichsgesetz*) Law on Equalization of Burdens

In effect from 1952 to 1970, the Law was intended to assist refugees from the former Soviet bloc. It provided compensation the form of pensions or lump sums for the loss of property (including unpaid or confiscated insurance policies) caused by flight from a defined area of expulsion in the East. Recipients were displaced persons, refugees and so called *Spätaussiedler* (late repatriates) as well as victims of religious, political, or racial persecution.

Legal Peace

The DM 10 billion that the German Foundation disbursed to persons who suffered under the Nazis was supposed to be the final installment of Germany's debt to them. The joint statement issued at the conclusion of the international consultation in Berlin on July 17, 2000, asserted that the amount was both a ceiling and the final amount, and that it would cover all payments made for loss of property and freedom. The governments, plaintiffs' lawyers, and representatives of the leading Jewish organizations agreed that it would be in their collective interest that the Foundation be the "exclusive remedy and forum for the resolution of all claims that have been or may be asserted against German companies arising out of the National Socialist era and WW II." They endorsed the principle that German companies were entitled to "receive all embracing and enduring legal peace."

London Debt Agreement

Under the London Debt Agreement of February 27, 1953, West Germany undertook to pay DM 13.73 billion to cover part of its prewar debt to some 70 countries as well as its postwar debt to the three western occupying powers. Claims for reparations were set aside pending a formal peace treaty. In fact, no treaty has even been signed. Instead, the so called "Two plus Four Treaty concerning the final agreement on Germany as a whole" put an end to all Allied privileges in Germany arising out of World War II.

Luxembourg Agreement

Under an agreement between the West Germany and the State of Israel signed on September 10, 1952, in Luxembourg, Germany undertook to pay DM 3 billion to Israel as global compensation for the material losses resulting from the crimes against the Jewish people. Israel used the money to resettle Jewish refugees in Israel.

Memorandum of Understanding (MOU)

The establishment of the International Commission on Holocaust Era Insurance Claims (ICHEIC) was based on a Memorandum of Understanding (MOU) endorsed by the principal parties affected. On board were U.S. insurance regulators, European insurance companies (Allianz, AXA, Generali, Winterthur and Zurich), as well as the World Jewish Restitution Organization, the Claims Conference and the State of Israel. ICHEIC was to create a claims and valuation process to settle and pay individual claims at no cost to the claimants.

Munich Pact

The Munich Pact refers to the agreement reached by the four Germany, Italy, Britain and France, on September 30, 1938, that led to the dismemberment of Czechoslovakia. Czechoslovakia was not invited to attend. The capitulation of Britain and France to Hitler's demands at Munich has become synonymous with craven appeasement.

NAIC

Members of the National Association of Insurance Commissioners (NAIC) are insurance regulators from the 50 states and the District of Columbia. It provides a forum for the development of a uniform policy when uniformity is in the best interests policyholders in each jurisdiction. NAIC also lobbies for shared objectives in financial market regulation.

Neumann's Zeitschrift für Versicherungswesen

A German periodical that dealt with the insurance business. Founded in 1877, over time, it became an influential and informative source of information on insurance the business in Germany and around the world. In 1943, this independent publication was merged with other journals into the *Deutsche Versicherung*, which ceased publication in 1944.

Nuremberg Laws

The Nuremberg Laws, the *Nürnberger Gesetze*, of September 15, 1935, packaged together 13 Nazi decrees issued earlier dealing with the denaturalization of German Jews based on a pseudo-scientific rationale for racial discrimination. (See *Reichsbürgergesetz*)

Paris Peace Conference, 1919

The Paris Peace Conference of 1919 was organized by the victorious World War I allies (the United States, Great Britain, France, Italy, and other allied states) to set the guidelines for peace treaties with the defeated Central Powers (Germany, Austria-Hungary, Bulgaria and the Ottoman Empire). The Paris Peace Conference set the stage for the following treaties, all of them negotiated in the absence of representatives of the Central Powers:

Treaty of Versailles

The Treaty of Versailles was the contract that formally ended World War I. The treaty required Germany to pay huge reparations and accept stringent restrictions on its military. It also mandated substantial territorial concessions: Alsace-Lorraine was returned to France; Belgium received Eupen and Malmedy; the

Saar region was placed under international administration up to 1935; Northern Schleswig was returned to Denmark after a plebiscite; Poland received most of the former German provinces of Posen (Poznan) and West Prussia, a "corridor" to the Baltic Sea and parts of Upper Silesia; Danzig was declared a "free city" within the Polish customs union; Czechoslovakia received the Hultschin district; Memel, a small strip of territory in East Prussia along the Baltic Sea, was ultimately placed under Lithuanian control. In all, Germany had to give up 13 percent of its territory in Europe, home to 10 percent of its population.

Treaty of Saint-Germain

The Treaty of St. Germain dissolved the Austro-Hungarian Empire. The new Republic of Austria consisted of most of the German-speaking part of the former Empire. Hungary, Czechoslovakia, Poland, and the Kingdom of the Slovenes, Croats and Serbs (later Yugoslavia) became independent.

Treaty of Neuilly

The Treaty of Neuilly dealt with Bulgaria. Bulgaria was compelled to recognize the independence of Yugoslavia and cede western Thrace to Greece and parts of Dobruja to Romania.

Treaty of Trianon

Under the Treaty of Trianon, Hungary had to cede most of its territory to Romania, Czechoslovakia and the Kingdom of Serbs, Croats and Slovenes. Hungary lost 71 percent of its territory and 63 percent of its inhabitants.

Treaty of Sèvres

This treaty, signed in 1920 and subsequently revised in Lausanne in 1923 forced the Ottoman Empire to cede Middle Eastern territories that later became British and French League of

Nations mandates; give up its Mediterranean coastline to Italy, its Aegean coast to Greece, accept international authority over the Dardenelles and the Sea of Marmara, and to recognize the Republic of Armenia in eastern Anatolia.

Poland

According to the 1931 census, Jews constituted 10 percent of Poland's population of 32 million, the second largest Jewish community in the world. About three million Polish Jews were murdered during World War II.

Reichsbürgergesetz — 1935 German Citizenship Law

This law divided Germans into nationals (*Staatsangehörige*) and citizens (*Reichsbürger*) and served as a point of departure for the subsequent persecution and extermination of German Jews. As defined in the First Regulatory Decree, dated November 1935, a Jew could not be a *Reichsbürger* but only a *Staatsangehörige*, with abridged civil rights.

Reichsfluchtsteuer Emigration Tax

The emigration tax was first introduced in 1918 to stem the outflow of capital. By 1934, German nationals who wanted to emigrate and whose assets exceeded RM 200,000 or had an annual income of at least RM 20,000, had to pay the *Reichsfluchtsteuer* of 25%. In 1934 the tax threshold was lowered to RM 50,000 and the tax raised to 65%. By 1936 the marginal tax was 81%, and, by September 1939, 96% of sums transferred abroad.

Reichsmark

Legal tender (symbol RM) in Germany from 1924 until June 20, 1948.

Relaxed Standards of Proof

The Relaxed Standards of Proof established by ICHEIC enabled claimants to submit non-documentary and unofficial documentary evidence to back up their case. The companies were not allowed to reject documents as being insufficiently probative if the evidence was plausible on the face of it. They also could not insist on the production of any document which more than likely had been destroyed, lost or rendered inaccessible to the claimant. (For details see Annex B of the Trilateral Agreement)

Reinsurance

The practice whereby insurers transfer portions of risk portfolios to other parties to protect themselves in the event of a large obligation. Reinsurance companies do not enter into contracts with insurance policyholders, but provide coverage for direct insurance companies.

Restitution (*See Wiedergutmachung*)

SJOA Foundation

The *Stichting Individuele Verzekeringsaanspraken Sjoa* (Sjoa Foundation for Individual Insurance Claims) originated in a 1999 agreement between the Dutch Association of Insurers (DAI) and the Central Jewish Board (CJO) in the Netherlands to settle Jewish life insurance policies that had not been paid out after the Second World War. A sum of 20 million Dutch florins was reserved for this purpose. The Sjoa Foundation will handle requests submitted before January 2010.

Thirteenth Regulatory Decree on the German Citizenship Law 1943

This decree deprived Jews of the protection of the courts, and suspicion of criminal activity was dealt with solely by the police.

Section 2 decreed that when a Jew dies, all his or her assets become the property of the Reich.

Transition Treaty

A convention promulgated in 1954 by the three Western Allies and Germany stipulated that all the restitution and compensation edicts issued by the Allies should remain in force, using the provisions set up in the U.S. Occupation Zone as the minimum standards. The German Federal Restitution Law and the German Federal Compensation Law were the offspring of the Transition Treaty.

Trilateral Agreement

The Trilateral Agreement committed the German Foundation, Remembrance, Responsibility and the Future, the International Commission on Holocaust Era Insurance Claims, and the German Insurance Association to work together to resolve the Holocaust insurance issue as it affected Germany. It set the guidelines for the settlement of individual claims on unpaid or Nazi confiscated policies of German insurance companies and the Foundation's part in financing ICHEIC's Humanitarian Fund.

Valuation Guidelines

The Trilateral Agreement laid down guidelines on how to calculate the current value of old insurance policies after inflation, war and economic upheaval. On a policy issued in Germany by a German company, a claimant with a valid claim received a minimum payment of $4,000 if he himself was a survivor of the Holocaust. Heirs received at least $3,000. Slightly lower minimums were paid on policies issued in Eastern Europe. If the valuation of a claim was below $100, the minimum payment was

$500; if the valuation was above $100, the minimum payment was $2,000 for survivors and $1,000 for heirs.

NS-Verfolgtenentschädigungsgesetz (Nazi Victims Law) and *Gesetz zur Regelung offener Vermögensfragen* (Victims Compensation Law)

These two laws established the right of persons living in the former East Germany to claim compensation for property which had been confiscated by the Nazis.

Vermögensverzeichnis(se) (Asset Declarations)

Under a decree issued April 26, 1938, the *Verordnung über die Anmeldung des Vermögens von Juden*, every German Jew with assets of more than 5,000 Reichsmarks, whether in Germany or abroad, had to declare it to the tax authorities no later than June 30, 1938. The decree was later applied to Austria and to the annexed areas of Czechoslovakia.

Wiedergutmachung

From its very start in 1949, the Federal Republic of Germany assumed responsibility for paying compensation for the crimes of the Nazi era. This effort became known as *Wiedergutmachung*, literally "making good again." It covered compensation benefits for the loss of life, health, freedom, professional damage and possession of property, slave labor and imprisonment in concentration camps or ghettoes. Stipends or lump sums were paid to Nazi victims, and whenever possible, wrongfully confiscated property was returned to their rightful owners or their heirs or successor organizations. German compensation laws and agreements included: *Bundesergänzungsgesetz* (BErgG); *Bundesentschädigungsgesetz* (BEG); *Bundesrückerstattungsgesetz* (BRüG); Equalization Fund; Lastenausgleichsgesetz (LAG); London Debt Agreement; Luxembourg Agreement between Israel and Germany of 1952; Hague Protocols Nos. 1 and 2; *NS-Verfolgtenentschädigungsgesetz* Transition Treaty.

Appendix I

ICHEIC Memorandum of Understanding (MoU)

1. It is agreed by the undersigned European insurance companies. United States insurance regulatory authorities, and Jewish and survivor organizations that a just process shall be established that will expeditiously address the issue of unpaid insurance policies issued to victims of the Holocaust.

2. It is agreed by the undersigned that an International Commission ("IC") will be established. The parties to this Memorandum of Understanding ("MOU") agree to actively and voluntarily pursue the goal of resolving insurance claims of Holocaust victims through the IC. The IC will be composed of twelve persons or their alternates: six persons designated by the United States regulators and the World Jewish Restitution Organization, together with the Conference of Jewish Material Claims Against Germany, and the State of Israel, and six persons designated by the undersigned European insurance companies and European regulators. Each group above that is a member of the IC will designate two alternates to attend in observer status. In addition, there will be three additional observers designated by the World Jewish Restitution Organization, together with the Conference of Jewish Material Claims Against Germany, and the State of Israel, one observer designated by the European Economic Commission and one observer designated by the United States Department of State. The twelve representatives will appoint an additional member who shall serve as the Chairperson. The Chairperson shall be independent and not affiliated with any of the persons, or groups represented on the IC. Members of the IC shall serve on a volunteer basis and without remuneration. The IC shall attempt to resolve all issues within two years from its formation.

3. Following the creation of the IC, insurance companies or their successors that issued policies to persons who were subsequently victims of the Holocaust and were not original signatories to this MOU will be given the opportunity to become signatories to this MOU and participate in the IC process. The IC process, at the discretion of the signatory companies, can be extended to affiliates of the signatories.

4. The IC shall initiate and conduct an investigatory process to determine the current status of those insurance policies issued to Holocaust victims during the period of 1920 to 1945 for which claims are filed with the IC. To assess the remaining unpaid insurance policies of Holocaust victims, a reasonable review will be made of the participating companies' files, in conjunction with information concerning Holocaust victims from Yad Vashem and the United States Holocaust Memorial Museum and other relevant sources of data. The

IC or its participating companies shall retain one or more internationally recognized auditing firms that operate in those countries where the above-referenced insurance companies are based and other experts as needed.

a. The IC shall promulgate an audit mandate implementing the goal of this MOU. This mandate shall outline a work program for the audit firm(s). In addition to establishing a framework for an overall work plan, the mandate shall also establish a mechanism whereby any investigatory or audit work already performed by the various insurance companies in this area is reviewed to determine whether it is consistent with the standards and goals of the mandate and if so, shall be incorporated into the work plan of the IC auditors. The insurance companies and insurance regulators that are parties to this MOU shall ensure that the respective auditing firm(s) and other experts have complete and unfettered access to any and all of their relevant books, records and file archives as is necessary to their audit activities. Such access shall be in cooperation with and in accordance with local insurance authorities and laws. Any documents reviewed or received by the IC will be maintained as strictly confidential.

b. As part of the audit mandate, the IC will address the issue of a full accounting by the insurance companies and publication of the names of Holocaust victims who held unpaid insurance policies. In addition, the IC shall establish a toll free mechanism to aid survivors, beneficiaries and heirs of Holocaust victims in the submission of claims and inquiries.

5. The IC shall establish a claims and valuation process to settle and pay individual claims that will be of no cost to claimants. The initial responsibility for resolving claims rests with the individual insurance companies, in accordance with guidelines to be promulgated by the IC. The signatory companies shall submit to the IC all claims received directly by the company within 30 days of receipt. The IC shall endeavor to integrate data already collected by the various U.S. states into the overall process. Such process shall include the establishment of relaxed standards of proof that acknowledge the passage of time and the practical difficulties of the survivors, their beneficiaries and heirs in locating relevant documents, while providing protection to the insurance companies against unfounded claims.

6. Such claims process shall also include the valuation of policies, including, but not limited to the establishment of standards and formulae to account for currency reforms, currency conversions and interest. In the case of insurance claims that were previously submitted for resolution through a post-war governmental restitution program, the IC shall examine the program, payments and payment calculations to determine if they were equitable and

adequate. To the extent an insurance policy was subject to a postwar governmental restitution program, the insurance company will receive credit for the amount paid out for the insurance policy against the value of the policy as determined by the IC. The IC process shall constitute an exclusive remedy. Claim awards shall be compensatory only.

7. Each insurance company that has agreed to voluntarily submit to this process shall establish its own dedicated account, sufficiently funded, to be used exclusively for the immediate payment of Holocaust related insurance claims which have been submitted to the IC and which are determined by the IC to be valid and attributable to each specific insurance company. No signatory insurance company shall be required to pay any claim that the IC determines to be attributable to an existing insurance company that has not signed this MOU.

8. The IC shall establish and administer a Special Fund consisting of two sections. Each signatory company will make an initial contribution to the two Specific Humanitarian Sections.

  A.   Specific Humanitarian Section:
       (1) This section shall provide relief to claimants who seek relief under policies that cannot be attributed to a particular insurance company as, well as to claimants who seek relief under policies issued by companies no longer in existence. These funds shall be separately maintained.
           (a) If the audit process develops additional, claims and if additional claims are received that fall into the category of paragraph (8)(A)(1) of this section and there are insufficient funds remaining in the segregated (8)(A)(1) account, each signatory company shall make additional contributions as the IC deems necessary to be assessed on an equitable basis taking into account both historic and current involvement.
       (2) In addition, each signatory company agrees to make an equitable contribution to this section, to be used to satisfy claims on any of its policies that were nationalized or any of its policies that were paid, as required by local law, to a governmental authority that was not the named beneficiary of the policy. The monies contributed by each signatory company shall be used to satisfy claims awards only against that company. These funds shall be separately maintained.
           (a) In the event the audit process develops additional claims and if additional claims are received that fall into paragraph (8)(A)(2) and there are insufficient funds remaining in the segregated (8)(A)(2) account, each signatory company shall contribute an additional amount to pay any monies awarded by the IC on that signatory company's paragraph (8)(A)(2) policies.

B. <u>General Humanitarian Section:</u> This section shall be used for the benefit of needy victims of the Holocaust and for other Holocaust-related humanitarian purposes. It is understood that the contributions made under this section give due consideration to the category of "heirless claims," i.e., unpaid policies issued by the signatory companies to Holocaust victims as to which there is no living beneficiary or other living person entitled to receive the proceeds. Each signatory company shall make an initial contribution to this fund, with subsequent contributions to be determined by the IC to be assessed on an equitable basis taking into account both historic and current involvement.

9. Upon execution of this MOU, the insurance companies will establish a fund to cover the expenses of the IC. Each signatory company shall make an initial contribution of $250,000.00. Thereafter, as the IC deems necessary, subsequent contributions will be assessed based on an equitable basis. The cost of auditing an individual company's books and records and any expenses relating to the processing or investigation of claims against an individual insurance company shall be borne by that insurance company. There shall be an annual budget for the operation of the IC administered by the Chairperson and an annual audit of the IC's expenses.

10. The IC signatories will work to achieve exemptions from related pending and future legislation and will work to resolve all pending litigation for those insurers that become signatories to this MOU and which fully cooperate with the processes and funding of the IC.

11. Upon agreement to the terms of this MOU, the respective parties shall announce the members of the IC and the Chairperson.

Appendix II

German-American Executive Agreement dated 17th July 2000

Agreement between
the Government of the Federal Republic of Germany
and
the Government of the United States of America
concerning the Foundation
"Remembrance, Responsibility and the Future"

****

The Government of the Federal Republic of Germany
and
the Government of the United States of America

Intending to shape relations between their two States in a spirit of friendship and cooperation for the future and to successfully resolve issues stemming from the past,

Recognizing that the Federal Republic of Germany has, building on Allied legislation and in close consultation with victims' associations and interested Governments, provided, in an unprecedented manner, comprehensive and extensive restitution and compensation to victims of National Socialist persecution,

Noting the historic announcement on February 16, 1999, made by the Federal Chancellor and German companies, in which the companies stated their intention to establish a foundation to compensate forced laborers and others who suffered at the hands of German companies during the National Socialist era and World War II,

Noting that, by means of the Foundation Initiative, its member companies wish to respond to the moral responsibility of German business arising from the use of forced laborers and from damage to property caused by persecution, and from all other wrongs suffered during the National Socialist era and World War II,

Recognizing as legitimate the interest German companies have in all-embracing and enduring legal peace in this matter, and further recognizing that such interest was fundamental to the establishment of the Foundation Initiative,

Noting that the two Governments announced that they welcomed and support the Foundation Initiative, Noting that the Federal Republic of Germany and German companies have since agreed on the creation of a single Foundation, "Remembrance, Responsibility and the Future" (the "Foundation"), formed under German federal law as an instrumentality of the

Federal Republic of Germany and funded by contributions from the Federal Republic of Germany and the German companies,

Recognizing that German business, having contributed substantially to the Foundation, should not be asked or expected to contribute again, in court or elsewhere, for the use of forced laborers or for any wrongs asserted against German companies arising from the National Socialist era and World War II,

Recognizing that it is in the interest of both parties to have a resolution of these issues that is non-adversarial and non-confrontational, outside of litigation,

Recognizing that both parties desire all-embracing and enduring legal peace to advance their foreign policy interests,

Noting in this regard the June 16, 2000, letter of the Assistant to the President of the United States for National Security Affairs and the Counsel to the President of the United States and the July 5, 2000, letter of the Foreign Policy and Security Advisor of the Chancellor of the Federal Republic of Germany, copies of which have been made public,

Having worked as partners, in consultation with other interested parties and governments, to assist German companies to achieve wide support for the total amount of funds and the eligibility criteria of the Foundation and for the establishment of all-embracing and enduring legal peace,

Noting that the Foundation will assure broad coverage of victims and broad participation by companies which would not be possible through judicial proceedings,

Believing that the Foundation will provide as expeditious as possible a mechanism for making fair and speedy payments to now elderly victims,

Having in mind that the Foundation covers, and that it would be in the interests of both parties for the Foundation to be the exclusive remedy and forum for addressing, all claims that have been or may be asserted against German companies arising from the National Socialist era and World War II,

Recalling that for the last 55 years the parties have sought to work to address the consequences of the National Socialist era and World War II through political and governmental acts between the United States and the Federal Republic of Germany,

Noting that this Agreement and the establishment of the Foundation represent a fulfillment of these efforts,

Recognizing that the German Government has tabled a Bill before the German Federal Parliament ("Bundestag") to establish the Foundation

Have agreed as follows:

Article 1

(1) The parties agree that the Foundation "Remembrance, Responsibility and the Future" covers, and that it would be in their interests for the Foundation to be the exclusive remedy and forum for the resolution of, all claims that have been or may be asserted against German companies arising from the National Socialist era and World War II.

(2) The Federal Republic of Germany agrees to ensure that the Foundation shall provide appropriately extensive publicity concerning its existence, its objectives and the availability of funds.

(3) Annex A sets forth the principles that shall govern the operation of the Foundation. The Federal Republic of Germany assures that the Foundation will be subject to legal supervision by a German governmental authority; any person may request that the German governmental authority take measures to ensure compliance with the legal requirements of the Foundation.

(4) The Federal Republic of Germany agrees that insurance claims that come within the scope of the current claims handling procedures adopted by the International Commission of Holocaust Era Insurance Claims ("ICHEIC") and are made against German insurance companies shall be processed by the companies and the German Insurance Association on the basis of such procedures and on the basis of additional claims handling procedures that may be agreed among the Foundation, ICHEIC, and the German Insurance Association.

Article 2

(1) The United States shall, in all cases in which the United States is notified that a claim described in article 1 (1) has been asserted in a court in the United States, inform its courts through a Statement of Interest, in accordance with Annex B, and, consistent therewith, as it otherwise considers appropriate, that it would be in the foreign policy interests of the United States for the Foundation to be the exclusive remedy and forum for resolving such claims asserted against German companies as defined in Annex C and that dismissal of such cases would be in its foreign policy interest.

(2) The United States, recognizing the importance of the objectives of this agreement, including all-embracing and enduring legal peace, shall, in a timely manner, use its best efforts, in a manner it considers appropriate, to achieve these objectives with state and local governments.

Article 3

(1) This agreement is intended to complement the creation of the Foundation and to foster all-embracing and enduring legal peace for German companies with respect to the National Socialist era and World War II.

(2) This agreement shall not affect unilateral decisions or bilateral or multilateral agreements that dealt with the consequences of the National Socialist era and World War II.

(3) The United States will not raise any reparations claims against the Federal Republic of Germany.

(4) The United States shall take appropriate steps to oppose any challenge to the sovereign immunity of the Federal Republic of Germany with respect to any claim that may be asserted against the Federal Republic of Germany concerning the consequences of the National Socialist era and World War II.

Article 4

Annexes A, B and C shall be an integral part of this Agreement.

Article 5

This Agreement shall enter into force on the date on which the parties agree by exchange of notes.

DONE at Berlin on the 17th day of July, 2000, in duplicate in the German and English languages, both texts being equally authentic.

For the Government of the
Federal Republic of Germany

For the Government of the
United States of America

Annex A
of the Agreement between
the Government of the Federal Republic of Germany
and
the Government of the United States of America
concerning the Foundation "Remembrance, Responsibility and the Future"

Principles Governing the Operation of the Foundation

Article 1(3) of the Agreement provides that the principles governing the operation of the Foundation will be set forth in Annex A. This Annex reflects key elements of the Foundation that form a basis for the Parties' mutual commitments in the Agreement.

1. The Foundation legislation will state that the purpose of the Foundation is to make payments through partner organizations to those who suffered as private and public sector forced or slave laborers and those who suffered at the hands of German companies during the National Socialist era and to establish a "Remembrance and Future Fund" within the Foundation. It will state that the permanent task of the "Remembrance and Future Fund" is to support projects that (a) serve to promote understanding between nations, and serve social justice and international cooperation in the humanitarian sector; (b) support youth exchange programs and keep alive the memory of the Holocaust and the threat posed by totalitarian, unlawful regimes and tyranny; and (c) also benefit the heirs of those who have not survived.

2. The Foundation legislation will provide for a Board of Trustees that consists of an equal number of members appointed by the German Government and German companies and by other governments and victims' representatives, except that the Chairman shall be a person of international stature appointed by the Chancellor of the Federal Republic of Germany. The Board may be reduced in size after four years, but the balance of the membership will continue, to the extent appropriate. The Board will adopt by-laws by a two-thirds majority vote. All Foundation operations will be transparent and by-laws and similar procedures will be made public.

3. The Foundation legislation will provide that the Foundation will be audited by the Federal Accounting Office and that all partner organizations will also be audited.

4. The Foundation legislation will provide that persons who were held in concentration camps as defined under the Federal Compensation Law ("BEG") or in another place of confinement or ghetto under comparable conditions and were subject to forced labor ("slave laborers") will be eligible to receive up to DM 15,000 each. The Foundation legislation will also provide that persons who were deported from their homelands into the territory of

185

the 1937 borders of the German Reich or to a German-occupied area, and were held in prison-like or extremely harsh living conditions ("forced laborers") not covered by the above definition will be eligible to receive up to DM 5,000 each. In addition, from the allocated funds to make payments to forced laborers, partner organizations will be authorized to make payments to others who were forced to work during the National Socialist era. These other forced laborers will receive up to DM 5,000 each. The eligibility of all laborers covered by the Foundation will be limited to survivors and heirs, as defined under paragraph 8, of those who died after February 15, 1999. In addition, victims of "other non-labor personal injury wrongs," including, but not limited to, medical experimentation and *Kinderheim* cases, will be eligible to receive payments, within the limits of the amount allocated for that purpose. Victims of medical experimentation and *Kinderheim* cases are given priority over other non-labor personal injury wrongs. The eligibility of a victim to receive benefits for all "other non-labor personal injury wrongs" will not be affected by whether or not he or she also receives benefits for forced labor. The funds allocated for "other non-labor personal injury wrongs" will constitute a separate allocation. The partner organizations will receive, review, and process applications for payments from the amount allocated for "other personal injury." At the request of a partner organization, the property committee referred to in paragraph 11 will appoint an independent arbitrator to review and process applications to the particular partner organization. The amount allocated will be distributed to each partner organization so that each approved applicant is provided a pro-rata amount of the total amount for all approved "other personal injury" applicants. The decisions of the partner organizations and any arbitrator that may be appointed will be based on uniform standards approved by the Board of Trustees. The Foundation legislation will provide that any costs associated with reviewing and processing applications, including those associated with an arbitrator (if selected), will be drawn from the allocations for each partner organization. Excess amounts in the labor category allocated to any partner organization under the distribution plan annexed to the Joint Statement will be reallocated to labor, with the aim of reaching equal levels of payments to former slave and forced laborers wherever they reside. The Board of Trustees will be entitled to authorize payments above per capita ceilings should circumstances warrant.

5. The Foundation legislation will provide that a slave or forced laborer will not be able to receive payments for the same injury or wrong from both the Foundation and the Austrian Foundation for Reconciliation, Peace and Cooperation.

6. The Foundation legislation will provide that persons who suffered loss of or damage to property during the National Socialist era as a result of racial

persecution directly caused by German companies are eligible to recover under the payment system set forth in paragraph 11. The eligibility of such persons will be limited to those who could not receive any payment under the BEG or Federal Restitution Law ("BRueckG") because they did not meet the residency requirement or could not file their claims by the deadline because they lived under a government with which the Federal Republic of Germany did not have diplomatic relations, those whose claims were rejected under the BEG or BRueckG where legal proof became available only after the reunification of the Federal Republic of Germany, provided the claims were not covered by post-reunification restitution or compensation legislation, and those whose racially-motivated property claims concerning moveable property were denied or would have been denied under the BEG or BRueckG because the claimant, while able to prove a German company was responsible for seizing or confiscating property, was not able to prove that the property was transferred into then-West Germany (as required by law) or, in the case of bank accounts, that compensation was or would have been denied because the sum was no longer identifiable, where either (a) the claimant can now prove the property was transferred into then-West Germany or (b) the location of property is unknown.

7. The Foundation legislation, by making available the amount of 50 million DM, will provide a potential remedy for all non-racially motivated wrongs of German companies directly resulting in loss of or damage to property during the National Socialist era. The Foundation will refer such matters for review and processing to the committee referred to in paragraph 11. All funds allocated to payment for property matters will be distributed within those categories.

8. The Foundation legislation will provide that the heirs eligible to receive payments under paragraphs 6 and 7 consist of the spouse or children. In the absence of the victim, spouse and children, then payments under these paragraphs will be available to grandchildren, if alive; if not, to siblings, if alive; and if there are neither grandchildren nor siblings, to the individual beneficiary named in a will.

9. The Foundation legislation will provide that all eligibility decisions will be based on relaxed standards of proof.

10. The Foundation legislation will provide that legal persons will be allowed to make claims on behalf of individuals when those individuals have given powers of attorney. The Foundation legislation will also provide that where an identifiable religious community has suffered damage to or loss of community property, as distinct from individual property, resulting directly from the wrongs of a German company, a duly authorized legal successor may apply for payment to the committee referred to in paragraph 11.

11. The Foundation legislation will establish a three-member committee for property matters (paragraphs 6 and 7). The United States and the Federal Republic of Germany will each appoint one member; these two members will appoint a Chairman. A secretariat will be largely responsible for the initial review of applications. The Foundation legislation will require the Committee to establish simplified procedures, including simplified and expedited internal appeals. The Committee will not have the authority to reopen any case that has been finally decided by a German court or administrative body, or that could have been decided by application in time, except as specified in paragraph 6. All of the Committee's expenses will be funded from the amount allocated for property claims and the funds will be subject to audit.

12. The Foundation legislation will provide that the Committee referred to in paragraph 11 will distribute the funds allocated to it on a pro-rata basis.

13. The Foundation legislation will make clear that receipt of payment from Foundation funds will not affect the recipient's eligibility for social security or other public benefits. There will be offsets for prior compensation payments made by German companies for forced labor and other National Socialist era injustices, even if made through third parties, but there will be no offsets for any prior Government payments.

14. The Foundation legislation will provide that each applicant for a Foundation payment will be required to state that, upon receipt of a payment from the Foundation, he or she will waive any and all alleged National Socialist era claims against German companies and all National Socialist era labor and property damage claims against the German Government. Such a waiver will not preclude applicants from being eligible to receive payments under the Foundation legislation for other wrongs, for example other personal injuries or loss of property, or any combination thereof. Such a waiver also will not preclude an applicant from bringing an action against a specific German entity (i.e., Government agency or company) for the return of a specifically identified piece of art if the action is filed in the Federal Republic of Germany or in the country in which the art was taken, provided that the applicant is precluded from seeking any relief beyond or other than the return of the specifically identified piece of art.

15. The Foundation legislation will provide that each partner organization will create an internal appeals procedure.

16. The Foundation legislation will require that the Foundation provide appropriately extensive publicity concerning the benefits that the Foundation will offer and how to apply. The Board of Trustees, in consultation with the partner organizations, will determine the form and content of such publicity.

17. The Foundation legislation will allow applications to be made to the partner organizations for at least eight months after the enactment of the Foundation law.

18. The Foundation legislation will authorize the Foundation and its partner organizations to receive information from German Government agencies and other public bodies that is necessary for the fulfillment of their responsibilities, in so far as this is not contrary to particular statutes or regulations or the legitimate interests of the persons concerned.

19. The Foundation legislation will enter into force no later than when the funds of the Foundation are made available to it.

Annex B
of the Agreement between
the Government of the Federal Republic of Germany
and
the Government of the United States of America
concerning the Foundation "Remembrance, Responsibility and the Future"

Elements of U.S. Government Statement of Interest

Pursuant to Article 2, Paragraph 1, the United States will timely file a Statement of Interest and accompanying formal foreign policy statement of the Secretary of State and Declaration of Deputy Treasury Secretary Stuart E. Eizenstat in all pending and future cases, regardless of whether the plaintiff(s) consent(s) to dismissal, in which the United States is notified that a claim has been asserted against German companies arising from the National Socialist era and World War II.

The Statement of Interest will make the following points:

1. As indicated by his letter of December 13, 1999, the President of the United States has concluded that it would be in the foreign policy interests of the United States for the Foundation to be the exclusive forum and remedy for the resolution of all asserted claims against German companies arising from their involvement in the National Socialist era and World War II, including without limitation those relating to slave and forced labor, aryanization, medical experimentation, children's homes/Kinderheim, other cases of personal injury, and damage to or loss of property, including banking assets and insurance policies.

2. Accordingly, the United States believes that all asserted claims should be pursued (or in the event Foundation funds have been exhausted, should timely have been pursued) through the Foundation instead of the courts.

3. As the President said in his letter of December 13, 1999, dismissal of the lawsuit, which touches on the foreign policy interests of the United States, would be in the foreign policy interests of the United States. The United States will recommend dismissal on any valid legal ground (which, under the U.S. system of jurisprudence, will be for the U.S. courts to determine). The United States will explain that, in the context of the Foundation, it is in the enduring and high interest of the United States to support efforts to achieve dismissal of all National Socialist and World War II era cases against German companies. The United States will explain fully its foreign policy interests in achieving dismissal, as set forth below.

4. The United States' interests include the interest in a fair and prompt resolution of the issues involved in these lawsuits to bring some measure of justice to the victims of the National Socialist era and World War II in their lifetimes;

the interest in the furtherance of the close cooperation this country has with our important European ally and economic partner, Germany; the interest in maintaining good relations with Israel and other Western, Central, and Eastern European nations, from which many of those who suffered during the National Socialist era and World War II come; and the interest in achieving legal peace for asserted claims against German companies arising from their involvement in the National Socialist era and World War II.

5. The Foundation is a fulfillment of a half-century effort to complete the task of bringing justice to victims of the Holocaust and victims of National Socialist persecution. It complements significant prior German compensation, restitution, and pension programs for acts arising out of the National Socialist era and World War II. For the last 55 years, the United States has sought to work with Germany to address the consequences of the National Socialist era and World War II through political and governmental acts between the United States and Germany.

6. The participation in the Foundation not only by the German Government and German companies that existed during the National Socialist era, but also by German companies that did not exist during the National Socialist era, allows comprehensive coverage of slave and forced laborers and other victims.

7. Plaintiffs in these cases face numerous legal hurdles, including, without limitation, justiciability, international comity, statutes of limitation, jurisdictional issues, forum non conveniens, difficulties of proof, and certification of a class of heirs. The United States takes no position here on the merits of the legal claims or arguments advanced by plaintiffs or defendants. The United States does not suggest that its policy interests concerning the Foundation in themselves provide an independent legal basis for dismissal, but will reinforce the point that U.S. policy interests favor dismissal on any valid legal ground.

8. The Foundation is fair and equitable, based on: (a) the advancing age of the plaintiffs, their need for a speedy, non-bureaucratic resolution, and the desirability of expending available funds on victims rather than litigation; (b) the Foundation's level of funding, allocation of its funds, payment system, and eligibility criteria; (c) the difficult legal hurdles faced by plaintiffs and the uncertainty of their litigation prospects; and (d) in light of the particular difficulties presented by the asserted claims of heirs, the programs to benefit heirs and others in the Future Fund.

9. The structure and operation of the Foundation will assure (or has assured) swift, impartial, dignified, and enforceable payments; appropriately extensive publicity has been given concerning its existence, its objectives, and the availability of funds; and the Foundation's operation is open and accountable.

Annex C
of the Agreement between
the Government of the Federal Republic of Germany
and
the Government of the United States of America
concerning the Foundation "Remembrance, Responsibility and the Future"

Definition of "German Companies"

"German companies," as used in Article 1(1) and Article 2(1), are defined as in Sections 12 and 16 of the legislation establishing the Foundation "Remembrance, Responsibility and the Future," as follows:

1. Enterprises that had their headquarters within the 1937 borders of the German Reich or that have their headquarters in the Federal Republic of Germany, as well as their parent companies, even when the latter had or have their headquarters abroad.

2. Enterprises situated outside the 1937 borders of the German Reich in which during the period between January 30, 1933, and the entry into force of the legislation establishing the Foundation "Remembrance, Responsibility and the Future," German enterprises as described in Sentence (1) had a direct or indirect financial participation of at least 25 percent.

3. "German companies" does not include foreign parent companies with headquarters outside the 1937 borders of the German Reich in any case in which the sole alleged claim arising from National Socialist injustice or World War II has no connection with the German affiliate and the latter's involvement in National Socialist injustice, unless there is pending a discovery request by plaintiff(s), of which the United States is provided notice by the defendant with copy to plaintiff(s), seeking discovery from or concerning World War II or National Socialist era actions of the German affiliate.

Appendix III

Joint Statement dated 17th July 2000

on occasion of the final plenary meeting concluding international talks on the preparation of the Foundation "Remembrance, Responsibility and the Future"

The Governments of the Republic of Belarus, the Czech Republic, the State of Israel, the Republic of Poland, the Russian Federation and Ukraine,

The Governments of the Federal Republic of Germany and the United States of America,

The German companies that founded the initiative to establish a foundation, which have since been joined by thousands of other German companies, and

As further participants, the Conference on Jewish Material Claims Against Germany, Inc. and the undersigned attorneys,

Recalling the proposal presented to the Chancellor of the Federal Republic of Germany by German companies on February 16, 1999, to send, as the century draws to a close, "a conclusive humanitarian signal, out of a sense of moral responsibility, solidarity and self-respect,"

Acknowledging the intention of both the Government of the Federal Republic of Germany and German companies to accept moral and historical responsibility arising from the use of slave and forced laborers, from property damage suffered as a consequence of racial persecution and from other injustices of the National Socialist era and World War II,

Recalling with appreciation the December 17, 1999, statement of the President of the Federal Republic of Germany paying tribute to those who were subjected to slave and forced labor under German rule, recognizing their suffering and the injustices done to them, and begging forgiveness in the name of the German people,

193

Affirming the consensus reached by all participants on December 17, 1999, at the 7th plenary meeting in Berlin on the establishment of the Foundation "Remembrance, Responsibility and the Future,"

Understanding that the Foundation is a sign of solidarity with the victims living in Central and Eastern European states and also a means of providing funds for victims from Central and Eastern Europe, most of whom benefited little from prior German compensation and restitution programs,

Understanding that insofar as the sum of 10 billion DM to be made available by the German public sector and the German companies for the Foundation "Remembrance, Responsibility and the Future" is concerned, that sum is both a ceiling and the final amount and that all payments made towards former National Socialist slave and forced laborers, for other personal injury, for damage to property and for the Future Fund envisaged as part of the Foundation, as well as other costs incurred in connection with the Foundation, shall be financed from this sum, from any contributions from others, and the interest thereon,

Understanding that additional contributions by others for use by the Foundation are welcomed,

Recognizing that the Foundation will provide dignified payments to hundreds of thousands of survivors and to others who suffered from wrongs during the National Socialist era and World War II,

Accepting the common objective that German companies (including parents and subsidiaries as defined in Annex A) receive all embracing and enduring legal peace,

Recognizing that it would be in the participants' interests for the Foundation to be the exclusive remedy and forum for the resolution of all claims that have been or may be asserted against German companies arising out of the National Socialist era and World War II,

Recognizing that the establishment of the Foundation does not create a basis for claims against the Federal Republic of Germany or its nationals,

Declare as follows:

1. All participants welcome and support the Foundation "Remembrance, Responsibility and the Future" and declare their agreement with its elements, including the annexed distribution plan (Annex B). The interests of the former forced laborers, other victims and heirs have been duly taken into account. Based on the circumstances, all participants consider the overall result and the distribution of the Foundation funds to be fair to the victims and their heirs. The Foundation opens up the prospect of payment being made, even if, 55 years after the end of the war, the wrong-doer can no longer be traced or is no longer in existence. The Foundation is also a means of providing funds for forced laborers in addition to payments made by Germany so far.

2. Given the advanced age of the victims concerned, the primary humanitarian objective of the Foundation "Remembrance, Responsibility and the Future" is to show results as soon as possible. All participants will work together with the Foundation in a cooperative, fair and non-bureaucratic manner to ensure that the payments reach the victims quickly.

3. Payments are to be made to applicants on behalf of the Foundation "Remembrance, Responsibility and the Future" irrespective of their race, religion and nationality. Insofar as the participants themselves distribute funds, they will base their decisions on the criteria of eligibility set out in the German law establishing the Foundation and will act justly in this regard.

4. The participating Governments and other participants will proceed as follows:

   a) The Government of the Federal Republic of Germany ("Germany") and the German companies shall each contribute DM 5 billion to the Foundation "Remembrance, Responsibility and the Future."

   b) Germany and the Government of the United States of America ("United States") will sign an Executive Agreement. Such agreement contains the obligation undertaken by the United States to assist in achieving all-embracing and enduring legal peace for German companies.

c) The Governments of the participating Central and Eastern European States and Israel will implement the necessary specific measures within the framework of their national legal systems to achieve all-embracing and enduring legal peace.

d) Assuming the request for a transfer referred to in paragraph (e) is granted, the DM 5 billion contribution of German companies shall be due and payable to the Foundation and payments from the Foundation shall begin once all lawsuits against German companies arising out of the National Socialist era and World War II pending in U.S. courts including those listed in Annex C and D are finally dismissed with prejudice by the courts. The initial portion of the DM 5 billion German Government contribution will be made available to the Foundation by October 31, 2000. The remainder of the German Government contribution will be made available to the Federal Foundation by December 31, 2000. Contributions from the German Government will begin earning interest for the benefit of the Foundation immediately upon being made available to the Foundation. The German Government may advance some of its contribution to the partner organizations for certain start-up costs before the lawsuits are finally dismissed. The German companies will make available reasonable advanced funding to provide appropriate publicity of the upcoming availability of Foundation benefits. German company funds will continue to be collected on a schedule and in a manner that will ensure that the interest earned thereon before and after their delivery to the Foundation will reach at least 100 million DM.

e) Counsel for German company defendants and counsel for plaintiffs (each seeking to assemble at least a substantial majority of defendants' and plaintiffs' counsel respectively) have filed requests with the Multidistrict Litigation Panel seeking a transfer under appropriate conditions to a mutually agreeable federal judge of the federal district court cases listed in Annexes C and D, for the purpose of implementing the other steps in this Joint Statement and in order to facilitate carrying out the objectives of the Executive Agreement by dismissing with prejudice the transferred cases and any later filed cases thereafter to be transferred as "tag-along" cases.

f) Germany will immediately establish a preparatory committee for the Foundation. The preparatory committee, after consulting with victims' representatives, will provide the publicity envisaged in paragraph (d) prior to the formal establishment of the Foundation, and, in consultation with partner organizations, prepare for the collection of applications for payment by the partner organizations.

g) The counsel for the plaintiffs will file motions or stipulations to dismiss with prejudice all lawsuits they have filed currently pending in U.S. courts against German companies arising out of the National Socialist era and World War II, including those listed in Annex C. They will also cooperate in seeking dismissal with prejudice by the courts of all other such lawsuits, including those listed in Annex D.

h) Germany and the United States will bring into force the Executive Agreement and the United States will thereupon file the Statement of Interest as provided therein.

i) The German Government will encourage German companies to open their archives relating to the National Socialist era and World War II.

Done at Berlin on the seventeenth day of July of the year Two Thousand in a single original, copies of which will be made available to interested parties.

For the Government of the Republic of Belarus

For the Government of the Czech Republic

For the Government of the State of Israel

For the Government of the Republic of Poland

For the Government of the Russian Federation

For the Government of Ukraine

For the Government of the United States of America

For the Government of the Federal Republic of Germany

For the Foundation Initiative of German Enterprises

For the Conference on Jewish Material Claims Against Germany, Inc.

Linda Gerstel
Lawrence Kill
for Anderson, Kill & Olick, P.C.

Edward W. Millstein
Stephen A. Whinston
for Berger and Montague, P.C

Irwin B. Levin
Richard E. Shevitz
for Cohen & Malad, P.C.

Michael D. Hausfeld
for Cohen, Milstein, Hausfeld & Toll, P.L.L.C.

Edward Fagan
for Fagan & Associates

Carey D'Avino

Barry Fisher
for Fleishman & Fisher

Dennis Sheils
Robert Swift
for Kohn, Swift & Graf, P.C.

Morris A. Ratner
for Lieff, Cabraser, Heimann & Bernstein, L.L.P.

Martin Mendelsohn
for Verner, Liipfert, Bernhard, Mc Pherson and Hand

Deborah M. Sturman
Melvyn I. Weiss
for Milberg, Weiss, Bershad, Hynes & Lerach, L.L.P.

J. Dennis Faucher
for Miller, Faucher, Cafferty & Wexler, L.L.P.

Burt Neuborne
New York University School of Law

Myroslaw Smorodsky

Melvyn Urbach

Stanley M. Chesley
for Waite, Schneider, Bayles & Chesley

Michael Witti

ANNEX A

to the
Joint Statement
on occasion of the final plenary meeting concluding international talks
on the preparation of
the Federal Foundation "Remembrance, Responsibility and the
Future",
done at Berlin, 17 July 2000

Definition of "German Companies"

"German companies" are defined as in Sections 12 and 16 of the legislation establishing the Foundation "Remembrance, Responsibility and the Future," as follows:

1. Enterprises that had their headquarters within the 1937 borders of the German Reich or that have their headquarters in the Federal Republic of Germany, as well as their parent companies, even when the latter had or have their headquarters abroad.

2. Enterprises situated outside the 1937 borders of the German Reich in which during the period between January 30, 1933, and the entry into force of the legislation establishing the Foundation "Remembrance, Responsibility and the Future," German enterprises as described in Sentence (1) had a direct or indirect financial participation of at least 25 percent.

3. "German companies" does not include foreign parent companies with headquarters outside the 1937 borders of the German Reich in any case in which the sole alleged claim arising from National Socialist injustice or World War II has no connection with the German affiliate and the latter's involvement in National Socialist injustice, unless there is pending a discovery request by plaintiff(s), of which the United States is provided notice by the defendant with copy to plaintiff(s), seeking discovery from or concerning World War II or National Socialist era actions of the German affiliate.

to the Joint Statement on occasion of the final plenary meeting concluding international talks on the preparation of the Federal Foundation "Remembrance, Responsibility and the Future," done at Berlin, 17 July 2000

Joint Chairmen's Proposal

LABOR	Suballocation Amount (Billion DM)	Amount (Billion DM)	Percentage of Amount for Labor	Overall Percentage	Supplemental Funds (Billion DM)	Suballocation Amount with Supplemental Funds[1a] (Billion DM)	Percentage of Amount for Labour with Supplemental Funds	Supplemental Funds Comments
Slave Labor	3.630 DM				0.100 DM			Swiss Fund
Forced Labor	4.420 DM							
Capital for Slave and Forced Labor		8.050 DM		80.50 %				
Suballocations (Slave and Forced Labor Combined)								
Partner Organizations[1]:								
Claims Conference[2]	1.812 DM		22.51 %		0.050 DM	1.812 DM	22.37 %	Interest Earned to CEEs
Republic of Poland	1.796 DM		22.31 %			1.812 DM	22.37 %	
Ukraine	1.709 DM		21.22 %			1.724 DM	21.29 %	
Russian Federation	0.828 DM		10.28 %			0.835 DM	10.31 %	
Republic of Belarus	0.687 DM		8.54 %			0.694 DM	8.56 %	
Czech Republic	0.419 DM		5.21 %			0.423 DM	5.22 %	
Rest of Eastern Europe & Rest of World (incl. Sinti and Roma)[3]	0.800 DM		9.94 %			0.800 DM	9.88 %	
Other Personal Injury Cases[4]		0.050 DM		0.50 %				

1. Amounts for each country foundation (Republic of Poland, Ukraine, Russian Federation, Republic of Belarus and Czech Republic) calculated using the same proportions (not percentages) as in January 31 CEE proposal.
1a. Amounts reflect reallocation of supplemental funds.
2. Amount includes payments to 120,800 slave laborers.
3. Includes up to 260 Mio. DM to be distributed by the Claims Conference to Jewish slave and forced laborers.
4. Other Personal Injury Cases (e.g., medical experimentation and other cases).

TOTAL CAPITAL FOR LABOR		8.100 DM	81.00 %	8.250 DM	
TOTAL CAPITAL FOR NON-LABOR		1.000 DM	10.00 %		
Banking Claims	0.150 DM				
Other Property Claims/Catch-all[5]	0.050 DM				
Banking Humanitarian	0.300 DM				
Insurance Claims[6]	0.150 DM			0.050 DM	Interest Earned
Insurance Humanitarian/ ICHEIC	0.350 DM				
FUTURE FUND		0.700 DM	7.00 %		
Programs for Heirs[7]					
Reserve for Insurance Claims[8]	0.100 DM				
ADMINISTRATION		0.200 DM	2.00 %		
TOTAL CAPITAL FOR NON-LABOR; FUTURE FUND AND ADMINISTRATION		1.900 DM		1.950 DM	
TOTAL FOUNDATION CAPITAL		10.000 DM	100 %		

5. "Catch-all" (property claims not otherwise covered).

6. Includes ICHEIC administrative expenses. Insurance claims in excess of DM 150 million allocation to be paid from interest earned (DM 50 million). Insurance claims in excess of DM 200 million to be paid from Future Fund reserve of DM 100 million.

7. 10 % (minimum) of Future Fund to be for programs for heirs.

ANNEX C

to the

Joint Statement

on occasion of the final plenary meeting concluding international talks on the preparation of
the Federal Foundation "Remembrance, Responsibility and the Future",
done at Berlin, 17 July 2000

List of known World War II and National Socialist era cases
against German companies pending in U.S. courts
filed by plaintiffs' counsel participating in the negotiations

No.	Status	Civil Action No.	Plaintiffs	Defendants	Plaintiffs' Attorneys	Court/Judge
1.	Filed 3/31/97; amended 6/26/97	97 CV 2262	(a) Marta Drucker Cornell; (b) Erna Gans; (c) Samuel Hersly; (d) Igor Kling; (e) Amalia Kranz Burstin; (f) Tibor Vidal; (g) Morris Weinman; (h) Martha Saraffian; (i) Rose Steg; (j) Margaret Zentner; (k) Socrates Fokas; (l) Ruth Hess; (m) Ivan Solti; (n) Renata Schwarz; (o) Henry Diamant; (p) Ernest Broderick; (q) Miriam Kohn Breiner; (r) Fritz Ehrlich; (s) Siegfried Herzfeld; (t) Leslie Keller; (u) Karl Loewenstein; (v) Maria Solt; (w) Georgina Feher Reich;	(1) Assicurazioni Generali S.p.A. Consolidated; (2) Allianz Elementar Versicherungs-AG (sued as Wiener Allianz Versicherungs-AG); (3) Riunione Adriatica di Sicurta S.p.A. (claim of Erna Gans dismissed without prejudice 5/24/99); (4) Allianz Lebensversicherungs-AG; (5) Der Anker Allgemeine Versicherungs AG; (6) Victoria Lebensversicherung AG (voluntarily dismissed without prejudice 7/29/99); (7) Basler Lebens-Versicherungs-Gesellschaft; (8) Gerling-Konzern	Edward Fagan (Fagan & Associates); Robert Swift, Joanne Zack (Kohn, Swift & Graf, P.C.); Michael Witti (Law Offices); Eugene Anderson, Lawrence Kill, Steven Cooper, Linda Gerstel (Anderson, Kill & Olick, P.C.)	S.D.N.Y./Mukasey

No.	Status	Civil Action No.	Plaintiffs	Defendants	Plaintiffs' Attorneys	Court/Judge
			(x) Henry Bauer; (y) Magdelena Kallan; (z) Rudy Rosenberg; (aa) George E. Strauss; (bb) Gitta Bron; (cc) Michael Jordan	Lebensversicherungs-AG; (9) Zürich Life Insurance Company (sued as Zürich Lebensversicherungs Gesellschaft); (10) Nordstern Lebensversicherungs-AG; (11) Union Des Assurances Generales de Paris *as Successor in Interest to* L'Union (dismissed 3/16/00); (12) Vereinte Lebensversicherung AG (sued as Vereinte Versicherung AG); (13) Mannheimer Lebensversicherung AG (dismissed without prejudice 10/26/98); (14) Winterthur Lebensversicherungs Gesellschaft; (15) Deutscher Ring Lebensversicherungs-AG, *as Successor in Interest to* STAR Life of Prague Insurance Company, Funnick, Österreichische Versicherungs Aktiengesellschaft, and Phonix and/or Phonix Österreichische Lebensversicherungs AG; (16) Adriavita S.p.A., f/k/a or *as Successor in Interest to* Trieste Adria (voluntarily dismissed without prejudice		

No.	Status	Civil Action No.	Plaintiffs	Defendants	Plaintiffs' Attorneys	Court/Judge
				10/20/97); (17) John Doe Corporation #1 *as a Successor in Interest to* Phonix Allgemeine Versicherungs Gesellschaft; (18) John Doe Corporation #2, *as Successor in Interest to* Phonix (Prague, The Czech Republic); (19) John Does Corporation #3 *as a Successor in Interest to* Feniks Life Insurance Company (In Bulgaria); (20) John Does Insurance Companies or Corporations 4-100		
2.	Filed 3/4/98; dismissed 9/13/99; opinion amended 10/29/99; appealed to 3d. Cir. 9/27/99	98 CV 959; CA-99-5832	Elsa Iwanowa	(1) Ford Motor Co.; (2) Ford Werke A.G.	Allyn Z. Lite, Joseph J. DePalma, Bruce D. Greenberg (Goldstein, Lite & DePalma, L.L.C.); Melvyn I. Weiss, Joseph Opper, Stephen Schwartz, Deborah M. Sturman (Milberg, Weiss, Bershad, Hynes & Lerach, L.L.P.); Michael D. Hausfeld, Paul T. Gallagher (Cohen, Milstein, Hausfeld & Toll, P.L.L.C.); Burt Neuborne (Of Counsel)	D.N.J./Greenaway; appealed to 3d. Cir.
3.	Filed 3/17/99 (consolidated complaint)	Master File No. 98 CV 3938 (as	After consolidation, recaptioned In Re Austrian and German Bank Holocaust	(1) Dresdner Bank AG; (2) Deutsche Bank AG; (3) Commerzbank AG; (4) Bayerische Hypo and	(a, g) Stephen A. Whinston (Berger & Montague, P.C.); Richard Appleby (Law Offices of Richard Appleby & Associates);	S.D.N.Y./Kram

No.	Status	Civil Action No.	Plaintiffs	Defendants	Plaintiffs' Attorneys	Court/Judge
		consolidated)	Litigation: (a) Bertysch Plaintiffs[1/]; (b) Bronner Plaintiff; (c) Duveen Plaintiffs; (d) Elkan Plaintiffs; (e) Haas Plaintiffs; (f) Hammerstein Plaintiffs; (g) Kahn Plaintiffs; (h) Mason Plaintiff; (i) Watman Plaintiffs; (j) World Council of Orthodox Jewish Communities, Inc. Plaintiff	Vereinsbank; (5) Creditanstalt AG (final order and judgment on class action settlement 1/18/00); (6) Bank Austria AG (final order and judgment on class action settlement 1/18/00); (7) Raiffeisen Zentralbank Österreich AG; (8) VIAG AG; (9) German and Austrian Banking Institutions 1 through 100	Marvin A. Miller, J. Dennis Faucher (Miller, Faucher, Cafferty & Wexler, L.L.P.); Mel Urbach (Law Offices of Mel Urbach); (b) Bernard Bronner (Law Offices of Bernard Bronner); (c, d) Melvyn I. Weiss, Joseph Opper, Deborah M. Sturman (Milberg, Weiss, Bershad, Hynes & Lerach, L.L.P.); Michael D. Hausfeld, Paul T. Gallagher (Cohen, Milstein, Hausfeld & Toll, P.L.L.C.); Irwin B. Levin, Richard E. Shevitz (Cohen & Malad, P.C.); Martin Mendelsohn (Of Counsel); Barry A. Fisher (Fleishman, Fisher & Moest); Robert L. Lieff, Elizabeth J. Cabraser, Caryn Becker, Morris A. Ratner, Karen J. Mandel (Lieff, Cabraser, Heimann & Bernstein, L.L.P.); Joseph D. Ament, Michael B. Hyman (Much, Shelist, Freed, Denenberg, Ament & Rubenstein, P.C.); Arthur Miller (Of Counsel); Burt Neuborne (Of Counsel); (e) James D. Silbert (Silbert, Hiller & Sena, L.L.P.); (f) James D. Silbert (Silbert, Hiller & Sena, L.L.P.); (h) Frederick P. Furth, Chris Micheletti (Furth, Fahrner & Mason); Elizabeth Berney;	

[1/] Gisela Bertysch and Greta Kleinman v. Bank Austria AG and Raiffeisen Zentralbank Oesterreich AG, 99 C.V. 302 (S.D.N.Y.) (Kram, J.) (filed 4/7/00; consolidated with 98 CV 3938, In Re Austrian and German Bank Holocaust Litigation, 2/19/99).

No.	Status	Civil Action No.	Plaintiffs	Defendants	Plaintiffs' Attorneys	Court/Judge
					(i) Linda Gerstel, Lawrence Kill (Anderson, Kill & Olick, P.C.); Edward D. Fagan, Carey D'Avino (Fagan & D'Avino); Robert A. Swift, Denis Shiels (Kohn, Swift & Graf, P.C.); William Marks (The Marks Law Firm); Michael Witti (Law Offices); (j) Stephen A. Whinston (Berger & Montague, P.C.); Mitchell R. Schrage (Mitchell R. Schrage & Associates, P.L.L.C.); Mel Urbach (Law Office of Mel Urbach)	
3A.	Filed 6/3/98; amended 10/5/98; consolidated with 98 CV 7793, 99 CV 190, 99 CV 302, 99 CV 387, 99 CV 388 and recaptioned as In Re Austrian and German Bank Holocaust Litigation, 98 CV 3938, 2/19/99; further consolidated with 99 CV 1065 and 99 CV 1067 3/11/99; consolidated class action complaint filed 3/17/99	98 CV 3938	(a) Harold Watman; (b) Ruth Abraham; (c) Michal Schonberger; (d) Rudolfine Schlinger; (e) Ernestine Schwarz Wasyl	(1) Deutsche Bank AG; (2) Dresdner Bank AG; (3) Creditanstalt AG; (4) Bank Austria AG; (5) German and Austrian Banking Institutions #1-100	Edward D. Fagan, Carey D'Avino (Fagan & D'Avino); Robert L. Lieff, Morris A. Ratner, Karen Mandel (Lieff, Cabraser, Heimann & Bernstein, L.L.P.); Robert Swift, Denis Shiels, Martin J. D'Urso (Kohn, Swift & Graf, P.C.); Irwin B. Levin, Richard E. Shevitz (Cohen & Malad, P.C.); Lawrence Kill, Linda Gerstel, Andrea Pincus (Anderson, Kill & Olick, P.C.); William Marks (The Marks Law Firm); Michael Witti (Law Offices); John M. Van Dyke (Law Offices); Mel Urbach (Law Offices)	S.D.N.Y./Kram
3B.	Filed in E.D.N.Y. 10/27/98; voluntarily	98 CV 6620; 99 CV 388	(a) Henry Duveen; (b) Bernard Lee; (c) Semmy Frenkel;	(1) Deutsche Bank AG; (2) Dresdner Bank AG; (3) Commerzbank AG;	Melvyn I. Weiss, Deborah M. Sturman (Milberg, Weiss, Bershad, Hynes & Lerach, L.L.P.);	E.D.N.Y./Glasser; S.D.N.Y./Kram

No.	Status	Civil Action No.	Plaintiffs	Defendants	Plaintiffs' Attorneys	Court/Judge
	dismissed without prejudice 2/24/99; refiled in S.D.N.Y. 1/15/99; consolidated with 98 CV 3938, In Re Austrian and German Bank Holocaust Litigation, 2/19/99		(d) Isaac Kaufman; (e) Siegfried Buchwalter; (f) Martin Lowenberg; (g) Lydia Milrod; (h) Stanley Gartska; (i) Margit Freidlander-Stuart; (j) Ruth Simon-Hamburger	(4) German Banking Institutions #1-100	Michael D. Hausfeld (Cohen, Milstein, Hausfeld & Toll, P.L.L.C.); Arthur Miller (Of Counsel); Burt Neuborne (Of Counsel); Robert L. Lieff, Morris A. Ratner, Elizabeth J. Cabraser (Lieff, Cabraser, Heimann & Bernstein); Irwin B. Levin, Richard E. Shevitz (Cohen & Malad, P.C.); Martin Mendelsohn (Law Offices); Barry A. Fisher (Fleishman, Fisher & Moest); Joseph D. Ament, Michael Hyman (Much, Shelist, Freed, Denenberg, Ament & Rubenstein, P.C.)	
3C.	Filed 10/30/98; consolidated with 98 CV 3938, In Re Austrian and German Bank Holocaust Litigation, 2/19/99	98 CV 7793	Johanna Mason	(1) Deutsche Bank AG; (2) Dresdner Bank AG; (3) Creditanstalt AG; (4) Bank Austria AG	Frederick Furth, Michael Lehmann (Furth, Fahrner & Mason)	S.D.N.Y./Kram
3D.	Filed in E.D.N.Y 11/9/98; voluntarily dismissed without prejudice 2/24/99; refiled in S.D.N.Y. 1/15/99; consolidated with 98 CV 3938, In Re Austrian and German Bank Holocaust Litigation, 2/19/99	98 CV 6996; 99 CV 387	(a) Marian Salomon Elkan; (b) Paul Schwarz; (c) Elisabeth Bishop; (d) Roman Neuberger; (e) Nathan Gutman	(1) Creditanstalt AG; (2) Bank Austria AG; (3) Deutsche Bank AG; (4) Dresdner Bank AG; (5) Austrian and German Banking Institutions #1-100	Robert L. Lieff, Morris A. Ratner, Elizabeth J. Cabraser, Karen Mandel (Lieff, Cabraser, Heimann & Bernstein, L.L.P.); Irwin B. Levin, Richard E. Shevitz (Cohen & Malad, P.C.); Martin Mendelsohn (Law Offices); Melvyn I. Weiss, Joseph Opper, Deborah M. Sturman (Milberg, Weiss, Bershad, Hynes & Lerach, L.L.P.); Michael D. Hausfeld, Paul T. Gallagher (Cohen, Milstein, Hausfeld & Toll, P.L.L.C); Barry A. Fisher (Fleishman, Fisher & Moest); Joseph D. Ament, Michael Hyman	E.D.N.Y./Glasser; S.D.N.Y./Kram

No.	Status	Civil Action No.	Plaintiffs	Defendants	Plaintiffs' Attorneys	Court/Judge
					(Much, Shelist, Freed, Denenberg, Ament & Rubenstein, P.C.); Arthur Miller (Of Counsel); Burt Neuborne (Of Counsel)	
3E.	Filed in E.D.N.Y. 11/19/98; dismissed without prejudice 3/2/99; refiled in S.D.N.Y. 2/11/99; consolidated with 98 CV 3938, In Re Austrian and German Bank Holocaust Litigation, 3/11/99	98 CV 7223; 99 CV 1067	(a) Gabriele Hammerstein; (b) Helen Nightengale; (c) Alice Nightengale Luhan	Deutsche Bank AG	Richard Hiller, Michael B. Sena (Silbert, Hiller & Sena, L.L.P.); Elizabeth Berney (Law Offices)	E.D.N.Y./Glasser; S.D.N.Y./Kram
3F.	Filed 1/5/99; transferred to S.D.N.Y. 3/16/99; consolidated with In Re Austrian and German Bank Holocaust Litigation, 98 CV 3938, 11/1/99	99 CV 0058; 99 CV 2165	Simon Bronner	Dresdner Bank AG	Bernard Bronner (Law Offices of Bernard Bronner)	E.D.N.Y./Glasser; transferred to S.D.N.Y. 3/16/99; reassigned to Kram 5/13/99
3G.	Filed 1/11/99; consolidated with 98 CV 3938, In Re Austrian and German Bank Holocaust Litigation, 2/19/99	99 CV 0190	(a) Bezalel Kahn; (b) Miriam Deutsch; (c) Ludwig Schaffer	(1) Deutsche Bank AG; (2) Creditanstalt AG	Richard Appleby (Law Offices of Richard Appleby); Stephen A. Whinston (Berger & Montague, P.C.); Mel Urbach (Law Offices of Mel Urbach); Marvin A. Miller, J. Dennis Faucher (Miller, Faucher, Chertow, Cafferty and Wexler)	S.D.N.Y./Kram
3H.	Filed 2/11/99;	99 CV 1065	Gerhard Haas and	Deutsche Bank AG	James D. Silbert (Silbert, Hiller & Sena,	S.D.N.Y./Kram

No.	Status	Civil Action No.	Plaintiffs	Defendants	Plaintiffs' Attorneys	Court/Judge
	amended 3/3/99; consolidated with 98 CV 3938, In re Austrian and German Bank Holocaust Litigation. 3/11/99		Charlotte Haas Schueller		L.L.P.)	
3l.	Filed 3/3/99; consolidated with 98 CV 3938, In Re Austrian and German Bank Holocaust Litigation	99 CV 1586	Gerhard Haas and Charlotte Haas Schueller	(1) Bayerische Hypo; (2) Vereinsbank (successor by merger to Bayerische Hypotheken U-Wechsel Bank)	James D. Silbert (Silbert, Hiller & Sena, L.L.P.)	S.D.N.Y./Kram
3l.	Filed 10/5/99; consolidated with 98 CV 3938, In Re Austrian and German Bank Holocaust Litigation. 11/1/99	99 CV 10258	World Council Of Orthodox Jewish Communities, Inc.	Deutsche Bank AG	Mitchell R. Schrage (Mitchell R. Schrage & Associates, P.L.L.C.); Mel Urbach (Law Offices Of Mel Urbach); Stephen A. Whinston (Berger & Montague, P.C.)	S.D.N.Y./Kram
4.	Filed 8/21/98; consolidated with 98 CV 5019, Vogel v. Degussa AG, for pre-trial purposes only 2/5/99; dismissed 9/13/99; opinion amended 9/21/99; appealed to 3d. Cir. 9/29/99	98 CV 3958; CA-99-5871	(a) Alice Burger-Fischer; (b) Michal Schonberger; (c) Goldie Hoffmen-Engel; (d) Hester Haskel	(1) Degussa AG; (2) Degussa Corporation	Edward Fagan (Fagan & Associates); Michael Magaril, Lawrence Kill, Linda Gerstel, Andrea Pincus (Anderson, Kill & Olick, P.C.); Irwin B. Levin, Richard E. Shevitz (Cohen & Malad, P.C.); Robert L. Lieff, Karen Karpen (Lieff, Cabraser, Heismann & Bernstein); Robert Swift, Martin D'Urso (Kohn, Swift & Graf, P.C.); Morris A. Ratner, Karen Mandel (Lieff, Cabraser, Heimann & Bernstein); William Marks (The Marks Law Firm); Michael Witti (Law Offices	D.N.J./Debevoise; appealed to 3d. Cir.
5.	Filed 8/30/98; amended 9/1/98	98 CV 5499	(a) Helene Pollack; (b) Tivka Jacobovitz	(1) Siemens AG; (2) Fried. Krupp AG	Edward Fagan, Carey D'Avino (Fagan & Associates);	E.D.N.Y./Glasser

No.	Status	Civil Action No.	Plaintiffs	Defendants	Plaintiffs' Attorneys	Court/Judge
			Slomovic; (c) Richard Friedemann; (d) Herman Sheppard; (e) Jack Sittsamer; (f) Olga Szabo Berkovitz; (g) Tibor Eisen; (h) Morris Newman; (i) Channa Weisel; (j) Tania Porzucki; (k) Bernard Roth; (l) Morris Elbaum; (m) Alan Black; (n) Magda Davis; (o) Harry Nieschawer; (p) George Gottlieb	Hoesch-Krupp; (3) Henkel KG a.A (dismissed as defendant 8/12/99); (4) Bayerische Motoren Werke AG; (5) Daimler-Benz AG; (6) Volkswagen AG; (7) Audi AG; (8) Leica Camera AG; (9) Württembergische Metallwarenfabrik AG; (10) MAN AG; (11) Corporate Does Nos. 1-100	Robert Lieff, Morris A. Ratner, Karen Mandel (Lieff, Cabraser, Heimann & Bernstein); Robert Swift, Martin J. D'Urso, Steven M. Steingard (Kohn, Swift & Graf, P.C.); Irwin B. Levin, Richard E. Shevitz (Cohen & Malad, P.C.); William Marks (The Marks Law Firm); Michael Witti (Law Offices); Jon Van Dyke (Law Offices); Mary Boies (Boies & McInnis, L.L.P.); Harlan A. Levy (Barrett, Gravante, Carpinello & Stern, L.L.P.)	
6.	Filed 8/31/98; amended 11/24/99; consolidated as lead case with 98 CV 4429, Rosenfeld v. Volkswagen AG, 6/15/99	98 CV 4104	(a) Elly Gross; (b) Lilly Lea Klein; (c) Emanuel Rosenfeld	(1) Volkswagen AG; (2) Volkswagen of America, Inc.	Allyn Z. Lite, Joseph J. DePalma, Bruce D. Greenberg (Lite, DePalma, Greenberg & Rivas, L.L.C.); Melvyn I. Weiss, Joseph Opper, Deborah M. Sturman (Milberg, Weiss, Bershad, Hynes & Lerach, L.L.P.); Arthur Miller (Of Counsel); Burt Neuborne (Of Counsel); Michael D. Hausfeld, Kristopher A. Kinkade (Cohen, Milstein, Hausfeld & Toll, P.L.L.C.); Martin Mendelsohn (Law Offices); (c) Peter S. Pearlman (Cohn, Lifland, Pearlman, Herrmann & Knopf)	D.N.J./Greenaway; reassigned to Bissell 4/1/99
6A.	Filed 9/23/98; consolidated with lead case 98 CV 4104, Gross v. Volkswagen AG 6/15/99	98 CV 4429	Emanuel Rosenfeld	Volkswagen AG	Peter S. Pearlman, Jeffrey W. Herrmann (Cohn, Lifland, Pearlman, Herrmann & Knopf, L.L.P.); Stephen A. Whinston, Joel M. Sweet (Berger & Montague, P.C.); Mel Urbach (Law Offices of Mel Urbach)	D.N.J./Greenaway; reassigned to Bissell 3/31/99
7.	Filed 9/9/98 consolidated with	98 CV 4252; CA-99-5917	Malka Lichtman	Siemens AG	Peter S. Pearlman, Jeffrey W. Herrmann (Cohn, Lifland, Pearlman, Herrmann &	D.N.J./Debevoise; appealed to 3d. Cir.

No.	Status	Civil Action No.	Plaintiffs	Defendants	Plaintiffs' Attorneys	Court/Judge
	98 CV 4468, Klein v. Siemens AG for pretrial purposes 4/15/99; dismissed by Burger-Fischer v. Degussa AG 9/13/99; opinion amended 9/21/99; appealed to 3d. Cir. 11/8/99				Knopf, L.L.P.); Stephen A. Whinston, Joel M. Sweet (Berger & Montague, P.C.); Mel Urbach (Law Offices of Mel Urbach)	
8.	Filed 9/11/98; administratively terminated 3/30/00	98 CV 4280	(a) Elizabeth Hirsch; (b) Gerry Blumenfeld	Fried. Krupp AG Hoesch-Krupp	Allyn Z. Lite, Joseph J. DePalma, Bruce D. Greenberg (Lite, DePalma, Greenberg & Rivas, L.L.C.); Melvyn I. Weiss, Deborah M. Sturman (Milberg, Weiss, Bershad, Hynes, & Lerach, L.L.P.); Arthur Miller (Of Counsel); Burt Neuborne (Of Counsel); Michael D. Hausfeld, Kristopher A. Kinkade (Cohen, Milstein, Hausfeld & Toll, P.L.L.C.); Martin Mendelsohn (Law Offices)	D.N.J./Greenaway
9.	Filed 9/11/98; administratively terminated pending MDL motion 4/20/00	98 CV 4299	(a) Erna Anolik; (b) Gaby Wilson; (c) Lily Klein; (d) Edith Hass; (e) Gary Bason	Fried. Krupp AG Hoesch-Krupp	Peter S. Pearlman, Jeffrey W. Herrmann (Cohn, Lifland, Pearlman, Herrmann & Knopf, L.L.P.); Stephen A. Whinston, Joel M. Sweet (Berger & Montague, P.C.); Mel Urbach (Law Offices of Mel Urbach)	D.N.J./Greenaway; reassigned to Bassler 3/31/99
10.	Filed 9/11/98; amended 4/27/99; amended 4/14/00	98 CV 4397	Chaje Grosz	(1) AEG Aktiengesellschaft; (2) Daimler-Benz AG; (3) DaimlerChrysler AG	Peter S. Pearlman, Jeffrey W. Herrmann (Cohn, Lifland, Pearlman, Herrmann & Knopf, L.L.P.); Stephen A. Whinston, Joel M. Sweet (Berger & Montague, P.C.); Mel Urbach (Law Offices of Mel Urbach)	D.N.J./Greenaway; reassigned to Barry 3/31/99; reassigned to Hochberg 12/16/99
11.	Filed 9/22/98	98 CV 4428	(a) Julean Jacobowitz;	Rheinmetall AG	Peter S. Pearlman, Jeffrey W. Herrmann	D.N.J./Greenaway;

No.	Status	Civil Action No.	Plaintiffs	Defendants	Plaintiffs' Attorneys	Court/Judge
			(b) Helen Feuerwerker		(Cohn, Lifland, Pearlman, Herrmann & Knopf, L.L.P.); Stephen A. Whinston, Joel M. Sweet (Berger & Montague, P.C.); Mel Urbach (Law Offices of Mel Urbach)	reassigned to Lifland 3/31/99
12.	Filed 9/24/98; dismissed by Burger-Fischer v. Degussa AG 9/13/99; opinion amended 9/21/99; appealed to 3d Cir. 9/27/99	98 CV 4468; CA-99-5848	(a) Martha Klein; (b) Zelig Preis	Siemens AG	Allyn Z. Lite, Joseph J. DePalma, Bruce D. Greenberg (Goldstein, Lite & DePalma, L.L.C.); Melvyn I. Weiss, Joseph Opper (Milberg, Weiss, Bershad, Hynes & Lerach, L.L.P.); Arthur Miller (Of Counsel); Burt Neuborne (Of Counsel); Michael D. Hausfeld, Kristopher A. Kinkade (Cohen, Milstein, Hausfeld & Toll, P.L.L.C.); Martin Mendelsohn (Law Offices)	D.N.J./Debevoise; appealed to 3d. Cir.
13.	Filed 9/30/98; administratively terminated 3/30/00	98 CV 4542	Malka Kohn	Diehl GmbH & Co. (now named Diehl Stiftung & Co.)	Peter S. Pearlman, Jeffrey W. Herrmann (Cohen, Lifland, Pearlman, Herrmann & Knopf, L.L.P.); Stephen A. Whinston, Edward W. Millstein (Berger & Montague, P.C.); J. Dennis Faucher, Patrick Cafferty, Michael Dell'Angelo (Miller, Faucher, Cafferty & Wexler, L.L.P.); Mel Urbach (Law Offices of Mel Urbach)	D.N.J./Greenaway
14.	Filed 10/2/98	98 CV 6054	(a) Piri Katz; (b) Piri Feinhandler	Wurttembergische Metallwarenfabrik AG	Richard Appleby (Law Offices); Stephen A. Whinston, Edward W. Millstein (Berger & Montague, P.C.); J. Dennis Faucher (Miller, Faucher & Cafferty, L.L.P.); Mel Urbach (Law Offices of Mel Urbach)	E.D.N.Y./Glasser

No.	Status	Civil Action No.	Plaintiffs	Defendants	Plaintiffs' Attorneys	Court/Judge
15.	Filed 10/16/98	98 CV 6335	(a) Jack Bressler; (b) Paul Krell; (c) Bernard Mueller; (d) Henry Wegner; (e) Gerhard Bochner; (f) David Fields; (g) Abraham Solnick	(1) Phillip Holzmann AG; (2) Leonhard-Moll AG; (3) Dyckerhoff & Widmann AG; (4) Corporate Does Nos. 1-100	Edward Fagan, Carey D'Avino (Fagan & D'Avino)	E.D.N.Y./Glasser
16.	Filed 11/3/98	98 CV 7834	Moses Mandelbaum	(1) Messerschmitt-Boelkow-Blohm GmbH; (2) Daimler-Benz AG	Richard Appleby (Law Offices); Stephen A. Whinston, Joel M. Sweet (Berger & Montague, P.C.); Mel Urbach (Law Offices) Marvin A. Miller (Miller, Faucher, Cafferty and Wexler, L.L.P.)	S.D.N.Y./Martin
17.	Filed 11/4/98; consolidated with 98 CV 3958 , Burger-Fischer v. Degussa AG, for purposes of pretrial discovery and dispositive motion practice only 2/5/99; dismissed by Burger-Fischer v. Degussa AG 9/13/99; opinion amended 9/21/99; appealed to 3d. Cir. 9/27/99	98 CV 5019; CA-99-5831	(a) Michael Vogel; (b) Maria Dorenblat; (c) Vernon Rusheen; (d) Maria Richman	(1) Degussa AG; (2) Degussa Corporation	Joseph J. DePalma, Allyn Z. Lite, Bruce D. Greenberg (Goldstein, Lite & DePalma); Robert L. Lieff, Morris A. Ratner, Karen Mandel (Lieff, Cabraser, Heimann & Bernstein, L.L.P.); Melvyn I. Weiss, Joseph Opper, Deborah M. Sturman (Milberg, Weiss, Bershad, Hynes & Lerach, L.L.P.); Irwin B. Levin, Richard E. Shevitz (Cohen & Malad, P.C.); Martin Mendelsohn (Law Offices); Joseph D. Ament, Michael Hyman (Much, Shelist, Freed, Denenberg, Ament & Rubenstein, P.C.); Michael D. Hausfeld, Paul T. Gallagher (Cohen, Milstein, Hausfeld & Toll, P.L.L.C.); Barry A. Fisher (Fleishman, Fisher & Moest); Arthur Miller (Of Counsel); Burt Neuborne (Of Counsel); Thomas F. Campion, Jr. (Drinker Biddle & Shanley, L.L.P.)	D.N.J./Debevoise; appealed to 3d. Cir.
18.	Filed 11/19/98;	98 CV 5248	Abraham Gluck	AGFA-Gevaert AG	Peter S. Pearlman, Jeffrey W. Herrmann	D.N.J./Greenaway

214

No.	Status	Civil Action No.	Plaintiffs	Defendants	Plaintiffs' Attorneys	Court/Judge
	amended 10/21/99; stayed and administratively terminated 3/30/00				(Cohn, Lifland, Pearlman, Herrmann & Knopf; Stephen A. Whinston, Edward W. Millstein (Berger & Montague, P.C.); J. Dennis Faucher (Miller, Faucher & Cafferty, L.L.P.); Mel Urbach (Law Offices of Mel Urbach)	
19.	Filed 11/19/98; amended 10/19/99; stayed and administratively terminated for 180 days or until further order 3/30/00	98 CV 5247	(a) Wilmos Spitzer; (b) Joseph Roth; (c) Abraham Gluck	Bayerische Motorenwerke AG	Peter S. Pearlman (Cohn, Lifland, Pearlman, Hermann & Knopf; Mel Urbach (Law offices of Mel Urbach)	D.N.J./Greenaway
20.	Filed 12/11/98	98 CV 5671	(a) Mark Stern; (b) Eugeniusz Ciszewski; (c) Leonard Lerer; (d) Alec Mutz; (e) Raymond Drillings	Heinkel Holding GmbH d/b/a and/or a/k/a Heinkel Management GmbH d/b/a and/or a/k/a Heinkel Apparatebau GmbH & Co., d/b/a and/or a/k/a Heinkel Industriezentrifugen GmbH & Co.	Allyn Z. Lite, Joseph J. DePalma, Bruce D. Greenberg (Goldstein, Lite & DePalma, L.L.C.); Robert L. Lieff, Elizabeth J. Cabraser, Morris A. Ratner, Karen Mandel (Lieff, Cabraser, Heimann, & Bernstein, L.L.P.); Irwin B. Levin, Richard E. Shevitz (Cohen & Malad, P.C.); Melvyn I. Weiss, Joseph Opper, Deborah M. Sturman (Milberg, Weiss, Bershad, Hynes & Lerach, L.L.P.); Michael D. Hausfeld, Paul T. Gallagher (Cohen, Milstein, Hausfeld & Toll, P.L.L.C.); Barry A. Fisher (Fleishman, Fisher & Moest); Joseph D. Ament, Michael Hyman (Much, Shelist, Freed, Denenberg, Ament & Rubenstein); Arthur Miller (Of Counsel); Burt Neuborne (Of Counsel)	D.N.J./Simandle

No.	Status	Civil Action No.	Plaintiffs	Defendants	Plaintiffs' Attorneys	Court/Judge
21.	Filed 12/30/98	98 CV 9186	(a) Walter Winters; (b) Ella Bernstein; (c) Herman and Samuel Rosenblatt; (d) Robert J. Ellyn and Alice Ellyn Bukantz; (e) Eugenia Schenker; (f) Henry Jacoby; (g) Inge Schlesinger; (h) Henry Shery	(1) Assicurazioni Generali S.p.A. Consolidated; (2) Allianz Versicherungs-AG; (3) Allianz Lebensversicherungs-AG; (4) Riunione Adriatica di Sicurta S.p.A.; (5) Der Anker, Allgemeine Versicherungs AG; (6) AXA Colonia Konzern AG; (7) Nordstern Allgemeine Versicherungs-AG; (8) Union Des Assurances de Paris-Vie, *also as Successor in Interest to* L'Union (dismissed without prejudice 3/15/00); (9) Victoria Lebensversicherung AG; (10) Gerling-Konzern Versicherungs-Beteiligungs-AG; (11) Wuerttembergische AG Versicherungs-Beteiligungs Gesellschaft (dismissed without prejudice 11/22/99); (12) Vereinte Lebensversicherung AG (sued as Vereinte Versicherung AG); (13) Mannheimer Lebensversicherung AG (dismissed without prejudice 8/9/99);	Melvyn I. Weiss, Barry A. Weprin, Deborah M. Sturman (Milberg, Weiss, Bershad Hynes & Lerach, L.L.P.); Michael D. Hausfeld, Paul T. Gallagher (Cohen, Milstein, Hausfeld & Toll, P.L.L.C.); Martin Mendelsohn (Law Offices); Irwin B. Levin, Richard E. Shevitz (Cohen & Malad, P.C.); Arthur R. Miller (Of Counsel); Burt Neuborne (NYU School of Law); Morris A. Ratner, Elizabeth J. Cabraser (Lieff, Cabraser Heimann & Bernstein, L.L.P.); Robert L. Lieff, Elizabeth J. Cabraser, Karen J. Mandel (Lieff, Cabraser, Heimann & Bernstein, L.L.P.); Joseph D. Ament, Michael B. Hyman (Much, Shelist, Freed, Denenberg, Ament & Rubenstein, P.C.); Barry A. Fisher (Fleishman, Fisher & Moest)	S.D.N.Y./Mukasey

No.	Status	Civil Action No.	Plaintiffs	Defendants	Plaintiffs' Attorneys	Court/Judge
				(14) Winterthur Lebensversicherungs-Gesellschaft; (15) Deutscher Ring Lebensversicherungs-AG, *also as Successor in Interest to* Star Life of Prague Insurance Company, Funnick, Österreichische Versicherungs AG, and Phonix and/or Phonix Österreichische Lebensversicherungs-AG; (16) Adriavita S.p.A., *also as Successor in Interest to* Trieste Adria (dismissed without prejudice 10/18/99); (17) Basler, Versicherungs-Gesellschaft; (18) Zürich Versicherungs AG; (19) Agrippina Versicherung AG; (20) Gothaer Versicherungsbank VVaG; (21) Hannover Rueckversicherungs-AG (dismissed without prejudice 9/23/99); (22) Münchener Rückversicherungs Gesellschaft AG; (23) Aachener und Münchener Versicherung AG, *also as Successor in*		

No.	Status	Civil Action No.	Plaintiffs	Defendants	Plaintiffs' Attorneys	Court/Judge
				Interest to Thuringia Versicherungs AG and Cosmos Allgemeine Versicherungs AG; (24) Albingia Versicherungs AG; (25) Kölnische Rückversicherungs-Gesellschaft AG; (26) ERC Frankona Rueckversicherungs AG; (27) ARAG Allgemeine Versicherungs AG; (28) Alte Leipziger Versicherung AG; (29) John Doe Corporation #1, *as Successor in Interest to* Phonix Allgemeine Versicherungs Gesellschaft; (30) John Doe Corporation #2, *as Successor in Interest to* Phonix (Prague, the Czech Republic); (31) John Doe Corporation #3, *as Successor in Interest to* Feniks Life Insurance Company (in Bulgaria); (32) John Doe Corporation #4 *as Successor in Interest to* Donau Allgemeine Versicherungs AG (Vienna); (33) John Doe Corporation #5, *as*		

No.	Status	Civil Action No.	Plaintiffs	Defendants	Plaintiffs' Attorneys	Court/Judge
				Successor in Interest to Rothenburger Lebensversicherungs AG (Goerlitz); (34) John Doe Insurance Companies or Corporations 6-100		
22.	Filed 1/8/99; stayed pending appeals 3/7/00	99 CV 385	Elizabeth Greenspan	Dynamit Nobel AG	Peter Pearlman (Cohn, Lifland, Pearlman, Hermann & Knopf); Mel Urbach (Law offices of Mel Urbach)	D.N.J./Lechner; reassigned to Hochberg 12/16/99
23.	Filed 1/28/99	99 CV 418	(a) Irving Kempler; (b) Irving Drilings; (c) Mania Richman; (d) Helen Prince; (e) Matilda Schwartz; (f) Louis Berman; (g) Steven Fenves; (h) Irving Dalesman	DaimlerChrysler AG	Allyn Z. Lite (Lite, DePalma, Greenberg & Rivas, L.L.C.); Melvyn I. Weiss (Milberg, Weiss, Bershad, Hynes & Lerach, L.L.P.)	D.N.J./Barry; reassigned to Hochberg 12/16/99
24.	Filed 1/28/99; amended 3/3/99	99 CV 392	(a) Marian Solarczyk; (b) Jozef Wolan; (c) Jerzy Skzypek; (d) Zbigniew Wiktor Wroblewski; (e) Edmund Majewski; (f) Tadeusz Dworakowski; (g) Tadeusz Biernacki; (h) Arnold Mostowicz; (i) Tadeusz Ludwik Pluzanski; (j) Jan Kazimierz Bokus; (k) Eugeniusz Szobski	(1) Bayer AG; (2) BASF AG; (3) Bayerische Motoren Werke AG; (4) Robert Bosch GmbH; (5) Continental AG; (6) Degussa-Huels AG; (7) Deutsche Bank AG; (8) Dresdner Bank AG; (9) DaimlerChrysler AG; (10) Diehl Stiftung & Co.; (11) General Motors Corporation; (12) Heinkel AG; (13) Hoechst AG; (14) Philipp Holzmann U.S.A. Inc.; (15) Fried. Krupp AG Hoesch-Krupp; (16) Magna International,	Allyn Z. Lite, Joseph J. DePalma, Bruce D. Greenberg (Goldstein, Lite & DePalma, L.L.C.); Melvyn I. Weiss, Joseph Opper (Milberg, Weiss, Bershad, Hynes & Lerach, L.L.P.); Michael D. Hausfeld, Paul T. Gallagher (Cohen, Milstein, Hausfeld & Toll, P.L.L.C.); Robert L. Lieff, Elizabeth J. Cabraser, Morris A. Ratner, Karen Mandel (Lieff, Cabraser, Heimann & Bernstein); Irwin B. Levin, Richard E. Shevitz (Cohen & Malad, P.C.); Barry A. Fisher (Fleishman, Fisher & Moest); Joseph D. Ament, Stuart M. Widman (Much, Shelist, Freed, Denenberg, Ament & Rubenstein, P.C.); Kenneth F. McCallion, Raj Sharma	D.N.J./Bassler

No.	Status	Civil Action No.	Plaintiffs	Defendants	Plaintiffs' Attorneys	Court/Judge
				Inc.; (17) MAN AG; (18) Mannesmann AG; (19) Rheinmetall Group; (20) Siemens AG; (21) Volkswagen AG; (22) Wuerttembergische Metallwarenfabrik AG; (23) German Doe Corporations 1-100; (24) Austrian Doe Corporations 1-100	(Goodkind, Labaton, Rudoff & Sucharow, L.L.P.); Arnold Levin (Levin, Fishbein, Sedran & Berman); Arthur Bailey (Law Offices of Arthur Bailey & Associates); Arthur Miller (Of Counsel); Burt Neuborne (Of Counsel)	
25.	Filed 2/17/99; stayed until 7/31/00	99 CV 0036	Eva Mozes Kor	Bayer AG	Irwin B. Levin, Richard E. Shevitz (Cohen & Malad, P.C.); Elizabeth J. Cabraser, Morris A. Ratner (Lieff, Cabraser, Heimann & Bernstein, L.L.P.); Melvyn I. Weiss, Barry A. Weprin, Deborah M. Sturman (Milberg, Weiss, Bershad, Hynes & Lerach, L.L.P.); Michael D. Hausfeld, Paul T. Gallagher (Cohen, Milstein, Hausfeld & Toll, P.L.L.C.); Martin Mendelsohn (Law Offices); Burt Neuborne (NYU School of Law); Joseph D. Ament, Michael B. Hyman (Much, Shelist, Freed, Denenberg, Ament & Rubenstein, P.C.)	S.D. Ind. (Terre Haute Div.)/McKinney
26.	Filed 2/19/99	99 CV 756	(a) Isaac Nittenberg; (b) Alex Feldman; (c) Zoltan Wieder	(1) Bayerische Motoren Werke AG; (2) BMW (US) Holding Corporation	Allyn Z. Lite (Lite, DePalma, Greenberg & Rivas, L.L.C.); Melvyn I. Weiss (Milberg, Weiss, Bershad, Hynes & Lerach, L.L.P.); Morris A. Ratner (Lieff, Cabraser, Heimann & Bernstein, L.L.P.); Martin Mendelsohn (Law Offices); Burt Neuborne (NYU School of Law)	D.N.J./Bissell
27.	Filed 3/31/99; removed to federal court	BC 302420; 99 CV 02503	(a) Simon Wiesenthal Center; (b) Gray Davis;	(1) Deutsche Bank AG; (2) Dresdner Bank AG; (3) Commerzbank AG;	Elizabeth J. Cabraser, Morris A. Ratner, Lisa L. Leebove, Karen J. Mandel (Lieff, Cabraser, Heimann & Bernstein,	Super. Ct. of Calif. (Co. of San Fran.)/ Quidachay;

No.	Status	Civil Action No.	Plaintiffs	Defendants	Plaintiffs' Attorneys	Court/Judge
	5/27/99		(c) Charlotte Lenga; (d) Pearl Lebovic; (e) Armin Lebovic; (f) Joseph Steinschriber; (g) Zoltan Klein; (h) Eva Szekely; (i) Marcel Baum	(4) Deutsche Lufthansa AG; (5) Ford Motor Company; (6) General Motors Corporation; (7) VIAG AG; (8) Does 1-100	L.L.P.); William S. Lerach, Melvyn I. Weiss, Deborah M. Sturman (Milberg, Weiss, Bershad, Hynes & Lerach, L.L.P.); Irwin B. Levin, Richard E. Shevitz (Cohen & Malad, P.C.); Martin Mendelsohn (Verner, Lipfert, Bernard, McPherson and Hand, Chartered); Arnold Levin, Craig D. Ginsburg, Daniel C. Levin (Levin, Fishbein, Sedran & Berman); Michael D. Hausfeld, Paul T. Gallagher (Cohen, Milstein, Hausfeld & Toll, P.L.L.C.); Joseph D. Ament, Michael B. Hyman (Much, Shelist, Freed, Denenberg, Ament & Eiger, P.C.)	removed to N.D. Cal./Illston
28.	Filed 4/14/99; amended 5/6/99	99 CV 2124	(a) Helen Honzatko; (b) Susan Karas	(1) Volkswagen AG; (2) Corporate Does #1-100	Carey R. D'Avino (Carey R. D'Avino & Associates); Edward D. Fagan (Fagan & D'Avino, L.L.P.)	E.D.N.Y./Glasser
29.	Filed 4/14/99; amended 5/6/99	99 CV 2122	(a) Eugene Lichtag; (b) Mordka Sauler; (c) Adele Reves	Thyssen Krupp AG	Edward D. Fagan (Fagan & D'Avino, L.L.P.)	E.D.N.Y./Glasser
30.	Filed 4/14/99	99 CV 2125	Leslie D. Edwards	(1) Siemens AG; (2) Corporate Does 1-100	Carey R. D'Avino (Carey R. D'Avino & Associates); Edward D. Fagan (Fagan & D'Avino, L.L.P.)	E.D.N.Y./Glasser
31.	Filed 4/20/99	99 CV 2238	Honorata Chmielewska	(1) Siemens AG; (2) Corporate Does 1-100	Carey R. D'Avino (Carey R. D'Avino & Associates); Edward D. Fagan (Fagan & D'Avino, L.L.P.)	E.D.N.Y./Glasser
32.	Filed 4/20/99	99 CV 2240	(a) Antoni Koziarski; (b) Halina Wozniak; (c) Blanka Lewinska; (d) Ryszard Czerski	(1) DaimlerChrysler AG; (2) Thyssen Krupp AG; (3) Henkel KG a.A.	Edward D. Fagan (Fagan & D'Avino, L.L.P.)	E.D.N.Y./Glasser
33.	Filed 4/26/99	99 CV 1892	(a) Josef Hirsz	Continental AG	Allyn Z. Lite (Lite, DePalma, Greenberg	D.N.J./Wolin

221

No.	Status	Civil Action No.	Plaintiffs	Defendants	Plaintiffs' Attorneys	Court/Judge
			Rozenberg; (b) Roger Joseph		& Rivas, L.L.C.); Melvyn I. Weiss (Milberg, Weiss, Bershad, Hynes & Lerach, L.L.P.)	
34.	Filed 5/4/99	99 CV 2527	(a) Denesne Polgar; (b) Imrene Sigeti; (c) Bela Sipos; (d) Gezane Meszaros; (c) Dezsonne Gancz; (d) Miklosne Becker; (e) Janos Acel; (f) Gabor Soltesz	(1) DaimlerChrysler AG; (2) Thyssen Krupp AG; (3) Henkel KG a.A.; (4) Corporate Does 1-100	Edward D. Fagan (Fagan & D'Avino, L.L.P.)	E.D.N.Y./Glasser
35.	Filed 5/4/99	99 CV 2528	(a) Gyulane Harmat; (b) Tiborne Vago; (c) Antalne Maschek	(1) Siemens AG; (2) Corporate Does 1-100	Edward D. Fagan (Fagan & D'Avino, L.L.P.)	E.D.N.Y./Glasser
36.	Filed 5/5/99	99 CV 0472	Anna Snopczyk	Volkswagen AG	Beth J. Kushner (von Briesen, Purtell & Roper); Michael D. Hausfeld, Lyn M. Rahilly (Cohen, Milstein, Hausfeld & Toll, P.L.L.C.); Martin Mendelsohn (Martin Mendelsohn); Arthur Bailey (Arthur N. Bailey & Associates); Irwin B. Levin (Cohen & Malad, P.C.); Gordon Ball (Law Offices of Gordon Ball); Arnold Levin (Levin, Fishbein, Sedran & Berman); Robert L. Lieff (Lieff, Cabraser, Heimann & Bernstein, L.L.P.); Robert A. Skirnick (Meredith, Cohen, Greenfoegel & Skirnick, P.C.); Melvyn I. Weiss (Milberg, Weiss, Bershad, Hynes & Lerach); Joy Rothenberg (Joy Rothenberg); Burt Neuborne (Neuborne Law Office)	E.D. Wis./Clevert
37.	Filed 5/5/99	99 CV 3285	Israel Spitzer	Philipp Holzmann AG	Richard Appleby (Law Offices of Richard Appleby); Stephen A. Whinston (Berger &	S.D.N.Y./Chin

No.	Status	Civil Action No.	Plaintiffs	Defendants	Plaintiffs' Attorneys	Court/Judge
					Montague, P.C.); Mel Urbach (Law Offices of Mel Urbach); Marvin A. Miller, J. Dennis Faucher (Miller, Faucher, Cafferty and Wexler); Peter S. Pearlman (Cohen, Lifland, Pearlman, Herrmann & Knopp, L.L.P.); William J. Cook (Ness, Motley, Loadholt, Richardson & Poole)	
38.	Filed 5/13/99	99 CV 2210	(a) Alex Feuer; (b) Erwin Marcus; (c) Helen Rappaport; (d) Pearl Puffeles	(1) Bayer AG; (2) Hoechst AG; (3) Schering AG	Allyn Z. Lite (Lite, DePalma, Greenberg & Rivas, L.L.C.); Melvyn I. Weiss (Milberg, Weiss, Bershad, Hynes & Lerach, L.L.P.)	D.N.J./Bassler
39.	Filed 5/17/99; consolidated as lead case with 99 CV 2229, *Michelin v. Adam Opel AG*, 6/4/99	99 CV 2228	(a) Felix Opatowski; (b) Hugo Schindler; (c) Emeric Lax	(1) Adam Opel AG; (2) Albert Ackermann GmbH & Co. KG (dismissed as defendant 2/3/00); (3) Alcatel Sel AG *as successor in interest to* Standard Elektronik Lorenz AG; (4) Bayer AG; (5) BASF AG; (6) Beiersdorf AG; (7) Robert Bosch GmbH; (8) Deutsche Lufthansa AG; (9) Diehl Stiftung & Co.; (10) Dunlop AG; (11) Durkopp Adler AG; (12) Franz Haniel & CIE; (13) General Motors Co.; (14) PFAFF Aktiengesellschaft; (15) Heidelberger Zement AG; (16) Henkel AG; (17) Hochtief;	Allyn Z. Lite, Joseh L. DePalma, Bruce D. Greenberg (Goldstein Lite & DePalma, L.L.C.); Melvyn I. Weiss, Deborah M. Sturman, Joseph Opper (Milberg, Weiss, Bershad, Hynes & Lerach, L.L.P.); Robert L. Lieff, Elizabeth J. Cabraser, Karen Mandel, Morris A. Ratner (Lieff, Cabraser, Heimann & Bernstein); Irwin B. Levin, Richard E. Shevitz (Cohen & Malad, P.C.); Barry A. Fisher (Fleishman, Fisher & Moest); Michael D. Hausfeld, Lyn M. Rahilly (Cohen, Milstein, Hausfeld & Toll, P.L.L.C.); Joseph D. Ament, Stuart M. Widman (Much, Shelist, Freed, Denenberg, Ament & Rubenstein, P.C.); Kenneth F. McCallion, Raj Sharma (Goodkind, Labaton, Rudoff & Sucharow); Arnold Levin (Levin, Fishbein, Sedran & Berman)	D.N.J./Barry; reassigned to Hochberg 12/16/99

No.	Status	Civil Action No.	Plaintiffs	Defendants	Plaintiffs' Attorneys	Court/Judge
				(18) Hoechst AG; (19) Philipp Holzmann AG; (20) Hugo Boss AG; (21) Leica Camera AG; (22) Magna International, Inc.; (23) MAN AG; (24) Mannesmann AG; (25) Miele & Co.; (26) Optische Werke G. Rodenstock; (27) Rheinmetall Group; (28) Thyssen AG; (29) Varta AG; (30) Wuerttembergische Metallwarenfabrik AG; (31) German Doe Corporations 1-100; (32) Austrian Doe Corporations 1-100		
39A.	Filed 5/13/99; consolidated with lead case 99 CV 2228, Opatowski v. Adam Opel, 6/4/99	99 CV 2229	(a) Gilbert Michelin; (b) Henry Rosmarin	(1) Adam Opel AG; (2) Albert Ackermann GmbH & Co. KG; (3) Alcatel Sel AG *as successor in interest to* Standard Elektronik Lorenz AG; (4) Bayer AG; (5) BASF AG; (6) Beiersdorf AG; (7) Robert Bosch GmbH; (8) Deutsche Lufthansa AG; (9) Diehl Stiftung & Co.; (10) Dunlop AG; (11) Durkopp Adler AG; (12) Franz Haniel & CIE; (13) General Motors Co.;	Allyn Z. Lite, Joseph L. DePalma, Bruce D. Greenberg (Goldstein, Lite & DePalma, L.L.C.); Melvyn I. Weiss, Deborah M. Sturman, Joseph Opper (Milberg, Weiss, Bershad, Hynes & Lerach, L.L.P.); Robert L. Lieff, Elizabeth J. Cabraser, Karen Mandel, Morris A. Ratner (Lieff, Cabraser, Heimann & Bernstein); Irwin B. Levin, Richard E. Shevitz (Cohen & Malad, P.C.); Barry A. Fisher (Fleishman, Fisher & Moest); Michael D. Hausfeld, Lyn M. Rahilly (Cohen, Milstein, Hausfeld & Toll, P.L.L.C.); Martin Mendelsohn; Joseph D. Ament, Stuart M. Widman	D.N.J./Hochberg

No.	Status	Civil Action No.	Plaintiffs	Defendants	Plaintiffs' Attorneys	Court/Judge
				(14) PFAFF Aktiengesellschaft; (15) Heidelberger Zement AG; (16) Henkel AG; (17) Hochtief; (18) Hoechst AG; (19) Philipp Holzmann AG; (20) Hugo Boss AG; (21) Leica Camera AG; (22) Magna International, Inc.; (23) MAN AG; (24) Mannesmann AG; (25) Miele & Co.; (26) Optische Werke G. Rodenstock; (27) Rheinmetall Group; (28) Thyssen AG; (29) Varta AG; (30) Wuerttembergische Metall Warenfabrik AG; (31) German Doe Corporations 1-100; (32) Austrian Doe Corporations 1-100	(Much, Shelist, Freed, Denenberg, Ament & Rubenstein, P.C.); Kenneth F. McCallion, Raj Sharma (Goodkind, Labaton, Rudoff & Sucharow); Arnold Levin (Levin, Feishbein, Sedran & Berman); Arthur N. Bailey (Law Offices of Arthur N. Bailey & Associates); Arthur Miller (Of Counsel); Burt Neuborne (Of Counsel)	
40.	Filed 5/17/99	99 CV 2270	(a) Vera Grossman Kriegel; (b) Gita Senderovic Duschnitzky	(1) Bayer AG; (2) Hoechst AG; (3) Schering AG	Allyn Z. Lite, Joseph DePalma, Bruce D. Greenberg (Goldstein, Lite & DePalma, L.L.C.); Elizabeth J. Cabraser, Morris A. Ratner (Lieff, Cabraser, Heimann & Bernstein, L.L.P.); Melvyn I. Weiss, Barry A. Weprin, Deborah M. Sturman (Milberg, Weiss, Berchad, Hynes & Lerach, L.L.P.)	D.N.J./Bassler
41.	Filed 8/11/99	99 CV 4671	(a) Evgeny Guminsky; (b) Matrena Rashina; (c) Natalia Manziy;	(1) Siemens AG; (2) Bayerische Motoren Werke AG;	Pyotr S. Rabinovich (Pyotr S. Rabinovich); Myroslaw Smorodsky (Smorodsky &	E.D.N.Y./Glasser; reassigned to Dearie 8/13/99

No.	Status	Civil Action No.	Plaintiffs	Defendants	Plaintiffs' Attorneys	Court/Judge
			(d) Raisa Savast'Yanova; (e) Ivan Shuvalov; (f) Alexander Boyko; (g) Nikolay Godun; (h) Fedor Lirskiy	(3) Adam Opel AG; (4) General Motors Corp.; (5) Fried. Krupp AG Hoesch-Krupp; (6) Volkswagen AG; (7) BASF AG; (8) Hoechst AG; (9) Bayer AG; (10) DaimlerChrysler AG; (11) MAN AG	Stawnychy); Danylo Kourdelchouk, Oleksandr Storozhuk, Ukriniurkolleguia (Ukranian Bar Association for Foreign Affairs)	
42.	Filed 2/22/00	00 CV 1287	(a) Nadia Matviivna Vydrygan; (b) Olga Mytrofanivna Zakharchuk; (c) Paraska Grigoryevna Forostyana; (d) Larisa Ryzhenko	(1) Commerzbank, AG; (2) Corporate Bank Does 1-100	Pyotr S. Rabinovich (Pyotr S. Rabinovich); Myroslaw Smorodsky (Smorodsky & Stawnychy); Danylo Kourdelchouk, Oleksandr Storozhuk, Ukriniurkolleguia (Ukranian Bar Association for Foreign Affairs)	S.D.N.Y./Preska

226

ANNEX D

to the

Joint Statement

on occasion of the final plenary meeting concluding international talks on the preparation of

the Federal Foundation "Remembrance, Responsibility and the Future",

done at Berlin, 17 July 2000

List of known World War II and National Socialist era cases

against German companies pending in U.S. courts

filed by plaintiffs' counsel not participating in the negotiations

No.	Status	Civil Action No.	Plaintiffs	Defendants	Plaintiffs' Attorneys	Court/Judge
1.	Filed 5/16/94 (formerly known as Nacher v. Dresdner Bank AG)	94 CV 10193	Mandowsky	Dresdner Bank AG	Paul E. Kerson (Leavitt, Kerson & Leffler)	N.Y. Sup. Ct. (Queens Co.)/Golia
2.	Filed 4/2/98; removed to federal court 5/6/98; amended 7/6/98; dismissed 10/15/98; appealed to 9th Cir. 11/16/98; remanded to C.D. Cal. 5/18/00	BC 178677; 98 CV 3490; CA-99-55012	(a) Sophie Stahl; (b) Gabriele Stahl Lansing; (c) Werner Stahl	(1) Victoria Holding AG, formerly Victoria Insurance Company of Berlin; (2) Ergo Versicherungsgruppe AG as Successor in Interest to Victoria Holding AG; (3) Does 1-100	(a-c) William M. Shernoff, Michael J. Bidart, Sharon J. Arkin, Ricardo Echeverria (Shernoff, Bidart, Darras & Arkin); (b, c) Lisa Stern (Law Office of Lisa Stern)	Super. Ct. of Calif. (Co. of L.A.); removed to C.D. Cal./Tevrizian; reassigned to Keller 7/30/98; appealed to 9th Cir. 11/16/98; remanded to C.D. Cal. 5/18/00
3.	Filed 12/8/98; amended 7/2/99	BC 201983	(a) Eugene Klein; (b) Adolf Klein; (c) Irving Klein; (d) Jolan Klein Berkowitz; (e) Regina Klein David; (f) Freda Klein Mandel; (g) Janina Terner; (h) Carmel Esther Terner;	(1) Riunione Adriatica di Sicurta S.p.A.; (2) Allianz Insurance Company; (3) Allianz Underwriters Insurance Company; (4) Fireman's Fund Insurance Company; (5) Does 1-100	William M. Shernoff, Michael J. Bidart, Ricardo Echeverria, Douglas Carasso (Shernoff, Bidart, Darras & Dillon); Lisa Stern (The Law Office of Lisa Stern)	Super. Ct. of Calif. (Co. of L.A.)/Otero

227

No.	Status	Civil Action No.	Plaintiffs	Defendants	Plaintiffs' Attorneys	Court/Judge
			(i) Jenny Berkovits Kaufman; (j) Susan Berkovits Berger			
4.	Filed 1/15/99; amended 10/26/99	99 CV 0316	(a) Bernard Blau, Esther Blau, and Gavriel Blau; (b) Eva Einhorn; (c) Vera Freund; (d) Lily Hirsch; (e) Rosa Kaszirer; (f) Margaret Kind; (g) Lou Klein; (h) Gitta Leser and Nissan Leser; (i) Nathan Mittleman and Olga Mittleman; (j) Sara Rosenberg; (k) Eva Spiegel; (l) Rivka Steinmetz; (m) Elizabeth Strauss; (n) Josef Weinberg	(1) Ford Motor Co.; (2) Siemens AG; (3) Ford Werke AG; (4) Volkswagen AG; (5) Volkswagen of America; (6) Thyssen Krupp AG; (7) Württembergische Metallwarenfabrik AG; (8) Bayerische Motoren Werke AG; (9) Henkel KG a.A. (dismissed without prejudice 6/29/99); (10) DaimlerChrysler AG; (11) Corporate Does 1-100	Stephen G. Rinehart, Shari K. Garelick (Parker Chapin, L.L.P.)	E.D.N.Y./Glasser; reassigned to Gleeson 4/27/99
5.	Filed 5/5/99	99 CV 2113	Elsa Michaels	Allianz Lebensversicherungs AG	Wallace C. Doolittle, Eric J. Kaufman (Law Offices of Wallace C. Doolittle)	N.D. Cal./Legge
6.	Filed 6/15/99	99 CV 4318	(a) Tatiana Aleksandrovna Zaitseva (on her own behalf and as heir of Natalia Aleksandrovna Kaukhova); (b) Olena Ovechkina	(1) Siemens AG; (2) DaimlerChrysler AG; (3) Bayer AG; (4) Thyssen Krupp AG; (5) Bayerische Motoren Werke AG; (6) Degussa-Hüls AG; (7) Continental AG; (8) Robert Bosch GmbH; (9) Heinkel AG; (10) Hoechst AG; (11) Philipp Holzmann AG; (12) Magna International	Jeffrey H. Squire (Kirby, McInerney & Squire, L.L.P.); Steve W. Berman, Jeffrey T. Sprung (Hagens Berman)	S.D.N.Y./Chin

No.	Status	Civil Action No.	Plaintiffs	Defendants	Plaintiffs' Attorneys	Court/Judge
				Inc.; (13) MAN AG; (14) Mannesmann AG; (15) Rheinmetall Group; (16) Volkswagen AG; (17) Wurttembergische Metallwarenfabrik AG; (18) German Doe Corporations 1-100		
7.	Filed 6/30/99; administratively closed 5/1/00	99 CV 1955	Savas Kardiasmenos	(1) Siemens AG; (2) Bayer AG; (3) BASF AG; (4) Bayerische Motoren Werke AG; (5) Robert Bosch GmbH; (6) Continental AG; (7) Degussa-Huels AG; (8) Deutsche Bank AG; (9) Dresdner Bank AG; (10) DaimlerChrysler AG; (11) Diehl Stiftung & Co.; (12) General Motors Corporation; (13) Heinkel AG; (14) Hoechst AG; (15) Philipp Holzmann USA, Inc.; (16) Fried. Krupp AG Hoesch-Krupp; (17) Magna International, Inc.; (18) MAN AG; (19) Mannesmann AG; (20) Rheinmetall Group; (21) Volkswagen AG; (22) Württembergische Metallwarenfabrik AG; (23) German Doe	Andreas N. Akaras, Nicholas G. Karambelas (Sfikas, Karambelas & Akaras, L.L.P.)	D. Md./Legg

No.	Status	Civil Action No.	Plaintiffs	Defendants	Plaintiffs' Attorneys	Court/Judge
				Corporations 1-100; (24) Austrian Doe Corporations 1-100		D.N.J./Barry; reassigned to Hochberg 12/14/99
8.	Filed 8/20/99	99 CV 3964	(a) Valentin Suvarov; (b) Sinaida Birkina; (c) Nina Stephanova; (d) Fedorova; Belgarodskaya; (e) Elena Zyablova; (f) Nadejda Guravieva; (g) Taisla Isakova; (h) Galina Novicova; (i) Alexander Petrov	(1) The Federal Republic of Germany; (2) German Doe Corporations 1-100; (3) Austrian Doe Corporations 1-100	Pompeyo Roa Realuyo (Law Offices); Lawrence Sucharow, Kenneth F. McCallion, Rajan Sharma (Goodkind, Labaton, Rudoff & Sucharow, L.L.P.); Mark S. Shane (Law Offices)	
9.	Filed 9/9/99; removed to federal court 10/8/99	BC 306265; 99 CV 4514	(a) Ingrid Fueloep-Miller; (b) Christian Fueloep-Miller; (c) Walter Lowendahl, Jr.; (d) Peter Cerf	(1) Deutsche Bank AG; (2) Dresdner Bank AG; (3) Does 1-20	Nicholas N. Nierengarten, Rick E. Kubler (Gray, Plant, Mooty Mooty & Bennett); Peter S. Modlin, Theodore A. Griffinger, Jr. (Landels, Ripley & Diamond, L.L.P.)	Super. Ct. of Calif. (Co. of San Fran.); removed to N.D. Cal. (San Fran. Div./ Chesney; reassigned to Illston 10/22/99
10.	Filed 10/5/99; amended 12/10/99	99 CV 6375	(a) Vera Delakowski; (b) Rosalia Dolak; (c) Taisa Pavloff; (d) Ana Rynchak	(1) The Federal Republic of Germany; (2) Bayer AG; (3) BASF AG; (4) Bayerische Motoren Werke, AG; (5) Robert Bosch GmbH; (6) Continental AG; (7) Degussa AG; (8) Deutsche Bank AG; (9) Dresdner Bank AG; (10) Daimler-Chrysler AG; (11) Diehl Stiftung & Co.; (12) Ford Motor Company; (13) Ford Werke AG; (14) General Motors Corporation;	Kenneth F. McCallion, Rajan Sharma (Goodkind, Labaton, Rudoff & Sucharow, L.L.P.); Pompeyo Roa Realuyo; Elena Khudiakova (Of Counsel)	E.D.N.Y./Korman

No.	Status	Civil Action No.	Plaintiffs	Defendants	Plaintiffs' Attorneys	Court/Judge
				(15) Heinkel AG; (16) Hoechst AG; (17) Philipp Holzmann USA, Inc.; (18) Fried. Krupp AG Hoesch-Krupp; (19) Magna International, Inc.; (20) MAN AG; (21) Mannesmann AG; (22) Rheinmetall Group; (23) Siemens AG; (24) Volkswagen AG; (25) Württembergische Metallwarenfabrik AG; (26) German Doe Corporations 1-100; (27) Austrian Doe Corporations 1-100		
11.	Filed 11/15/99; stayed until 9/28/00 on 5/17/00 (except plaintiffs must give de bene esse depositions before 7/28/00)	99 CV 4938	(a) Ryszard Staniszewski; (b) Lucyna Janczenia; (c) Eugeniusz Konecki; (d) Tadeusz Pludowski	(1) Bayer AG; (2) DaimlerChrysler AG; (3) Thyssen Krupp AG; (4) Siemens AG; (5) BASF AG; (6) Hoechst AG; (7) German Doe Corporations 1-100	Jeffrey H. Squire, Jill M. Manning, Mark Strauss (Kirby, McInerney & Squire, LLP); Steven W. Berman, Jeffrey T. Sprung (Hagens Berman)	N.D. Cal./Alsup
12.	Filed 4/7/00; removed to federal court	BC 227931; 00 CV 4405	Josef Tiber Deutsch	(1) Turner Corporation; (2) Hochtief AG; (3) Kitchell Corporation, USA; (4) Does 1-100	Barry Fischer	Super. Ct. of Calif. (Co. of L.A.)/Lefkowitz; removed to C.D. Cal./Wilson
13.	Filed 5/00	BC 229586	Bernd Givon	(1) Nordstern Lebensversicherungs-AG; (2) Nordstern Service International; (3) AXA	Shernoff Bidart Darras & Dillon	Super. Ct. of Calif. (Co. of L.A.)

Appendix IV

Agreement between the German Foundation "Remembrance, Responsibility and the Future," the "International Commission on Holocaust Era Insurance Claims" and the "German Insurance Association (GDV)" concerning Holocaust Era Insurance Claims dated 16th October 2002

This Agreement is entered into by and among the Foundation "Remembrance, Responsibility, and Future" (hereinafter referred to as the "Foundation"), the International Commission on Holocaust Era Insurance Claims (hereinafter referred to as "ICHEIC"), and the German Insurance Association (hereinafter referred to as the "GDV") regarding the settlement of individual claims on unpaid or confiscated and not otherwise compensated policies of German insurance companies in connection with National Socialist injustice and by the Foundation and ICHEIC regarding payments to the Humanitarian Fund of ICHEIC.

WHEREAS, on July 17, 2000 an Executive Agreement was executed between the Government of the Federal Republic of Germany and the Government of the United States of America concerning the Foundation (hereinafter referred to as the "Executive Agreement"); and

WHEREAS, on July 17, 2000 a Joint Statement was executed between the Government of the Federal Republic of Germany, the Government of the United States of America and the Government of Israel, among others, (hereinafter referred to as the "Joint Statement"); and

WHEREAS, effective August 12, 2000 the Federal Republic of Germany enacted the German Federal Law to establish the Foundation (hereinafter referred to as the "Foundation Law"); and

WHEREAS, the parties to this Agreement:

-Recognizing the political and moral responsibility of Germany for the victims of the genocide and other severe human rights violations committed against the Jewish people and people of other nations;

-Recognizing that German insurance companies wish to respond to their moral and historical responsibility arising from their participation in the injustices of the National Socialist Regime. These injustices resulted in the suffering and losses of their policyholders during the Holocaust era;

-Recognizing the heavy losses of property, financial and other assets belonging to the Jewish people and other victims of the National Socialist Regime, including the proceeds of insurance policies;

-Recognizing that the Federal Republic of Germany has provided comprehensive and extensive restitution and compensation for material wrongs caused by the National Socialist persecution, including damage to property and losses of insurance policies;

-Recognizing the legitimate interest German insurance companies have in all embracing and enduring legal peace in this matter;

-Recognizing that German insurance companies, having contributed substantially to the financing of all the Foundation's objectives, including compensation of unpaid or confiscated and not otherwise compensated insurance policies, cannot be expected to contribute again to the compensation of any wrongs committed during the National Socialist era and World War II;

-Recognizing that it is in the interest of all parties to this Agreement to have a resolution of the outstanding issues in a non-adversarial and non-confrontational way;

-Confident that ICHEIC, the Foundation and the GDV will provide a just and expeditious mechanism for making payments on individual claims on unpaid or confiscated and not otherwise compensated policies.

The parties have agreed as follows:

Section 1. Scope of the Agreement

(1) The parties to this Agreement agree to work together in a close and trustful cooperation in order (i) to compensate unpaid or confiscated and not otherwise compensated insurance policies of German insurance companies (ii) to ensure that the terms of this Agreement are followed in full by all parties and (iii) to make the claims processing efficient, effective and responsive to claimants.

(2) For this purpose 76,693,784 Euro (150 million Deutschmark) pursuant to Section 9, Paragraph 4, Sentence 2, Number 3, of the Foundation Law and an additional 25,564,594 Euro (50 million Deutschmark) from interest earned by the Foundation's capital pursuant to Section 9, Paragraph 5 of the Foundation Law shall be made available to cover this compensation and the costs as set out in Section6 (1). Monies from those funds may also be used for the other purpose in each case.

(3) In the event that the funds of 102,258,376 Euro (200 million Deutschmark) should not be completely drawn down after all approved claims and the agreed costs pursuant to Section 6 (1) have been met, the monies not used shall be transferred to the Humanitarian Fund of ICHEIC as created in Section 9, Paragraph 4, Sentence 2, Number 5 of the Foundation Law (hereinafter referred to as the Humanitarian Fund).

(4) If approved claims against German insurance companies cannot be covered by the funds pursuant to Section 9, Paragraph 4, Sentence 2, Number 3 and Paragraph 5 of the Foundation Law, the Foundation shall make available up to 51,129,188 Euro (100 million Deutschmark) from the Fund "Remembrance and the Future" to meet those claims.

(5) The payment of 178,952,160 Euro (350 million Deutschmark) to the Humanitarian Fund pursuant to Section 9, Paragraph 4, Sentence 2, Number 5 of the Foundation Law shall be effected according to the provisions in Section 7 of this Agreement.

Section 2. Eligible Claims

(1) A claim concerning a life insurance policy is eligible for compensation, if

(a) the claim relates to a life insurance policy in force between January 1,

1920 and May 8, 1945 and issued by or belonging to a specific German company and which has become due through death, maturity or surrender; and

(b) the insurance policy was not paid or not fully paid as required by the insurance contract or was confiscated by the German National Socialist Regime or by the government authorities as specified in the definition of Holocaust victim in Section 14; and

(c) the policy (or policies) in question was not covered by a decision of a German restitution or compensation authority. A policy or policies will be considered as having been covered by a decision of a German restitution or compensation authority, where the decision covers the same specific policy or policies as those referred to in the claimant's claim form, except in cases where:

- the claim was rejected by the German restitution or compensation authorities due to their own lack of jurisdiction; or
- the claim was rejected by the German restitution or compensation authorities due to the fact that the claim was made by a person not entitled to claim; or
- the claim was not timely filed; or
- documentary evidence that would have led to a decision in favor of the claimant was previously unavailable but subsequently became available (such as opening of company or government archives);

and

(d) the claimant is, in the following order of priority:

- the policy beneficiary or his heir pursuant to the Succession Guidelines (Annex C);
- the policyholder or his heir pursuant to the Succession Guidelines;
- the insured or his heir pursuant to the Succession Guidelines;

and

(e) the policy beneficiary or the policyholder or the insured life, who is named in the claim, was a Holocaust victim; and

(f) the claim was lodged before a date mutually agreed by the parties to this Agreement. This date, once agreed, will be appropriately publicized by the parties.

(2) A claim concerning non-life insurance is eligible for compensation, if

(a) the insured event occurred while the policy was in force at the time of the event. Notwithstanding the above, a non-life insurance claim shall not be eligible if it was caused by war unless it can be attributed to racial or religious persecution; and

(b) the claimant is entitled as policyholder or as rightful heir of the policyholder to benefits of the policy notwithstanding the statutes of limitation; and

(c) the benefits of the policy were not paid out, because the policyholder became a Holocaust victim before an original insurance claim could be lodged, or if lodged before it could be settled or the benefits were confiscated by the German National Socialist Regime or by the government authorities as specified in the definition of Holocaust victim in Section 14; and

(d) the damage from the insured event was not compensated or restituted; and

(e) the claim was lodged before a date mutually agreed by the parties to this Agreement. This date, once agreed, will be appropriately publicized by the parties.

(3) For the processing of a claim concerning a non-life insurance policy ICHEIC will send, where necessary, a questionnaire to the claimants requesting the following information:

(a) the name of the German company that issued the policy;

(b) the type of insurance which was issued;

(c) where and when the insurance had been issued and whether the insurance policy was still in force at the time the loss occurred;

(d) who took out the insurance and who might have been entitled to proceeds under the policy;

(e) when and how the damage or loss happened or the injury occurred which the claimant believes was covered by the insurance policy;

(f) in the case a business was insured, the type of business, legal entity and/or name under which the business was carried out; and

(g) whether any claim for restitution or compensation dealing with the insured property has been filed by the claimant or claimant's relatives.

(4) Where there is a claim on an insurance policy which meets all the criteria in this section, but where the company determines that the proceeds of the policy was or is deemed to have been paid into a blocked account, the provisions of Section 20 of Annex A will apply. Any appeal will name the GDV as the relevant party.

Section 3. Processing of application

(1) ICHEIC shall forward claims to the GDV to be processed by them and the companies in accordance with this Agreement.

Section 4. Appeals Procedure

(1) Pursuant to Section 19 of the Foundation Law and the attached Appeal Guidelines (Annex E) ICHEIC shall—with the consent of the Foundation—set up an independent appeals body (the Panel).

(2) The Panel shall consist of three members: Judge William Webster, Judge Abraham Gafni and Dr. Rainer Faupel. The three members shall select a Chairman from among themselves. If it becomes necessary, for any reason, to fill a vacancy on the Panel, the Chairman of ICHEIC and a member of the board of the Foundation shall consult.

(3) An applicant may file an appeal to the Panel for a fresh review of (i) a German insurance company's decision to deny his claim or, (ii) whether the Valuation Guidelines have been correctly applied in calculating an offer made to the claimant. Any such appeal must be filed within 120 days of the

receipt of the company's decision.

(4) The decisions of the Panel are not open to legal challenge.

(5) All claims decisions, including provisional claims decisions, taken by the German MOU companies prior to the signing of this Agreement will be eligible for the ICHEIC appeals process. All claims decisions taken by all of the German companies after the signing of this Agreement will be eligible for the appeals process specified in this Agreement (Annex E).

Section 5. Procedure for payment of awarded compensation

(1) Claimants with approved claims shall be paid on the basis of the following procedure, which rests on the principles of fairness, justice, security, speed and cost-effectiveness.

(2) The Foundation will pay companies for any payments they make to claimants in accordance with the provisions of this Agreement. The companies should record the names of claimants of the approved claims, and submit them, following receipt of the signed consent and waiver forms, to the GDV. The GDV will compile a comprehensive list and forward the list in electronic format to the Foundation. Once the Foundation has the appropriate information in respect of claims, the Foundation will prefund the companies to pay the submitted claims. The submission of requests for payment and the payment to the claimant must be completed within four weeks.

(3) Each insurance company, in the case of a claim that names the company or is otherwise matched with the company, will provide ICHEIC, the Foundation and the GDV with a copy of each of the following information: (i) each decision letter, both offers and denials, and copies of all relevant documents as specified in Annex A, paragraph 18, sent to a claimant, (ii) for each offer that is accepted, a copy of the consent and waiver forms (the original version goes to the Foundation as required in Section 16, paragraph 2 of the Foundation Law), properly signed by the claimant, together with the ICHEIC claim number, the claimant's family name and the first name and the amount of the agreed offer. The Foundation will inform ICHEIC of the claims accepted and of the payments it makes to the companies.

(4) The Foundation may at any time ask the BAFin to make checks regarding the correct processing of claims by a given company through sampling. The reasons for such checks could be, inter alia: The company was not covered by the auditing described in Annex I, or the company has received a considerable amount of claims, or there are reasons to assume that the company has not respected the agreed claims handling procedure.

(5) Each company, either directly or through the GDV shall cooperate and respond to any reasonable inquiry from ICHEIC having regard to speed and efficiency, regarding any decisions with respect to a claim mentioned in Section 5(3).

(6) If at any time during the claims process the Chairman of ICHEIC informs the Foundation in writing that he has reason to believe that in taking their decisions one or more companies are, or may be, failing to comply with any of the requirements of this Agreement, the Foundation shall ask the BAFin to investigate the possible failures of compliance either in the course of carrying out the checks referred to in paragraph 4 above on the company

concerned or, if necessary because the matters in question need to be resolved urgently, by carrying out a special investigation immediately. The BAFin shall carry out both the checks referred to in paragraph 4 and any special investigations under this paragraph having regard to paragraphs 3 to 7 of the Audit procedure set out in Annex I and with the participation of ICHEIC observers as provided in paragraphs 9 and 10 of Annex I. Should significant irregularities be found in the claims process, the BAFin shall require the company in question to remedy those irregularities. In cases of disagreement between the BAFin and the ICHEIC observers, the procedures set out in paragraphs 11 to 23 of Anne x I will apply.

(7) Payments to claimants will be on the basis that no fees will be charged to the claimant.

Section 6. Distribution of Foundation Funds

(1) The payments and costs to be met from within the 102,258,376 Euro (200 million Deutschmark) ceiling calculated in accordance with Section 9, paragraph 4, sentence 2, number 3 and Section 9, paragraph 5 of the Foundation Law, are as follows:

ICHEIC will receive, upon the signing of this Agreement, 102,258,376 Euro (200 million Deutschmark) for the payment of claims and a portion of ICHEIC's operating expenses. The uses of the 102,258,376 Euro (200 million Deutschmark) will be:

- To fund 50% of all actual operating expenses of ICHEIC from January 1, 2001 until the termination of ICHEIC'S claims process (with the exception of expenses associated with the Generali Trust and the administration of the Humanitarian Fund). These actual operating expenses are not to exceed $60 million, including a provision for financing the publication of lists, paying banking fees incurred by the companies for payments to claimants and a contingency reserve. If, due to unforeseen circumstances, operating expenses exceed the $60 million amount, there will be consultation between ICHEIC and the Foundation on providing additional funds from the 102,258,376 Euro (200 million Deutschmark) to ensure completion of ICHEIC's claims process. Any additional contribution would require the agreement of the Foundation.
- To prefund German insurance companies for claims to be paid by them (including approved claims on confiscated policies and approved claims against expropriated German insurance companies and their subsidiaries) from the date of signing of, and in accordance with, this Agreement.
- To reimburse the German MOU companies for ICHEIC claims paid by them prior to the signing of this Agreement in compliance with ICHEIC's Memorandum of Understanding.
- Should there be any funds remaining at the end of the life of ICHEIC, they will be used for humanitarian purposes, at ICHEIC's discretion.

(2) Prior to the signing of this Agreement, ICHEIC will have established banking arrangements, with the agreement of the Foundation, to enable the

Foundation to withdraw funds from the 102,258,376 Euro (200 million Deutschmark) account to prefund the German insurance companies for payments to claimants approved in accordance with Section 5 and the banking charges incurred by them in making the payments through a bank selected by ICHEIC based upon the lowest cost.

(3) No German MOU companies or any other German entities will be entitled to any offsets or any reimbursements (other than as provided in Section 6 (1) above), including costs of peer review audits.

(4) There will be no payments from the 102,258,376 Euro (200 million Deutschmark) or from the 178,952,160 Euro (350 million Deutschmark) to any costs incurred by the GDV or individual German companies in investigating claims.

(5) The German MOU companies will have no further financial obligation to cover ICHEIC's operating and other expenses (other than peer review audit) after this Agreement is signed.

(6) Any interest earned on the sums transferred to ICHEIC from the 102,258,376 Euro (200 million Deutschmark) and the 178,952,160 Euro (350 million Deutschmark) Humanitarian Fund in accordance with Section 1(2) and Section 1(5) above shall, from the date of the transfers, accrue to ICHEIC and may thereafter be freely used by ICHEIC for any legitimate purpose permitted by its Memorandum of Understanding. Any interest earnings that are used for the purpose of financing ICHEIC's administrative expenses shall not be regarded as part of the Foundation's 50% contribution to ICHEIC's future operating expenses as specified in Section 6 (1) above.

(7) If approved claims against German insurance companies cannot be covered by the 102,258,376 Euro (200 million Deutschmark) fund, the Foundation shall make available up to 51,129,188 Euro (100 million Deutschmark) from the Fund "Remembrance and the Future" to meet those claims.

Section 7. Humanitarian Fund of ICHEIC

The Foundation and ICHEIC have agreed between themselves on the following provisions:

(1) According to Section 9, Paragraph 4, sentence 2, number 5 of the Foundation Law, 178,952,160 Euro (350 million Deutschmark) will be transferred to the ICHEIC, upon the signing of this Agreement.

(2) These funds will be used for the following purposes:

- At the discretion of ICHEIC, for the payment of claims against unknown or no longer existing insurance companies and their subsidiaries (Section 8A1 of the MOU);
- For the payment of claims on insurance policies whose proceeds were transferred to blocked accounts;
- For the payment of the difference between the calculated value according to the BEG method and the minimum payment as described in Section 2(3) of the Valuation Guidelines;
- At the discretion of ICHEIC, for the benefit of needy victims of the Holocaust and for other Holocaust-related humanitarian and educational purposes;

238

- At the discretion of ICHEIC, for the payment of costs related to administration of the funds. Any such administrative costs shall be minimized to the maximum extent possible.

(3) Prior to the signing of this Agreement, ICHEIC will have established banking arrangements, with the agreement of the Foundation, to enable the Foundation to withdraw funds from the 178,952,160 Euro (350 million Deutschmark) Humanitarian Fund to prefund (i) the German insurance companies for the payment of the difference between the BEG calculated value and the minimum value on approved claims (ii) the GDV for the payment on policies transferred to blocked accounts and (iii) the banking charges incurred by the companies or the GDV in making such payments through a bank selected by ICHEIC based upon the lowest cost.

(4) The administrator of the Humanitarian Fund will inform the Foundation by 1 April every year about the usage of the funds in the previous year.

Section 8. Liability

If any employee or executive of one of the contracting parties violates their contractual obligations, either willfully or through gross negligence, the liable party shall compensate the other party or parties for any resulting damage.

Section 9. Duration of contract, termination

(1) This Agreement shall remain in effect until all obligations under this Agreement have been satisfied.

(2) This Agreement may be terminated through written notification by any party upon the gross violation of its provisions by one of the other parties, but only after the failure of the notified party to correct such violation within 30 days from the receipt of such notification and subject to the arbitration provisions of Section 11(4).

Section 10. Audit and the preservation of records

(1) ICHEIC is required to comply with Swiss accounting standards and shall maintain its records in accordance with generally accepted good practices. The ICHEIC shall keep the 178,952,160 Euro (350 million Deutschmark) Humanitarian Fund in a separate account for ease of administration and audit. ICHEIC will provide the Foundation, one month after the end of each semi-annual period, with a statement of its expenses as referred to in Section 1(2) during that period under each of its main subject headings. In addition ICHEIC will provide annual reports of its expenses related to administering the Humanitarian Fund. ICHEIC shall provide the Foundation with a copy of its audited accounts for each fiscal year together with its audited financial statement, including the auditor's report, as soon as such accounts and financial statement are available. The Foundation may make a reasoned request to ICHEIC to provide further information about ICHEIC's expenses and its budget process, where such information is needed in order to satisfy the Foundation that the funds provided to ICHEIC by the Foundation have been applied solely for the purposes set forth in this Agreement. Such request will be timely met. ICHEIC agrees that, upon receipt of a reasonable notice and written request, the Foundation, and its authorized auditing firm (which shall be an internationally

recognized auditing firm), shall have access, at the Foundation's expense, to ICHEIC's Chief Financial Officer and external auditors for the purpose of obtaining information to enable the Foundation to determine whether the funds provided by the Foundation to ICHEIC have been applied by ICHEIC solely for the purposes set forth in this Agreement.

(2) If on examination it is determined that ICHEIC has incorrectly applied the funds paid by the Foundation for ICHEIC administration, ICHEIC, shall, from other sources, restore to the appropriate fund the amount which has been incorrectly applied.

(3) ICHEIC shall ensure that the records generated during the processing of the claims and the appeals process are kept for at least a year after all claims have been processed and appeals concluded. If ICHEIC no longer wishes to retain these records, it shall offer them to the Foundation for further safekeeping.

Section 11. Choice of law clause, place of jurisdiction and arbitration

(1) This agreement shall be subject to Swiss law.
(2) The place of jurisdiction for all legal disputes arising from this Agreement shall be Geneva, Switzerland.
(3) The parties shall endeavor in good faith to resolve any dispute in relation to the interpretation or application of this Agreement amicably by negotiations between the parties.
(4) Any dispute, controversy or claim arising out of or relating to this Agreement, or the breach, termination or invalidity thereof, which cannot be settled by amicable agreement between the parties, shall be settled by arbitration in accordance with the UNCITRAL Arbitration Rules.

Section 12. Legal Peace

ICHEIC will use its best efforts to achieve an all embracing and enduring legal, regulatory, legislative and administrative peace for German insurance companies which are in compliance with this Agreement.

Section 13. Final Provisions

(1) This Agreement constitutes a final settlement between the three parties. No further verbal or written agreements between the three parties to this Agreement have been reached.

(2) This Agreement supersedes, for German MOU companies, the procedures established under the MOU, except that German MOU companies will remain subject to ICHEIC audit procedures including, at their own expense, the phase two peer review audits as provided in Annex J, the monitoring processes provided in Annex K and the appeals provisions as provided in Section 4 (5). The MOU companies will cooperate directly with ICHEIC in resolving any problems identified through the claims process.

(3) In light of ICHEIC's continued responsibility to ensure the implementation of the claims process, ICHEIC may make future decisions and arrangements as deemed necessary, provided that such decisions are consistent with this Agreement. Should there be any disagreement (1) as to whether a future ICHEIC decision is consistent with this Agreement or (2) otherwise pertaining to the interpretation of this Agreement, it should be addressed by

a high level representative of (i) ICHEIC, (ii) the Foundation, (iii) the GDV, (iv) US insurance regulators and (v) Jewish organizations participating in ICHEIC with the aim of finding a reasonable resolution of the dispute.

(4) A member of the Board of Directors of the Foundation or the Chairman of the ICHEIC or the Managing Director of the GDV may each at any time, by written notice, inform the other two parties of any amendment which it considers should be made to this Agreement. The other two parties shall, in such case, agree to discuss the amendment(s) proposed at a meeting to take place not more than one calendar month after receipt of the written notice. In order to become effective any amendment to this Agreement must be agreed by all three parties and must be made in writing.

(5) Should one or several of the provisions of this Agreement be or become ineffective this shall not affect the remaining provisions. If one of the provisions becomes ineffective the parties shall nevertheless endeavor to achieve the aim of the clause in question as far as this is legally permissible.

(6) This Agreement is executed in two languages (English and German). Each version is equally authentic.

(7) The following Annexes are attached and form an integral part of this Agreement:

Annex	**Subject**
Annex A	Claims Handling Procedure
Annex B	Relaxed Standards of Proof
Annex C	Succession Guidelines
Annex D	Valuation Guidelines
Annex E	Appeal Guidelines
Annex F	Consent and Waiver
Annex G	Appeal Form
Annex H	Agreement on Publication of Lists
Annex I	Agreements on Audits
Annex J	ICHEIC Stage II Peer Review Audit
Annex K	ICHEIC – Monitoring Group – Terms of Reference

Section 14. Glossary

Definitions—words used in this Agreement have the following meanings:

Agreement: means both this Agreement and its Annexes, as they may be amended from time to time.

Appeal: means the request by a Claimant for a fresh review of a decision made by a German Company in connection with the handling of insurance claims under this Agreement and that is submitted by the Claimant to the Appeals Panel for resolution.

Appeal Form: is the written document attached as Annex G.

Arbiter: means a suitably qualified person, with the necessary independence and impartiality, skills, and experience, appointed by the Panel to determine an Appeal or Appeals.

BAFin: means the German Bundesanstalt für Finanzdienstleistungsaufsicht, which is the federal agency for the supervision of financial services.

BEG: means the Bundesentschädigungsgesetz, which is the federal compensation law.

Blocked Account: means a bank account from which the owner was constrained in withdrawing the proceeds due to the legal restrictions on the account from 1933 to 1945 imposed by the German National Socialist Regime and other relevant governments.

BZK: means Bundeszentralkartei, which is the federal central filing agency.

Claimant: is an individual or representative of any individual(s) who has submitted an insurance claim covered by this Agreement.

Claims Handling Procedures: means the procedures laid out in Annex A.

Confiscated Policy: a policy the proceeds of which were paid as required by local law in the relevant countries (or are deemed to have been under the Valuation Guidelines) directly to a governmental authority that was not the named beneficiary of the policy.

Foundation: means the German Foundation "Remembrance, Responsibility and the Future" established under the German Foundation Law effective on August 12th, 2000.

GDV: means Gesamtverband der Deutschen Versicherungswirtschaft, which is the German Insurance Association.

German Company or **Company:** as defined in Annex C of the Executive Agreement means those enterprises that had their headquarters within the 1937 borders of the German Reich or that have their headquarters in the Federal Republic of Germany, as well as their parent companies, even when the latter had or have their headquarters abroad. Enterprises situated outside the 1937 borders of the German Reich in which during the period between January 30, 1933, and the entry into force of the legislation establishing the Foundation "Remembrance, Responsibility and the Future," German enterprises as described in the first sentence had a direct or indirect financial participation of at least 25 percent. "German companies" does not include foreign parent companies with headquarters outside the 1937 borders of the German Reich in any case in which the sole alleged claim arising from National Socialist injustice or World War II has no connection with the German affiliate and the latter's involvement in National Socialist injustice, unless there is pending a discovery request by plaintiff(s), of which the United States is provided notice by the defendant with copy to plaintiff(s), seeking discovery from or concerning World War II or National Socialist era actions of the German affiliate.

German MOU Company: means Allianz AG and its affiliates and the branches and affiliates of AXA, Zurich Financial Services, Winterthur Lebensversicherungs-Gesellschaft and Assicurazioni Generali, which meet the definition of a German company.

Holocaust victim: for the purposes of this Agreement means anyone who, as a result of racial, religious, political or ideological persecution by organs of the German National Socialist Regime, was deprived of his/her life or freedom; suffered damage to his/her mental or physical health; was deprived of his/her economic livelihood; suffered loss or deprivation of financial or other assets; or suffered any other loss or damage to his/her property. For the purpose of this definition, persecution by governmental authorities of the following countries for the period in brackets until the end of the Second World War in the following countries is considered equal to persecution by the organs of the German National Socialist Regime: Bulgaria (1941), Vichy France (1940),

Slovakia (1939), Italy (1939), Hungary (1939), Romania (1940), and Croatia (1940).

ICHEIC: means the International Commission on Holocaust Era Insurance Claims.

Insurance Claim: means a claim to an insurance policy submitted to the claims process.

Life Insurance Policy: means all forms of life insurance, including annuities, endowments and dowries.

MOU: means the Memorandum of Understanding dated August 25, 1998 creating ICHEIC which was signed by certain European insurance companies, certain non-governmental Jewish organizations, the State of Israel and certain insurance regulators.

Panel: means the body comprising three Panel Members which is the supreme decision making body for determining an Appeal or Appeals.

Panel Member: is one person of the Panel who may make a decision on an Appeal or Appeals as the case may be.

Relaxed Standards of Proof: means the Relaxed Standards of Proof as annexed to the this Agreement as Annex B.

Serious Irregularity: means an irregularity by the Panel, Panel Member or Arbiter which is likely to cause substantial injustice to the claimant by reason of (1) the Panel, Panel Member or Arbiter exceeding their powers (other than by exceeding their substantive jurisdiction), (2) failure of the Panel, Panel Member or Arbiter to conduct the proceedings in accordance with the Appeal Guidelines, or to deal with the issues put to them, and (3) the decision being obtained by fraud or in a manner which is contrary to public policy.

Succession Guidelines: means the guidelines determining the rights of the Claimant to succeed to the benefits of an insurance policy as annexed to this Agreement as Annex C.

Valuation Guidelines: means the guidelines assigning values to the proceeds of Holocaust era insurance policies as annexed to this Agreement as Annex D.

Executed in Washington, DC this 16 day of October, 2002, to be effective upon the signature of all parties.

for INTERNATIONAL COMMISSION ON HOLOCAUST ERA INSURANCE CLAIMS

By: _____/s/_____
    Lawrence S. Eagleburger

for FOUNDATION "REMEMBRANCE, RESPONSIBILITY AND FUTURE"

By:_____/s/_____   By:_____/s/_____
    Michael Jansen   Hans Otto Bräutigam

for GERMAN INSURANCE ASSOCIATION (GDV)

By: _____/s/_____
    Bernd Michaels

By: _____/s/_____
    Jörg Freiherr Frank von Fürstenwerth

ANNEX A
CLAIMS HANDLING PROCEDURES

Mailing forms to claimant

1) The ICHEIC helpline sends the claims form, the introductory letter, and the declaration of consent to the claimant (by mail). The claims form will be available in nine languages, including English and German and the claimant may indicate which version he prefers. The claimant will be asked to fill in the form in German or English, if possible, but may complete the claims form in any language.

Return of forms to the ICHEIC office

2) The answer of the claimant (completed questionnaire, signed declaration of consent, proof of identity and copies of existing documents in the possession of the claimant) is sent , by mail, to ICHEIC.

Work of call center

3) An information package will be sent to each cla imant who calls the helpline. If a claimant still cannot fill in the form, the call centre, using specially trained staff, will be available to assist claimants, free of charge, to complete the necessary forms correctly and completely. Where possible, each organisation will attempt to provide assistance within its current infrastructure and budget. However, if additional assistance is required, ICHEIC may fund the cost of the provision of these services.

Examination of returned forms by ICHEIC

4) The ICHEIC office examines the documents submitted by the claimants. If the claim form is in the Hebrew or Cyrillic alphabet, Capita London Market Services (CLMS) will transliterate names into the Latin alphabet using accepted and consistent transliteration standar ds and will translate the text into English. If the claim form is in German or English it will not be translated. Any other language will be translated into English.

5) CLMS will acknowledge receipt of the claim within 14 days and assign a claim number to it.

Named company claims

ICHEIC action

6) If the claimant names the company that issued the policy, CLMS will send the claim in electronic format to the GDV, provided that the following sections on the claim form (which are marked in bold) have been filled out (responses such as "do not know" or "not applicable" are adequate responses for sections 6.3 to 6.15, 7 and 8).

a) 1, eligibility
b) 2.1, 2.2 , 2.4, 2.7, 2.10, information about the claimant
c) 3.1 name of insurance company (which will be sent by official company number)
d) 6.1, 6.2, 6.4, 6.8, 6.11, information about the policyholder
e)7.1, 7.2, 7.4, 7.8, 7.11, information about the insured
f) 8.1, 8.2., 8.4, 8.8, 8.11, information about the beneficiaries
g) 9.1, compensation or restitution
h) Declaration of Consent and proof of identity

If the above mentioned essential information is missing, CLMS will ask the claimant to provide it before sending the claim to the GDV. If any other information (not regarded as essential) is missing, then it will be assumed that the claimant answered "I do not know" to those questions.

The GDV will check the information recorded on the electronic extracts. If any of the following sections have no information, the GDV will return the claim to CLMS as incomplete:

2.1, 2.2, 2.7, 3.1, 6.1, 6.2 and 6.8 (for 6.8 any variant of "I do not know" will be shown as 00/00/00). CLMS will contact the claimant for the missing information.

---

7) If companies require further information while pr ocessing a claim, companies will contact claimants directly with copies to ICHEIC.

---

8) The declaration of consent has to be signed. If this is not the case ICHEIC sends the declaration of consent back to the claimant and asks him to complete the declaration of consent.

---

9) Proof of identity of the claimant must also be provided. If it is not, CLMS will contact the claimant, but will not hold up the transmission of the claim while doing so.

Distribution of claim forms by ICHEIC

---

10) The ICHEIC office examines the contents of the claimant's answer in order to ascertain which company is concerned by the claim. If ICHEIC decides that the claim is covered by this Agreement , ICHEIC's claims processor (CLMS) will send to the GDV all information in electronic format of all claims (named and unnamed claims separately) and in the case of named company claims, will send hard copies of the claim form with relevant attachments directly to named companies. Where necessary, in cases of uncertainty about the company responsible for processing the claim, ICHEIC will consult BAFin. CLMS will send all new claims weekly.

11) ICHEIC informs the claimant that the claim has been sent to the GDV (NOTE: a text of the letter to the claimant will be agreed with the GDV)

Examination of named claims by the GDV and German compensation/restitution archives

12) The procedure for checking for compensation/restitution before named company claims are sent to companies is as follows:

---

i) GDV sorts out enquiries, checks if they have been made before,

ii) GDV records names, etc in database iii) GDV passes lists of named claims to BZK

iv) BZK investigates names within its file cards

v) BZK notifies GDV of match/no-match between the claimant or policyholder and its records of claimants for compensation

vi) GDV informs companies of "no match" or "match" with compensation/restitution archives

vii) BZK sends to the local archives details of the claims that "match"

viii) Local archives check if the BEG record relates to insurance and that the restitution or compensation proceedings related to the policy(ies) that are subject to the ICHEIC claim. The questions that local archives will be invited to answer include:
a) Was an insurance policy part of the compensation/restitution decision?
b) If so, what was the file reference in the archive?
d) If so, what was the policy number and which company issued the policy? (if known)
e) Was compensation /restitution paid? If so how much and to whom?
f) If compensation was not paid, what were the reasons for the rejection?

ix) Local archives inform the GDV accordingly with the answers to the questions

x) GDV passes the information to the relevant company

xi) Where the named insurance company does not belong to the GDV, the GDV shall forward the claim to that insurance company inviting it to process the claim in accordance with the Agreement. If the non-member insurance company agrees to do so, the claim is then treated like any other named claim. If the non-member insurance company refuses to investigate the claim or has not replied within 3 months, the GDV will process the claim itself on the basis of any information provided by the claimant and the named insurance company and sends the claimant its decision. In these cases the claimant will have a right of appeal against the GDV's decision.

Action by companies

13) The company informs the claimant with a copy to ICHEIC and the German Foundation if a restitution/compensation decision has been taken relating to the specific policy claimed, including a copy of the answers to the questions from the archive and of any relevant documents provided by the archive. Subject to the exceptions in Section 2 (1) (c) of the Agreement, in cases where a restitution/compensation decision was taken relating to the specific policy claimed, the claim will be denied.

14) The companies shall not search further in the compensation/restitution archives unless they need to do so to check whether a policy was compensated before making an offer to a claimant or where it is in the interest of the claimant to do so in order to match a claim.

15) Once checks for compensation are completed, the company will inform the claimant which company is investigating the claim. The company will carry out the research and processing of the claims in accordance with ICHEIC standards as agreed with the German Foundation and the GDV.

16) The company will provide the claimant with a status report on named claims within 90 days of receipt and, if necessary, every six months thereafter until a decision has been taken.

17) The company analyses the results of the investigation and makes a decision on the claim according to the relaxed Standards of Proof agreed with the Foundation (Annex B) and the Succession Guidelines (Annex C). Payment offers are based on the standards regarding valuation and interest established by ICHEIC and agreed with the Foundation (Annex D).

18) The company sends its decision directly to the claimant and adds copies of all relevant documents relating to the claim. This letter will also advise the claimant of his right to appeal the company's decision and the procedure for doing so. The company sends copies of the letter together with copies of all relevant documents relating to the claim to ICHEIC and informs the GDV accordingly.

19) If the company makes an offer to the claimant, its letter will include a document of waiver and release (Annex F). It will also include copies of all documents relevant to the claim and a valuation sheet showing how the sum has been calculated.

20) Where an insurance company determines, during the claims handling process, that the proceeds of the policy were paid or deemed to have been paid into a "blocked account" according to Annex D (Valuation Guidelines), the company shall inform the GDV. The GDV shall notify the claimant with a copy to ICHEIC that, although the claim concerns a policy that was properly paid by the insurance company, he/she is entitled, according to Annex D (Valuation Guidelines), to a humanitarian payment of the same amount as if the policy had remained unpaid. Along with the notification, the GDV shall offer the claimant a compensation payment, calculated according to Annex D (Valuation Guidelines). Once the offer is accepted, the GDV shall be prefunded by the Foundation from the ICHEIC Humanitarian Fund and shall pay the claimant directly. The GDV shall inform the claimant that he has a right of appeal in respect of the offer.

Procedure for handling unnamed company claims

Examination by ICHEIC

21) If the claimant did not name a company, CLMS will follow the same procedure as for named claims (in Paragraph 6) except that, if information about the company, the insured or the beneficiaries is missing, the claim will be handled as if the claimant had answered "I do not know" to those questions.

22) In these cases CLMS will only contact the claimant for additional information if requested by the GDV. If the Declaration of Consent is missing or incomplete, CLMS will only ask the claimant to provide it, if any company confirms that it has a match. The Declaration of Consent must then be provided by the claimant for all further processing.

23) If ICHEIC decides that the claim may be covered by the Agreement the

ICHEIC's claims processor (CLMS) will send to the GDV all information in electronic format of all claims (unnamed claims separately).

Action by GDV and companies

24) The GDV will distribute the electronic information on unnamed company claims to all relevant companies. The companies will check their records for any matches. Once a match is found, the company will inform the GDV, who will notify CLMS of the match and follow the procedure for named company claims (from Paragraph 12 onwards). Other companies will continue to search their records for other policies related to the original claim. If no match is found with any relevant company, the GDV will inform CLMS who will inform the claimant -if it cannot be researched any further.

Queries from claimants and handling delays

25) Claimants who request information from ICHEIC (or the company) about the handling of their claim will be sent a letter (or orally if they telephone the ICHEIC call centre), explaining that there may be some time before they receive a final decision on their claim. [Note: the draft of such a letter will be agreed with the GDV]

26) If the claimant provides fresh information (either in response to a request, or voluntarily) this will be sent by CLMS (in electronic format if possible) to the GDV who will inform the relevant company.

27) When CLMS finds a match between a claim and a record in the ICHEIC research database or a match is found in accordance with Annex H, Exhibit 3 CLMS will inform the respective company through the GDV using the same procedure as for fresh information. In such cases, the procedures for named company claims, including appeals, will apply.

28) If the claimant (through ICHEIC) or ICHEIC request information about a particular offer or denial the ICHEIC will contact the GDV. The company will provide the information in accordance with Section 5 (5) of the Agreement.

Appeals

29) All claims decisions, including provisional claims decisions, taken by the German MOU companies prior to the signing of this Agreement will be eligible for the ICHEIC appeals process. All claims decisions taken by all of the German companies after the signing of this Agreement will be eligible for the appeals process specified in this Agreement.

30) In the company's decision letter the claimant will be told of his rights to appeal and the procedure for doing so. Should a claimant file an appeal the company will follow the appropriate procedure as specified in Paragraph 29 above.

ANNEX B

RELAXED STANDARDS OF PROOF FOR LIFE INSURANCE POLICIES*

PART A

The Foundation "Remembrance, Responsibility and Future", the International Commission on Holocaust Era Insurance Claims (ICHEIC) and the German Insurance Association establish the following Relaxed Standards of Proof for use by German insurance companies (insurance companies) to assess the validity of unpaid life insurance claims from the Holocaust-era. The insurance companies will review claims pursuant to Relaxed Standards of Proof based on the information provided by the claimant as well as information discovered during the insurer's investigation of its files, records and archives, together with documents and records recovered during the search of appropriate archives by ICHEIC. The Relaxed Standards of Proof have been established to make it as easy as possible for a claim to be assessed, taking into account all relevant information.

A   In making a claim related to an insurance policy issued to a victim of the Holocaust, a claimant:

   1   shall show that it is plausible, in the light of all the special circumstances involved, including but not limited to the destruction caused by World War II, the Holocaust and the lengthy period of time that has passed since the insurance policy in question was obtained, that the claimant is entitled, either in whole or in part, to the benefits of the insurance policy under consideration.

   2   shall submit all relevant documentary and non-documentary evidence in the claimant's possession or under the claimant's control that may reasonably be expected to be submitted in view of the circumstances and the years that elapsed, of that particular claim, including but not limited to the history of the claimant and the claimant's family, the history of the policy-holder/beneficiary/insured (if they are not the claimant), and whether or not the policyholder, insured or claimant was a victim of the Holocaust;

   3   shall submit a copy or reproduction of any original document about the insurance contract within the claimant's possession or control;

   4   shall disclose whether the claimant or, to the claimant's knowledge, any other person has applied for, or received, any payment, compensation, reparations or restitution from any government or organisation in respect of the policy under consideration;

   5   shall disclose the identity of any person known to the claimant whom the claimant believes or may have reasonable grounds to believe may have a valid claim to the benefits of the policy under consideration; and

   6   shall not submit any evidence in support of a claim which the claimant knows is falsified, forged or materially misleading.

B   In assessing a claim by a claimant, the participating insurance companies have agreed:

---

* The eligibility criteria for non-life insurance policies is set out in Sections 2(2) and (3) of the Agreement.

1   not to reject any evidence as being insufficiently probative of any fact necessary to establish the claim if the evidence provided is plausible in the light of all the special circumstances involved, including but not limited to the destruction caused by World War II, the Holocaust and the lengthy period of time that has passed since the insurance policy under consideration was obtained;

2   not to demand unreasonably the production of any document or other evidence which, more likely than not, has been destroyed, lost or rendered inaccessible to the claimant;

3   to consider all information submitted by the claimant together with all information recovered by the insurers and ICHEIC during their search of insurer and other appropriate archives and at all times to consider the difficulties of proving a claim after the destruction caused by World War II, the Holocaust and the lengthy period of time that has passed since the insurance policy under consideration was obtained.

C   The existence of an insurance policy[1] will be considered adequately substantiated by any one of the following:

1   an original or copy of an insurance policy;

2   original or copies of premium receipts for an insurance policy;

3   information in the records of an insurer that verifies the existence of an insurance policy;

4   written correspondence between the insurer or agent or representative of the insurer and the claimant that verifies the existence of an insurance policy;

5   records held or maintained by any governmental body that verify the existence of an insurance policy;

6   records of any governmental body held by the claimant that verify the existence of an insurance policy.

The review process shall also consider whether any other document or statement, or combination of documents or statements, are sufficient to substantiate the existence of an insurance contract ("catch-all" provision).

D   Evidence of details of the insurance contract, the contract's history, information on any payment made to the policyholder, on blocked accounts or any government by the insurer and details of any payment, compensation, restitution, reparations, as well as nationalisation shall be considered adequately substantiated by any of the following documents, including but not limited to:

1   correspondence with an insurer or the agent or representative of an insurer;

2   information in the records of an insurer;

3   records held or maintained by any governmental body that verify the above mentioned details surrounding the insurance contract;

4   records of any governmental body held by the claimant that verify the above mentioned details surrounding the insurance contract.

The review process shall consider whether any other document or statement, or combination of documents or statements, are sufficient to substantiate the above-

---

1. Please note: The existence of an insurance policy does not automatically mean that the claim is valid.

mentioned details surrounding the insurance contract. ("catch-all" provision)

Information about personal circumstances may be gathered from the following documents, including but not limited to:

1   photographs;
2   maps;
3   reports or notices published in any newspaper, gazette or other journal;
4   diaries and personal letters;
5   family histories or tree;
6   birth or death certificates;
7   employment or school records;
8   military records;
9   a sworn or affirmed statement or affidavit, made by the claimant or by any person having relevant knowledge or authority;
10   immigration or emigration records;
11   letters, written evidence;
12   mortgages;
13   any other evidence that the claimant may wish to add to his file.

PART B

There can be no question that there has to be sufficient and adequate evidence of a contractual relationship with an insurance company. In the first instance the claimant is invited to provide whatever evidence he has. But whatever evidence the claimant can offer—and even if there is none—the companies will, as part of the claims process, carry out a thorough investigation of their records and where, deemed appropriate by the company, a search of outside archives, to help the claimants find evidence of the contractual relationship, even if they themselves have none. Satisfaction of that requirement will be determined in accordance with these Relaxed Standards of Proof, which are to be interpreted liberally in favour of the claimant; all parties agree to this basic concept. There is intentionally built into the Relaxed Standards of Proof wide latitude and flexibility. Indeed it is understood that, under the catch-all provisions, non documentary evidence, as well as other documentary evidence not specifically mentioned or contemplated in the Relaxed Standards of Proof, will be considered in determining the existence of a policy.

When the existence of the contract has been established, the burden shifts to that company. At this point the relevant details of the contract (e.g. type of insurance, value insured, premium and duration) need to be determined. This will be done using evidence from the claimant, the company or other outside sources.

Once the existence and details of the contract or claim are established, the company must establish the status of the contract, i.e. what, if any, adjustments are to be made to the value of the claim (i.e. loans, forfeitures, redemptions, payment of insured benefits, etc.). Most importantly the company will have to demonstrate, either from its own records or from external documentary evidence that it has fulfilled its contractual obligations.

A company's ability to satisfy this burden will depend, in part, on the adequacy of the records available to it. It is understood that some company records have been destroyed, either during the war or in the normal course of business, making it impossible to state with complete certainty whether any particular claim was paid or otherwise reduced in value. A company may present any evidence from its own records or external sources, which would prove that a payment was made to the proper insured or a beneficiary.

If a company is unable to demonstrate that a policy has been paid or that the value should otherwise be adjusted, the full payment of the sum insured under the policy, as calculated under the Valuation Guidelines (Annex D) will be offered.

Decisions based on these factors, like all other decisions, will be subject to the appeals procedure. Those hearing and deciding the appeals will be authorised to make fresh reviews of the record (including evidence offered under the catch-all provisions). This procedure will insure that those with strong evidence of a claim, even if purely nondocumentary, as well as those with less persuasive evidence, will be given an appropriate and fair review while maintaining the integrity of the process. The named companies will be afforded the opportunity to show that payments and adjustments were made, but claimants will not be unduly prejudiced by a lack of records or a presumption of payment where proof is unavailable.

In short, the process established in the Relaxed Standards of Proof allows the claimant to bring non documentary and unofficial documentary evidence for assessment, and guarantees that any claim (irrespective of what evidence the claimant can produce) will be thoroughly researched to see if conclusive evidence of the contract can be found. But it also avoids the risk to the integrity of the review process which would arise if payments were made on the basis of non documentary or unofficial documentary evidence, irrespective of its strength and plausibility.

PART C

Relaxed Standards of Proof will also apply where the burden of proof lies with the insurance company in accordance with Section D of Part A of this document. Under the Relaxed Standards of Proof the companies may use any evidence available to them from their own records or external archives to prove the status of the policy. In this context so-called "negative evidence" (eg, an inference from the absence of a policy from certain company registers that the policy did not exist or was cancelled or paid) is in principle admissible in determining a claim and in an appeal, subject to sufficient supporting evidence being available from the audit process and elsewhere, to show that the company records in question are trustworthy and comprehensive. However, where the Agreement provides for the use of "deemed dates" to determine whether a policy had been confiscated or paid into a blocked account, the "deemed dates" must also apply to such negative evidence. Accordingly, "negative evidence" from a company register showing that a policy had been paid after the "deemed date" would, in the absence of other evidence, create a presumption that the payment had been made into a blocked account or confiscated (see the provisions in the Valuation Guidelines Annex D, Sections 4 and 5), and the converse would apply before a "deemed date".

ANNEX C

SUCCESSION GUIDELINES

1   In matters concerning the right of the Claimant to succeed to or inherit the benefits of an insurance policy (the "Proceeds") from the person who was entitled to the Proceeds at the insured event (the "Deceased Person"), the Panel, Panel Member and Arbiters shall apply the following Succession Guidelines:

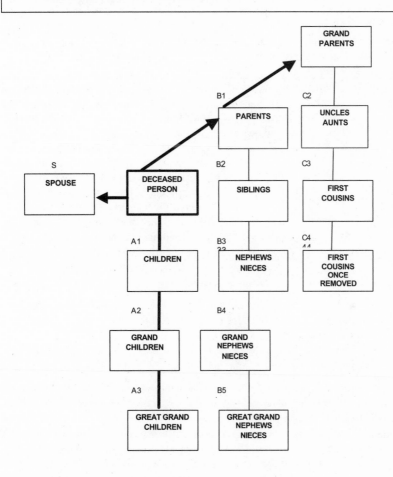

Category	Relationship to Deceased Person	Distribution of Proceeds
S	Spouse and no issue or other relatives	All Proceeds to spouse.
S + A1 – A3	Spouse and issue	$50,000 and half the residue of the Proceeds to spouse, balance to any issue as provided in Paragraph 2(i).
A1 – A3	Issue and no spouse	All Proceeds to issue as provided in Paragraph 2(i).
B1	One or both parents, no spouse, no issue	Proceeds to surviving parent or parents.
B2 – B5	Siblings, and no spouse, issue or parent	All Proceeds to the siblings and their issue as provided in Paragraph 2(i).
C1 – C4	One or more grand-parents or their issue, no spouse, issue, parents or siblings	1. Half of the Proceeds to the paternal grandparents. If none survives, half to their issue as provided in Paragraph 2(i). 2. Half of the Proceeds to the maternal grandparents. If none survives half to their issue as provided in Paragraph 2(i). 3. If the paternal or maternal grandparents and their issue do not survive the Deceased Person, the whole of the Proceeds to the surviving grandparents on the other side or their issue as provided in Paragraph 2(i).

2   For all purposes of these Succession Guidelines:

    (i)   Where the Proceeds or part of the Proceeds are to be divided in accordance with this Paragraph 2(i), those Proceeds shall be divided into as many equal shares as there are:
        (a)   living members of the nearest generation of issue then living; and
        (b)   deceased members of that generation who leave issue then living.

    (ii)   Each living member of the nearest generation receives one share and the share of each deceased member of that generation who leaves issue shall be divided in the same manner.
        (a)   The Deceased Person's relatives of the half blood shall be treated as if they were relatives of the whole blood.
        (b)   Distributees of the Deceased Person conceived before his or her death but born alive thereafter take as if they were born in his or her lifetime
        (c)   An adopted child shall take under this Succession Guidelines as if such adopted child were a natural child.
        (d)   Where one or more persons, Claimants, or the estates, heirs, legatees, descendants, survivors, beneficiaries, or other such successors-in-

interest (as limited by these Succession Guidelines), is entitled to the Proceeds, each such person shall take the proportion of the Proceeds to which he or she is properly entitled under these Succession Guidelines.

3   If the person who was entitled to the Proceeds at the date when the policy matured left a written will that has been provided to the Panel, Panel Member and Arbiters, as the case may be, the Panel, Panel Member and Arbiters shall distribute the Proceeds among the beneficiaries named in the will applying the Succession Guidelines to any question of succession to any person named in the will.

4   Where the sequence of demise between any persons is unknown, the older person shall be deemed to have predeceased the younger. Where the respective ages of such persons are unknown, they shall be deemed to have passed away at the same time.

5   Where no claim is submitted by a successor to the Deceased Person, the successors to the policyholder or, if none, to the insured may succeed to the Proceeds. In such cases, references to the Deceased Person shall be read as references to the insured or the policyholder as appropriate.

6   In cases where the application of the Succession Guidelines would be inappropriate because of special circumstances that would make their application contrary to the principles of justice, the Panel shall endeavour to reach a fair settlement.

In any decision of the Panel, Panel Member or Arbiter, the obligation of any particular company is limited to one payment of the proceeds of the policy, which may be divided between one or more persons as decided by the Panel, Panel Member or Arbiter.

ANNEX D

VALUATION GUIDELINES

1 INTRODUCTION

1.1 Annex D, as agreed between ICHEIC and the Foundation and which will be applied by German insurance companies, is intended as a guideline for those assigning values to valid claims on Holocaust era life insurance policies and for those advising on the offers made by companies on such policies.

1.2 The valuation of a claim includes two phases. The first is the assignment of a base value to a policy, depending on the terms of the contract, the history of the payment of premiums etc and the circumstances of the insured event (death of the insured or maturity of the policy).

1.3 The base value of a policy is the value that the policy would have had at the date of the insured event (on death of the insured person or on maturity at the end of the policy). The second phase in the valuation of a claim is the application of appropriate multipliers to the base value to produce the current value.

1.4 A policy shall be valued as unpaid if a claim on the policy is proved to be valid according to the Agreement and the relaxed Standards of Proof (Annex B) and there is no evidence that the policy was paid.

1.5 Rules for determining the treatment of policies paid during the Holocaust but where the proceeds were either confiscated or paid into a blocked account or where it is deemed likely that they were confiscated or paid into a blocked account are set out in Sections 4 and 5 below.

2 POLICIES ISSUED IN GERMANY

2.1 For policies issued in Germany (within the boundaries of 1937) and denominated in German currency, for which the Federal Republic of Germany established programmes of compensation after the war under the Bundesentschaedigungsgesetz (the BEG) or other programmes of compensation or restitution, the company shall assess the claim (both the base value and the valuation up to 1969) as if it had been submitted to the BEG, using the same methods of valuation, and apply a multiplier to this value of 8X.

2.2 For offers made from January 2001 the value will be updated by reference to the appropriate multiplier (see Schedule 2).

2.3 As agreed between ICHEIC and the Foundation, each claimant shall receive in respect of any valid claim on a policy issued in Germany by a German company at least a minimum payment of $ 4000, if he is himself a survivor of the Holocaust or $3000 for other valid claims. The company will determine the value of the policy according to Sections 2.1 and 2.2 of this Annex. No maximum limit should be applied. The differences between the calculated value according to Sections 2.1 and 2.2 and the minimum payment shall be met from the Humanitarian Fund. The total payment to the claimant shall be made by the company after the corresponding amounts have been provided by the Foundation.

2.4 If a claim is on a policy where the German Compensation or Restitution Authorities had rendered a decision on that specific policy then such a decision cannot be considered further in the claims process, subject to the exceptions provided in Section 2 (1) (c) of the Agreement.

3 DETERMINING BASE VALUES (Not Germany)

Policies relating to those who died during the Holocaust era

3.1 **Date of death:** If the company or the claimant has evidence of the date of death or deportation of the policyholder or the insured, this shall be used as relevant in assessing the base value. If there is no evidence, the dates for deemed death shown in Schedule 1, shall be used.

3.2 **Base value at death:** If the insured person or the policyholder died during the Holocaust era (see Schedule 1), the base value at the date of the insured event is the full sum insured minus any specific deduction (unless the company can demonstrate that the policy had been voluntarily converted to "paid up" status by the policyholder). (Paid up value is defined as a new sum insured at a lower value according to the terms of the policy, or as assessed by the company).

3.3 The **specific deductions** are for:

3.3.1 loans taken out during the life of the policy but before the beginning of the Holocaust era and not repaid;

3.3.2 premiums not paid, subject to the following conditions:

- If premiums stopped after the date of deportation (from the evidence) or the start of the Holocaust era (using Schedule1), the company shall deduct those unpaid premiums from the full sum insured, up to a maximum of two years.
- If premiums ceased before start of the Holocaust era given in schedule 1, the offer shall be based on the "paid up" value.
- Only if the company has evidence of unpaid premiums shall it make a deduction. If the company has no records it shall make no deduction.

and

- **3.3.3** compensation related to the specific policy and paid under post war arrangement (other than in Germany by governments or any other state entities. (Section 2 (1) (c) of the Agreement).

3.4 **Policies converted to paid up status:** In cases where there is evidence that the policy was formally converted to paid up status, the following rules apply:

- If conversion was before the start of the Holocaust era, base value equals paid up value.
- If conversion was in or after the year of the start of the Holocaust era, and the company can show that this was made voluntarily by the policyholder in writing, then the base value equals the paid up value.
- If conversion was made in or after the year of the start of the Holo-

caust era, but the company cannot show that this was made voluntarily by the policyholder in writing, then the base value equals the full sum insured, less any deductions for unpaid premiums in accordance with paragraph 3.3.2).

- From all base values any further adjustments required by paragraphs 3.3.1 and 3.3.3 should be applied.

Policies of survivors

3.5 If the insured person and the policy holder survived after 1945 (and premiums had not been paid), the base value is the "paid up" value of the policy as assessed by the company (which will deem premium payments to have stopped in 1945) and subject to any further adjustments required by paragraphs 3.3.1. and 3.3.3.

4 CONFISCATED POLICIES

4.1 Policies that were paid, as required by local law, to a government authority that was not the named beneficiary of the policy shall be given the same valuation as applied to unpaid claims. Payments shall be financed from money allocated for claims.

4.2 In the absence of evidence to the contrary produced either by the claimant or the company, a payment should be treated as confiscated if it was in or after the year given for the respective country in the table in Schedule 1 Column (iii).

4.3 Conversely, where a company can demonstrate that the proceeds of the policy were paid before the deemed date, it should be assumed, in the absence of evidence to the contrary, that the payment was made to the rightful beneficiary.

4.4 For France, any claim that a policy was confiscated will be considered under the procedures in paragraph 5.3 below for blocked accounts in France. [1]

5 BLOCKED ACCOUNTS

5.1 Where there is evidence that policies were paid, but the payment was into a blocked account, these policies shall be given the same valuation as applied to unpaid claims. As agreed between ICHEIC and the Foundation pursuant to Section 7 Paragraph 2 of the Agreement, payments shall be financed from money allocated for the Humanitarian Funds. The payment to the claimant shall be made by the GDV after the corresponding amounts have been provided by the Foundation.

5.2 A payment on a policy will be deemed paid into a blocked account if it was during the years given for the respective country in the table in Schedule 1 Column (ii), unless there is evidence that it was not paid into a blocked account.

5.3 For policies issued in France, where there is a scheme for the compensation of bank accounts that were blocked, the claim will be referred to the relevant authority.

5.4 For policies issued in Austria, the payment is deemed to be made into a blocked account if it was made to the policyholder from March 1938

---

1. Note: Procedures on Belgian policies are under consideration.

through the end of 1939 unless there is evidence that the payment was not made into a blocked account.

5.5 For policies issued in Germany the following rules shall apply:

5.5.1 During the period from the start of 1933 through to the end of 1937:

5.5.1.1 The payment is deemed to be made into a blocked account, if there is evidence according to the Relaxed Standards of Proof that:

the policyholder emigrated or was deported or was otherwise deprived in that period of his freedom as a Holocaust victim (as defined in Section 14 of the Agreement)

or

that a policyholder attempted to emigrate or was arrested or detained.

unless there is evidence that the payment was not made into a blocked account.

5.5.1.2 Conversely, if there is no evidence that the policyholder emigrated, attempted to emigrate, was arrested or detained or was deprived of his freedom as a Holocaust victim (as defined in Section 14 of the Agreement), then it can be assumed that payment was not made into a blocked account and was properly paid.

5.5.2 During the period from the start of 1938 through the end of 1939, the payment is deemed to be made into a blocked account if it was made to the policyholder or beneficiary, unless there is evidence that the payment was not made into a blocked account.

6 DETERMINING CURRENT VALUES

The current value of a policy is in the base value increased by agreed factors to allow for changes in currency, economic circumstances and interest during the years from the insured event to the present day. The factors for each country are designed to give a present day value to the base values, while taking account of the many economic and monetary events which disturbed the purchasing power of currencies in wartime and post-war Europe. For policies issued in Eastern Europe account has also been taken of the fact that insurance companies were nationalised or liquidated under the instructions of the post war governments.

6.1 Western European countries including Germany

The current value of offers on policies issued in these countries is calculated in accordance with the steps outlined in Schedule 2.

6.2 Eastern European countries

Offers on policies issued in these countries are in US dollars. The current value is determined in accordance with the steps outlined in Schedule 2. For policies issued in dollars and not converted into the local currency, the base value remains in dollars.

7 OTHER ISSUES

7.1 Unknown values

If a claimant satisfies the Relaxed Standards of Proof that a policy existed which was unpaid and names the company that issued the policy, but the amount of the policy cannot be determined, the offer shall be based on a multiple of three times (3X) the average value for policies in the respective country (shown in Schedule 3). The appropriate multipliers should then be applied but the payment offered should not exceed $6,000 per policy.

7.2 Minimum payments for policies issued in Eastern Europe

If the valuation of a claim on a policy issued in Eastern Europe is below $100, the minimum payment is $500; if the valuation is above $100, the minimum payment is $2,000 for survivors and $1,000 for other proven claimants.

7.3 Policies denominated in currencies other than the country of issue

If a policy was issued in a currency of another country (e.g. Swiss Francs) and subsequently converted into the local currency, in accordance with a law of general application, the current value is determined according to the rules for that country. For Western European countries, if the policy was not converted (e.g. a cross-border sale) the valuation is according to the multipliers in Schedule 4. For policies issued in Eastern Europe and not converted, the procedure in Schedule 2 from Step 2 (for East European claims) should be followed. Policies issued with a link to the price of gold should be treated as if they had been issued in the nominal currency.

Prior settlement by companies

7.4 Any claim settled between a claimant and an insurance company after the war will not be reopened, even if the claimant would be entitled to a larger amount under the Valuation Guidelines.

7.5 Cancelled policies

7.5.1 For policies that were cancelled or suspended for non-payment of the premiums after the payment of the first premium, if any unpaid premiums were due in years on or after the start of the Holocaust era in the country of issue and if the insured or the policyholder died during the Holocaust era, the policy shall be deemed to be valid for the full sum insured (less any specific deductions under paragraphs 3.3.1 and 3.3.3) at the date of the insured event.

7.5.2 If the policyholder and the insured survived the Holocaust era and did not reinstate the policy, the policy shall be valued as a paid up policy on the assumption that premiums had been paid until 1945.

8 FINAL PROVISION

All offers shall include a schedule showing how the calculation of the offer has been made.

Dates for determining the deemed dates of events, if not otherwise known, for
(i)   the start of the Holocaust or Nazi persecution in each country,
(ii)   payments into blocked accounts
(iii)   the start of confiscation of the proceeds of insurance polices and
(iv)   year of death,

	(i) Start of Holocaust Era/NS persecution	(ii)Dates of deemed payment to blocked account	(iii) Dates for start of deemed confiscation	(iv) Deemed death
Austria	1938	1938-1939	1940	1941
Belgium	1940	1941- 1944		1942
Bulgaria	1941		1942	1942
Croatia	1940		1940	1941
Czechoslovakia - Sudetenland	1938		1938	1941
Czechoslovakia -Bohemia Moravia and Slovakia	1939		1939	1941
France	1940	1941-1944		1942
Germany	1933	1933-1939	1940	1945
Greece	1941		1943	1943
Hungary	1939		1942	1944
Italy	1939		1943	1943
Netherlands	Sjoa		Sjoa	Sjoa
Poland	1939		1939	1941
Romania	1940		1941	1941
Yugoslavia	1941		1941	1941

TABLE OF VALUATION FACTORS
Western European Claims

Step 1
Multipliers to be used in step 1 as described in the valuation guide from the date of the insured event.
All multipliers to 2000

Year of insured event	Austria	Belgium	France*	Italy
1938	69.1	61.1		1335.2
1939	68.5	58.2	1.696	1271.4
1940	65.8	55.5	1.547	1144.4
1941	63.4	53.3	1.408	1035.1
1942	61.6	51.3	1.280	936.8
1943	60.2	49.3	1.163	679.9
1944	58.6	47.5	1.058	247.1
1945	54.3	45.7	0.961	163.6
1946	42.4	43.9	0.874	146.4
1947	28.4	42.0	0.795	109.2
1948	16.2	40.1	0.722	102.5
1949	12.8	38.3	0.657	97.0
1950	10.7	36.7	0.597	91.7
1951	8.2	35.1	0.543	86.4
1952	7.1	33.4	0.493	81.6
1953	7.1	31.8	0.464	77.0
1954	6.7	30.4	0.436	72.6
1955	6.3	29.0	0.411	68.3
1956	5.9	27.7	0.388	64.0
1957	5.5	26.2	0.362	59.9
1958	5.2	24.8	0.337	56.1
1959	4.8	23.6	0.316	53.1
1960	4.5	22.4	0.299	50.6

*The multipliers for France incorporate the currency reform of 1960 when 100 Old Francs were replaced by 1 New Franc.

Step 2

For offers made after 2001, an addition will be made to the value in Step 1 in respect of 2001 to reflect interest at the rate of 5.4% for the full year 2001 and an addition will be made at the rate of so many twelfths of 5%, including the month in which the offer is made, plus two twelfths, (for example, an offer in June 2002 will add a further 8/12ths of 5%).

1. **Netherlands** The arrangements for valuing and paying claims on policies issued in the Netherlands will be a matter for the Sjoa Foundation following the agreement with them.

2. For **Greece** , the policy sum insured should be converted to Italian lire at the average rate of exchange for the year of issue of the policy, any deductions would be made at the exchange rate for the appropriate year. The net sum due from the insured event has the multipliers for Italy applied to it. The exchange rates between the drachma and the lira are shown in Schedule 5.

3. For **Germany**, companies should use the method employed by the BEG to value claims up to the end of 1969 (the closure date for West German compensation claims). The values are then multiplied by 8, to bring the end 1969 value up to year 2000 values. For the year 2001 and later years the same multiplier is used as for Western Europe. The minimum payment on valid claim on a German policy will be $4,000 for claimants who are survivors and $3000 for other valid claimants. No maximum limit should be applied.

East European Claims

Step 1 - Exchange Rates
Convert the claims expressed in local currency to US dollars at the discounted exchange rates shown below.

Country	Currency	1 unit = US$
Bulgaria	Lev	US$ 0.00863
Czechoslovakia:	Koruna	US$ 0.024
Czechoslovakia: Sudetenland	Reichsmark	US$ 0.2807
Hungary	Pengo	US$ 0.1376
Poland	Zloty	US$ 0.1323
Romania	Lei	US$ 0.00509
Yugoslavia	Dinar	US$ 0.01594

Step 2

Multiply the dollar value by 11.286. This gives a value up to the end of the year 2000.

Step 3

For offers made after 2001, an addition will be made to the value in Step 2 in respect of 2001 to reflect interest at the rate of 5.4% for the full year 2001 and an addition will be made at the rate of so many twelfths of 5%, including the month in which the offer is made, plus two twelfths, (for example, an offer in June 2002 will add a further 8/12ths of 5%).

SCHEDULE 3

Average life insurance policy sums insured

The table below shows the average sums insured for each market in 1938 (1937 for Czechoslovakia), in local currency.

Average sum insured1938 (local currency)

Austria	Sch. 1246
Belgium	BFrs. 5730
France	FFs.20,744
Germany	RM. 841
Italy	L. 9355
Neth'lnds	G 309
Bulgaria	L. 26,559
Czech	Kcs. 12,070
Hungary	P. 827
Poland	Z. 2425
Romania	L.60,638
Yugoslavia	D. 24,080

The base value for qualifying claims (see paragraph 7.1 of the guidelines) would be a multiple of three times (3X) the averages shown above

Indices of bond yields and multipliers for UK, Switzerland & USA								
United Kingdom: Pound Sterling			Switzerland Swiss Francs			US dollars		
	bond yields	index	multi-pliers	bond yields	index	multi-pliers	bond yields	index	multi-pliers
1937	3.28			3.41			2.41		
1938	3.38	100.0	78.8	3.24	100	11.2	2.26	100.00	29.3
1939	3.72	103.7	76.0	3.76	103.8	10.8	2.05	102.05	28.7
1940	3.4	107.2	73.5	4.06	108.0	10.3	2.26	104.36	28.1
1941	3.13	110.6	71.2	3.39	111.6	10.0	2.05	106.50	27.5
1942	3.03	114.0	69.1	3.15	115.1	9.7	2.46	109.12	26.8
1943	3.1	117.5	67.1	3.32	119.0	9.4	2.47	111.81	26.2
1944	3.14	121.2	65.0	3.27	122.9	9.1	2.48	114.58	25.6
1945	2.92	124.7	63.2	3.29	126.9	8.8	2.37	117.30	25.0
1946	2.6	128.0	61.6	3.1	130.8	8.5	2.19	119.87	24.4
1947	2.76	131.5	59.9	3.17	135.0	8.3	2.25	122.56	23.9
1948	3.21	135.7	58.1	3.42	139.6	8.0	2.44	125.56	23.3
1949	3.3	140.2	56.2	2.94	143.7	7.8	2.31	128.46	22.8
1950	3.55	145.2	54.3	2.67	147.5	7.6	2.32	131.44	22.3
1951	3.64	150.4	52.4	2.95	151.9	7.4	2.57	134.81	21.7
1952	4.26	156.9	50.2	2.84	156.2	7.2	2.68	138.43	21.2
1953	3.94	163.0	48.3	2.55	160.2	7.0	2.92	142.47	20.6
1954	3.55	168.8	46.7	2.62	164.4	6.8	2.52	146.06	20.1
1955	4.32	176.1	44.7	2.97	169.3	6.6	2.8	150.15	19.5
1956	5.16	185.2	42.5	3.12	174.6	6.4	3.06	154.74	18.9
1957	5.49	195.4	40.3	3.65	180.9	6.2	3.54	160.22	18.3
1958	5.48	206.1	38.2	3.19	186.7	6.0	3.48	165.80	17.7
1959	5.19	216.8	36.3	3.08	192.4	5.8	4.13	172.64	17.0
1960	5.77	229.3	34.4	3.09	198.4	5.6	4.06	179.65	16.3
1989	9.58	3656.5	2.2	5.2	729.5	1.5	8.5	1534.41	1.9
1990	11.08	4061.6	1.9	6.68	778.2	1.4	8.55	1665.60	1.8
1991	9.92	4464.5	1.8	6.35	827.6	1.3	7.86	1796.51	1.6
1992	9.12	4871.7	1.6	5.48	873.0	1.3	7.01	1922.45	1.5
1993	7.87	5255.1	1.5	4.05	908.3	1.2	5.82	2034.34	1.4
1994	8.05	5678.1	1.4	5.23	955.8	1.2	7.11	2178.98	1.3
1995	8.26	6147.1	1.3	3.73	991.5	1.1	6.58	2322.35	1.3
1996	8.1	6645.0	1.2	3.63	1027.5	1.1	6.44	2741.91	1.2
1997	7.09	7116.2	1.1	3.08	1059.1	1.1	6.35	2628.88	1.1
1998	5.45	7504.0	1.1	2.39	1084.5	1.0	5.26	2767.16	1.1
1999	5	7879.2	1.0	3.02	1117.2	1.0	5.87	2929.59	1.0

Greece: Drachma to Lira rates
Following decision memo of 6 July 2000

1	2 US cents per drachma	3 US cents per lira	4 value of 1 drachma in lire	5 value of 1 lira in drachma
1915	19.0862	15.5287	1.229	0.814
1916	19.5296	15.2674	1.279	0.782
1917	19.7837	13.3181	1.485	0.673
1918	19.4195	12.7195	1.527	0.655
1919	12.223	11.26	1.086	0.921
1920	12.223	4.97	2.459	0.407
1921	5.0261	4.2936	1.171	0.854
1922	3.3059	4.7559	0.695	1.439
1923	1.7141	4.6016	0.373	2.685
1924	1.79	4.358	0.411	2.435
1925	1.5614	3.9776	0.393	2.547
1926	1.2579	3.8894	0.323	3.092
1927	1.3173	5.156	0.255	3.914
1928	1.3044	5.2571	0.248	4.030
1929	1.2934	5.2334	0.247	4.046
1930	1.2959	5.2374	0.247	4.042
1931	1.2926	5.2063	0.248	4.028
1932	0.832	5.1253	0.162	6.160
1933	0.7233	6.7094	0.108	9.276
1934	0.9402	8.5617	0.110	9.106
1935	0.9385	8.2471	0.114	8.788
1936	0.9289	7.2916	0.127	7.850
1937	0.9055	5.2607	0.172	5.810
1938	0.8958	5.2605	0.170	5.872
1939	0.8153	5.1959	0.157	6.373

Source: "Banking and Monetary Statistics" Board of Governors of
the Federal Reserve System November 1943

The valuation of drachma policies would convert the
policy value to lire, using the above exchange rates, for
the year in which the policy was taken out. (multiply
drachma value by figure from col.4)
No rates exist for Drachma - $ for the years 1919 and
1920. The rates shown are the average of 1918 and 1921.

ANNEX E
<u>APPEAL GUIDELINES</u>

1 Scope of These Guidelines

1.1   The Agreement and its Annexes, including these Appeal Guidelines ("Guidelines") shall govern the resolution of all appeals submitted to the Panel, Panel Member and Arbiters.

1.2   These Guidelines, in their entirety, apply only to appeals of decisions on life insurance policies.

1.3   In reaching decisions on appeals of decisions on non-life insurance policies, the Panel, Panel Member and Arbiter shall apply the rules set out in Section 2 (2) of the Agreement and in other respects shall follow these Guidelines to the extent possible, making adjustments as required (mutatis mutandis).

2 Jurisdiction

2.1   The Panel, Panel Member and Arbiters appointed pursuant to these Guidelines shall have jurisdiction over all issues raised in or by an appeal and shall make a fresh review of all information and evidence available to them and may uphold, amend or reverse the decision of the German company subject of the appeal.

2.2   The Panel, Panel Member and Arbiters shall have no jurisdiction over any of the following:

2.2.1   the validity of these Guidelines save that the Panel shall have jurisdiction to determine whether the Guidelines were applied correctly in any particular case;

2.2.2   claims concerning policies which are considered to have been covered by a decision rendered by a German restitution or compensation authority in accordance with Section 2 (1) (c) of the Agreement;

2.2.3   claims in which the claimant does not name a specific German company and where, upon subsequent investigation and research within the agreed claims handling procedures including Annex H, Exhibit 3, no policy was identified as being issued by or belonging to a specific German company;

2.2.4   claims concerning general humanitarian payments, as foreseen in Section 9 (4) No. 5 of the Foundation law (the Humanitarian Fund) except where, pursuant to Section 2 (4) of the Agreement, the appeal relates to, or appears to relate to, the issue as to whether the proceeds of an insurance policy were paid into a blocked account and in that case an appeal to the Panel or Panel Member or Arbiter will proceed. Where the appeal relates to, or appears to relate to, any other issue relating to a blocked account, the appeal will also proceed to the Panel, Panel Member and Arbiters. In any event, the Panel, Panel Member and Arbiter will direct, or order, that any sums to be paid to the claimant shall be paid, not by the German company, but instead according to Section 2 (4) of the Agreement.

3 Appointment and Organization of the Panel

3.1   Appeals are decided by a Panel.

3.2   The Panel shall consist of the following three members:

> Judge William Webster
>
> Judge Abraham Gafni
>
> Dr. Rainer Faupel

In the event of a vacancy occurring, the Chairman of ICHEIC and a Member of the Board of Directors of the Foundation shall consult.

3.3   The three members shall select a Chairman from among themselves.

3.4   The Panel shall not determine any appeal and is not properly constituted until all the members to be appointed as aforesaid are appointed.

3.5   Every Panel Member shall be and remain impartial and independent of the parties to each appeal to which he or she is appointed. No Panel Member shall accept an appointment to serve as a member of the Panel in an appeal involving a German company or claimant, with which Panel Member has any connection or relationship or where there are other facts or circumstances that are of such a nature as to call into question his or her independence or impartiality.

3.6   When nominating a Panel Member the nominating parties shall take into account the Panel Member's impartiality, availability, language skills, expertise, experience and the attendant costs associated with the nomination.

3.7   The Panel shall organize itself and may promulgate any rule of practice and/or internal guidelines necessary to the efficient and consistent processing of appeals, provided such rules or guidelines are consistent with these Guidelines and are approved by the Foundation and ICHEIC.

3.8   To assist the Panel in deciding appeals, a pool of Arbiters shall be established. The selection of the potential Arbiters shall be as follows:

3.8.1   Names of potential Arbiters may be supplied by ICHEIC (and its constituent members), the Foundation, the GDV (and its constituent members) and members of the Panel. There shall be a period of thirty (30) days from written notice by the Panel for these names to be submitted to it.

3.8.2   Thereafter the Panel shall circulate the list of names to ICHEIC and the GDV to be forwarded to their respective members and to the Foundation, each of whom shall have the right, for a period of forty-five (45) days, reasonably to reject any name from the list.

3.8.3   The Panel shall then review each name on the revised list and all eligible Arbiters shall be unanimously approved by the Panel.

3.9   When the Panel has determined by majority decision that its initial tranche of decisions have created a range of reliable precedents, it may decide to authorize the Chairman to transfer the decision on any appeal case to a single member of the Panel or an appointed Arbiter. The Chairman will appoint an Arbiter from the approved list of Arbiters.

3.10   In determining the allocation of appeals between the Panel itself and individual Panel members and Arbiters, the Chairman will seek to balance the objectives of speed and cost effectiveness with the need to ensure consistency of decision making. The Panel will reserve to itself appeals which it determines are complex or novel.

3.11   Where the decision is rendered by a Panel Member or Arbiter it shall be regarded as a decision of the whole Panel.

3.12   The Panel shall simultaneously submit to the Foundation, the GDV and ICHEIC quarterly written reports on its appeals processing. These reports shall include the activities and the conduct in general and the expenses, costs and fees that it has incurred.

4 Administration of the Panel

4.1   The Panel shall determine its internal administrative procedures, whic h include the establishment of an appeals office, and accordingly enact its internal rules and administrative procedures after approval of the Foundation and ICHEIC. The Panel shall appoint an appeals office in an appropriate venue, having regard for cost, convenience and efficiency.

5 Challenge and Replacement of Panel Members and Arbiters

5.1   Any Panel Member may be challenged by any party to an appeal on grounds that there are circumstances which give rise to justifiable doubts as to the independence and impartiality of the Panel Member challenged. Any challenge shall be submitted to the Chairman of ICHEIC and the Board of Directors of the Foundation specifying the facts and circumstances upon which the challenge is based as soon as possible after the challenging party becomes aware of such circumstances.

5.2   If the Panel Member contests the challenge, the Chairman of ICHEIC and a Member of the Board of Directors of the Foundation shall decide if there are justifiable doubts as to the independence and impartiality of the Panel Member.

5.3   Where the Chairman of ICHEIC and a Member of the Board of Directors of the Foundation, decide, in any case, that there are justifiable doubts as to the independence and impartiality of the Panel Member, the Panel Member shall be disqualified from determining that appeal.

5.4   Any Arbiter may be challenged by any party to an appeal on grounds that there are circumstances which give rise to justifiable doubts as to the Arbiter's independence and impartiality. Any challenge shall be submitted to the Panel specifying the facts and circumstances upon which the challenge is based as soon as possible after the challenging party becomes aware of such circumstances.

5.5   If the Arbiter contests the challenge, the Panel shall decide if there are justifiable doubts as to the independence and impartiality of the Arbiter.

5.6   Where the Panel decides, in any case, that there are justifiable doubts as to the independence and impartiality of the Arbiter, the Arbiter shall be disqualified from determining that appeal.

5.7   Any Panel Member or Arbiter shall immediately resign from the appeal if any facts or circumstances arise during the course of the appeal which are of such a nature as to call into question his or her independence and impartiality.

5.8   A Panel Member may only be replaced by agreement between the Chairman of ICHEIC and a Member of the Board of Directors of the Foundation due to a grave and weighty reason or in case of a gross neglect of duty.

5.9 An Arbiter shall be replaced with another Arbiter by the Panel, if the Panel decides that the Arbiter is prevented by law or other circumstances from fulfilling his functions as an Arbiter.

5.10 In case of dismissal or voluntary resignation of an Arbiter, a new Arbiter shall be appointed by the Panel, if necessary.

5.11 Following the dismissal or voluntary resignation of a Panel Member or an Arbiter, the newly appointed Panel Member or Arbiter shall determine if and to what extent any prior steps in any unresolved proceedings shall be repeated before the new Panel Member or Arbiter.

6 Venue of the Appeals Hearings

6.1 The official seat of the Appeals Panel shall be in Geneva, Switzerland.

6.2 The Panel or Panel Member may deliberate and hold hearings in any location that is appropriate for practical reasons, utilizing such modes of communication as is deemed necessary.

7 Filing Appeals

7.1 Each German company shall, upon the completion of its processing of the claimant's claim send to the claimant;

    7.1.1 the determination regarding the claimant's entitlement to the claimed insurance policy;

    7.1.2 all documents relevant to the claim and to the company's decision;

    7.1.3 notice that an appeal against the determination is possible and on the time within which an appeal shall be filed;

    7.1.4 an Appeal Form (Annex G) should the claimant want to appeal against the German company determination; and

    7.1.5 a copy of these Guidelines.

7.2 A claimant wishing to file an appeal shall sign the Appeals Form and submit it by post to the Panel. Together with the form the claimant shall file the following:

    7.2.1 a written statement of the grounds and reasons for making the appeal; and

    7.2.2 any information or evidence supporting the appeal not already submitted to the claims process.

7.3 Any new information or evidence shall be forwarded to the German company and the GDV. In light of the new information or evidence the German company has the opportunity to make an offer to the claimant.

7.4 The appeal shall not be processed by the Panel, Panel Member or Arbiter before 30 working days have expired from the date the German company received the new evidence or information.

8. Powers of the Panel

8.1 Upon receipt of the Appeal Form, as specified in Section 7.2 of these Guidelines the Panel shall request the relevant German company to produce to the Panel all documents relating to the claim.

8.2 If the Panel or Panel Member or Arbiter determines that additional documents or evidence or information is needed from a German company or a claimant in order to properly evaluate the appeal, it shall request such documents, evidence or information from that party.

8.3   If any party to the proceedings fails to provide any requested existing documents, evidence or information the Panel, Panel Member or Arbiter may, after taking all relevant facts into account, including the failure to provide such requested documents, continue the proceedings and render such decision as it deems just and fair in the circumstances.

8.4   Where the Panel, when determining an appeal, in an exceptional circumstance, has a substantial basis for believing that the German company has not complied with its claims handling obligations under this Agreement in its investigation of the claimant's claim, the Panel may request that the BAFin investigate the German company's handling of the claim.

8.5   Where a Panel Member or Arbiter, when determining an Appeal, in an exceptional circumstance, has a substantial basis for believing that the German company has not complied with its claims handling obligations under this Agreement in its investigation of the claimant's claim, the Panel Member or Arbiter may certify to the Panel, and the Panel may request, that the BAF in investigate the German company's handling of the claim.

8.6   If the BAFin upon completion of its investigation of the German company's handling of the claim is of the opinion, and so certifies in writing to the Panel that the German company is not in compliance with its claims handling obligations under this Agreement, the Panel may find for the claimant or may direct the Panel Member or Arbiter to find for the claimant and in all cases may fix compensation to be paid to the claimant in accordance wit h the Valuation Guidelines.

8.7   The Panel, Panel Member or Arbiter shall, wherever possible, determine the substance of any dispute, matter or issue raised in an appeal on the basis of this Agreement. If a matter or an issue is not covered by this Agreement, they shall determine the substance of any dispute in a fair and just way, after reviewing the relevant documents and evidence including the insurance contract.

8.8   The Panel, Panel Member or Arbiter shall make every effort to resolve each appeal within six months from the date it is filed. In extraordinary situations the resolution of an Appeal may extend beyond the six-month period, provided that the claimant is given timely notice that the decision will not be rendered within the agreed period.

9 Confidentiality

9.1   All documents, evidence or information and materials produced by or provided to any party for the purposes of an appeal by any party shall be kept confidential by all parties and persons involved in the appeal.

10 Conduct of Proceedings

10.1   The Panel, Panel Member or Arbiter shall conduct the proceedings in a fair, impartial and claimant friendly manner so as to facilitate the fully in-formed participation of all parties taking into account their age, language, residence, resources and whether or not they are represented in the proceedings by lawyers or other professionals.

10.2 The proceedings shall be conducted on a documents only basis, unless an oral hearing is requested by the claimant or the German company. The Panel may order that such a hearing be conducted by recorded telephone or videoconference. The Panel, Panel Member or Arbiter shall give the parties reasonable notice of all hearings. The parties may attend any oral hearing at their own expense.

10.3 All decisions and orders shall be in writing.

10.4 The Panel shall decide by majority. Members of the Panel may not abstain from voting. Decisions shall record the majority opinion only.

10.5 A decision shall be made in writing and signed by all Panel Members, in the case of a decision by the Panel; or by the Panel Member or Arbiter in the case of a decision by the Panel Member or Arbiter who has issued the decision.

10.6 Each decision shall contain:

10.6.1 the designation of the parties; and

10.6.2 a description of the parties' submissions, the factual findings and any applicable law in the dispute; and

10.6.3 the decisions on the merits and the reasons why the decisions were reached; and

10.6.4 the date of the decision.

11 Language and Translation

11.1 The appeal procedures shall be conducted in English or German unless the parties and the Panel, Panel Member or Arbiter agree on another language. The original version and language of any documents shall prevail in matters of construction and interpretation.

11.2 Where the Panel, Panel Member or Arbiter deems it appropriate, he shall arrange for the translation of any documents and the oral translation of any oral hearing, procedure or other oral communication.

12 Communications

12.1 The parties to an appeal and the Panel, Panel Member or Arbiter shall direct any correspondence or communication to be in writing or other means of telecommunication.

12.2 The last address or fax number notified to the Panel, Panel Member or Arbiter shall be deemed to be a valid address for delivery of any notice or communication.

13 Time Limits

13.1 Unless inappropriate to do so, any time limit or deadline shall be expressed by reference to a specific date.

13.2 Where a time limit or deadline is not expressed by reference to a specific date, counting of days shall commence on the day following the day upon which any notice of the deadline is received.

13.3 Unless special circumstances are shown, requests for extensions of time shall be made to the Panel before the expiry of the deadline. Requests for extensions of time shall be determined by the Panel, Panel Member or Arbiter having regard to the rights of other parties and to the need of expedient settlement of appeals. The Panel, Panel Member or Arbiter is entitled to extend any deadline as they see fit.

14 Multi-Party Proceedings

14.1 The Panel, Panel Member or Arbiter may, if he considers it appropriate, join, consolidate, order concurrent hearings or order a multi-party proceeding of all related appeals. For the purpose of these Guidelines "related appeals" are claims submitted by persons who appear to be related to each other or share the same family background or appeals submitted by the same claimant but relating to different policies.

14.2 Any claimant reviewing information relating to another appeal obtained by him as a result of an exchange of documents or information in a multi-party proceeding shall keep such information confidential and shall only use such information for purposes directly connected with the appeal.

14.3 Where, from information available to the Panel, Panel Member or Arbiter, it appears that the just and fair resolution of an appeal requires the participation in the appeal of a claimant or German company not already a party, they shall invite such claimant or German company to follow such other directions and orders as the Panel, Panel Member or Arbiter considers appropriate.

15 Representation

15.1 Although not required, any party may be represented by an attorney, counsel, lawyer, advocate or any other person of their choice at the party's own expense.

16 Costs

16.1 The appeals process is free of cost to the parties. However, each party shall bear, at its own expense, all costs for communication and all costs, fees and expenses incurred in connection with any representation or assistance it chooses to obtain in accordance with Section 10.2 and this Section.

17 Entitlement

17.1 The Panel, Panel Members or Arbiters shall admit all evidence, including information, statements and documents presented by the parties and any other information available and shall weigh the evidence applying the Relaxed Standards of Proof (Annex B) of the Agreement, bearing in mind the circumstances of each case, the difficulties of tracing documents and information and of proving or disproving the validity of a claim after the destruction caused by the Second World War and the Holocaust and the long time that has elapsed since the insurance policies were issued. In all claims and appeals processing, it is contemplated that German companies, the Panel, Panel Member or Arbiter shall apply the same Relaxed Standards of Proof.

17.2 In accordance with the Agreement, to succeed in an appeal the claimant must establish, based on the Relaxed Standards of Proof, that it is plausible;

17.2.1 that the claim relates to a life insurance policy in force between

273

1 January 1920 and 8 May 1945, and issued by or belonging to a specific German company (as defined in Section 14 of the Agreement) and which has become due through death, maturity or surrender;

17.2.2 that the claimant is the person who was entitled to the proceeds of that policy upon the occurrence of the insured event, or is otherwise entitled in accordance with Section 2 (1) (d) of the Agreement and pursuant to the Succession Guidelines (Annex C); and

17.2.3 that either the policy beneficiary or the policyholder or the insured life who is named in the claim was a Holocaust victim as defined in Section 14 of the Agreement.

17.3 Where the claimant has satisfied the burdens in Section 17.2 above, the relevant German company has a defense in accordance with the Agreement and under the same relaxed Standards of Proof and the claimant is not entitled to payment from the Foundation funds if;

17.3.1 the policy was cancelled before the insured event occurred and before the beginning of the Holocaust in the relevant country, in accordance with Section 7.5.1 of the Valuation Guidelines; or

17.3.2 the insurance policy in question was fully paid as required by the insurance contract. However, where it appears that the policy was paid or surrendered into a blocked account the provisions of Section 5 of the Valuation Guidelines shall apply; or

17.3.3 another person other than the claimant, who has submitted a claim, has a higher entitlement to the proceeds of the policy in accordance with Section 2 (1) (d) of the Agreement or the Succession Guidelines; or

17.3.4 the policy (or policies) in question are considered to have been covered by a decision of a German restitution or compensation authority in accordance with Section 2 (1) (c) of the Agreement.

18 Taking of Evidence

18.1 The Panel, Panel Member or Arbiter may accept relevant oral statement where written evidence, signed statement or statutory declarations are not available or appropriate.

18.2 The Panel may hear parties or other persons as unsworn witnesses or accept affirmations.

19 Panel, Panel Member and Arbiter Decisions

19.1 Based on the Valuation Guidelines (Annex D), the Panel, Panel Member or Arbiter may render an award for smaller or larger amounts than claimed, provided that no award shall be for a sum lower than any sum already offered to the claimant by the relevant German company, unless a fraudulent claim was brought.

19.2 Where it appears to the Panel, Panel Member and Arbiter that a third person may be entitled to part of the proceeds of an insurance policy claimed in the appeal, the decision shall reflect any such entitlement and the Panel may order the payment of the appropriate amount to any such third person out of the sum awarded by the Panel.

20 Correction of Decisions

20.1   The Panel, Panel Member or Arbiter, may on his own initiative or upon the application of a party:

20.1.1 correct a decision to remove any clerical mistake or error or clarify or remove any ambiguity in the decision, or

20.1.2 make an additional award in respect of any claim which was presented to the Panel, Panel Member or Arbiter but which was not dealt with in the decision, or

20.1.3 correct a decision in the case another person is entitled.

20.2   The powers afforded by the preceding paragraph shall not be exercised without affording the parties affected by the decision a reasonable opportunity to make representations to the Panel, Panel Member or Arbiter.

21 Interest

21.1   The Panel may order that interest be paid on an award in the following circumstances:

21.1.1 where the claimant appeals a decision by the relevant German company which is a denial not upheld on appeal and the Panel or Panel Member or Arbiter makes an award to the claimant.

21.1.2 where the claimant appeals a decision by the relevant German company which is an offer and the Panel, Panel Member or Arbiter, makes an award to the claimant.

21.2   In the circumstances referred to in Sections 21.1.1 and 21.1.2 interest shall be credited from the date of the relevant German company's decision to the date of the decision of the Panel, Panel Member and Arbiter at the rate equivalent to the interest rate referenced in the Valuation Guidelines for the year in which the decision is made.

22 Finality

22.1   Save as provided in Section 20, any decision, order or award, made by the Panel, Panel Member or Arbiter shall be final.

23 Settlement

23.1   It is the duty of the parties to notify the Panel, Panel Member or Arbiter immediately if the claim is settled or otherwise terminated by the mutual agreement of all parties.

23.2   Upon receipt of notification of a settlement or a termination the Panel, Panel Member or Arbiter shall terminate the proceedings and, if so requested by the parties, record the settlement or termination in the form of a consent order which shall have the same status as any other decision made by the Panel.

23.3   A consent order may only be entered if the Panel, Panel Member or Arbiter is satisfied that the settlement reached by and between the parties does not contain oppressive provisions, or provisions which adversely affect the rights of any third person.

24 Publication of Panel Decisions

24.1   The Panel shall notify the parties to the appeal as well as the GDV, the Foundation and ICHEIC of its decision in writing within 14 days of the date of the decision. ICHEIC and the Foundation will seek to arrange regular exchanges of information on a reciprocal basis about decisions taken on appeals respectively by the German Appeals Panel, the ICHEIC Appeals Tribunal, the Generali Trust Fund and the Sjoa Foundation.

25 Immunity

25.1   The Panel, Panel Members or Arbiter shall not be liable to any party for any act or omission in connection with the Panel work, except that they may be liable to a party for serious irregularity as defined in Section 14 of the Agreement and as interpreted and governed by Swiss law.

25.2   The claimant waives, by signing the Appeal Form (Annex G), all potential malpractice claims against the Panel, Panel Member or Arbiter. However, the waiver does not extend immunity to the Panel, Panel Member or Arbiter for any serious irregularity affecting the Panel, Panel Member or Arbiter, the proceedings or the decision. In this context serious irregularity is defined in Section 14 of the Agreement.

ANNEX F

<u>CONSENT AND WAIVER</u>

I accept the offer of _____ (the Payment) from _____ (the Company) for the one or more policies described on Exhibit A attached hereto (collectively, the Policy) and agree to waive my rights on this Policy as follows:

(a) Upon the receipt of the Payment, I irrevocably waive and release any and all rights and benefits, including the right of appeal, which I might now have or ever had, up to the date of this release, relating to, or in any way connected with, any of the following:

(i) The Policy or any claims related to it; and

(ii) Any claims outside of the German Foundation Act against both (a) the Federal Republic of Germany, German Federal States and other German public institutions relating to slave labor, forced labor and property losses, and (b) German companies relating to all claims connected with National Socialist (Nazi) injustice.

This release and waiver specifically does not apply to other insurance policies which are not described in this document or claims for other types of compensation or restitution under the German Foundation Act (such as slave labor). Any of these additional claims must be made within the framework of the German Foundation law; provided, however, that this waiver does not apply to any claims for the return of artwork. The claimant must pursue a claim for artwork either in Germany or in the country from which the artwork was taken.

(b) Neither I, nor to the best of my knowledge, any other claimant, has received any payment related to the Policy from the Company or any German reparation or compensation organization.

(c) I attest that the information provided in support of my claim is true and made to the best of my knowledge. I am aware that false information may lead to action for the return of any payment made and further legal action.

(d) I acknowledge that if new or additional facts are subsequently discovered relative to the Policy or the subject matter of this Consent and Waiver, the release and waiver of my rights will still continue in full force and effect.

(e) In consideration of the Payment, I undertake and agree that in the event that one or more other entitled claimants make(s) a claim under the Policy, or otherwise seek(s) payment or compensation in connection therewith, I shall share the Payment with such other entitled claimant(s) on a pro rata basis, in the absence of another mutually agreed basis.

(f) I agree that in connection with the processing and checking of this claim, my data and any other data relating to the Policy will be kept in a central database.

Please sign and date this official Consent and Waiver form where indicated and have your signature confirmed or notarized by a notary public, bank, German consulate or a Jewish social service agency possessing a seal. If you are homebound, your signature may be witnessed by an attending physician.

Signature of Claimant_____ **Date**_____

Print Name: _____

Address: _____

_____

_____

Confirmation or Notary

Subscribed, witnessed or sworn before me on the date stated above. An identification card or passport has proven the applicant's identity.

Signature of Witness or Notary_____ **Date** _____

CONSENT AND WAIVER

EXHIBIT A

DESCRIPTION OF INSURANCE POLICIES

Name of Insured	Name of Policyholder	Insurance Company	Amount of Insurance Coverage

APPEAL FORM

FOR SUBMISSION OF AN
APPEAL TO THE GERMAN FOUNDATION APPEALS PANEL

Established under an Agreement made between the Foundation "Remembrance Responsibility and Future", the International Commission on Holocaust Era Insurance Claims, and the German Insurance Association

A CLAIMANT	Your name
	Your claim number
	Your phone number Fax number

| **B GERMAN INSURANCE COMPANY** | Company that issued the decision   Date of decision (Day/Month/Year) |

| **C REASON FOR APPEAL OF DECISION** | Restate the basis for your claim and explain why you believe your claim has been wrongfully decided |
| **(If you need more space than provided, please attach additional paper.)** | |

INSTRUCTIONS TO THE CLAIMANT

To appeal the decision you have received on your claim from a German insurance company, you need to complete, sign and mail this Appeal Form within 120 days of receiving the company's decision.

You should be aware that by signing and submitting this Appeal Form:

1.) you provide notice that you do not agree with the German insurance company decision made on your claim;

2.) you acknowledge and agree that an Appeals Panel decision is final and that you waive any right to appeal such decision to any court whether on a question of law or fact;

3.) you acknowledge and agree that decisions, orders or awards of the Appeals Panel may be published, providing that such publication does not reveal the identity of any party; and

4.) you agree to be bound by the Appeal Guidelines.

To complete this Appeal Form:

- In A, please provide your name, your claim number, your phone number and a fax number, if available.

- In B, please provide the name of the German insurance company which issued the decision that you seek to appeal. Please also provide the date of the German insurance company's decision. (Again, please note that you must complete and submit this Appeal Form within 120 days of the date of the German insurance company's decision.)

- In C, please describe your claim and explain why you believe the German insurance company was wrong in its decision to deny your claim. (Add additional paper if the space provided above is not sufficient.)

- Please sign your name and date below.

- When you have completed the Appeal Form, please send it, with any additional pages you may have added in explaining the basis of your appeal, or any additional material not previously sent with your claim, to:

Attention—The German Foundation Appeals Panel
[TNT, 000/00000/000
Int Antwoordnummer,
C.C.R.I. Numero 5120
3000 VB Rotterdam,
Pays-Bas, NEDERLAND.]

CLAIMANT's **SIGNATURE**	Please sign here	Date (Day/Month/Year)

ANNEX H

Agreement by the German Insurance Association, ICHEIC, and the Foundation Regarding the Publication of a Holocaust-related List of Possible Policyholders

The German Insurance Association (GDV), on behalf of the participating German insurance companies, the Foundation and ICHEIC agree to work together with a view to publishing as comprehensive a list as possible of holders of insurance policies issued by German companies who may have been Holocaust victims. To this end, they agree as follows:

I. **Comprehensive database of Jewish residents who lived in Germany between 1933 and 1945**

1   The Foundation commits itself to generate as comprehensive as possible an electronic database of Jewish residents in Germany in the period of January 1, 1933 to May 30, 1945 within approximately 3 months after the signing of this agreement. As a starting point, the Foundation will use a list of Jews living in Germany compiled by the Federal Archives (Bundesarchiv). This list was extracted from a national census in 1939. The Foundation commits itself to supplement this list with names from Memorial Books, emigration and deportation lists and other registers of German Holocaust victims. A list of the archive sources to be searched has been agreed and will be evaluated by the team of experts appointed by the Bundesarchiv and ICHEIC (the advisory group). This list is attached as Exhibit 1. If further archive sources likely to yield significant numbers of additional names, which can be searched within the approximately 3month period at a reasonable cost, become known to and approved by the advisory group, the Foundation will add them to the list.

2   The Foundation will entrust the Bundesarchiv as the competent German agency to compile the electronic database of Jewish residents in Germany in the period of January 1, 1933 to May 30, 1945. The advisory group, in accordance with the written recommendations of the experts at a meeting in Berlin on May 6–7, 2002 (the "Berlin Meeting"), will guide the work of the Bundesarchiv on the archive sources to be researched at the outset of the project and will regularly be informed and consulted by the Foundation and ICHEIC on the work as it progresses.

3   The database of Jewish residents in Germany produced from the research of the archives in Exhibit 1 will be screened electronically to remove any duplicate names.[1] Care will be taken in identifying duplicate names to ensure that duplicates are only removed when it is sufficiently certain the same person is referred to. The advisory group will advise and assist the Bundesarchiv in this task.

4   It is expected that the list of Jewish residents in Germany will usually contain family name, first name and the complete date of birth. Where available from the archival sources, additional information such as maiden name, place of birth, place of residence, and occupation will be

---

1. In carrying out this screening, regard will be given to the written recommendations of the experts given in the Berlin Meeting.

incorporated into the list.

5   The Foundation will recommend to the Government of the Federal Republic of Germany that copies of the list of Jewish residents in Germany should be made available as soon as possible subsequent to the matching exercise to Yad Vashem in Jerusalem, the US Holocaust Memorial Museum in Washington, the Jüdisches Museum in Berlin and the Conference on Jewish Material Claims Against Germany onthe basis of agreements between the respective parties.

II.   List of policyholders of German insurance companies

1   All German insurance companies with existing electronic databases, both those companies which did not sign the ICHEIC MOU (non-MOU companies) and those companies which signed the ICHEIC MOU will provide out of their German portfolio a consolidated list with available electronically existing information regarding policyholders from the era between 1920 and 1945, independent of whether the policies were paid or unpaid, compensated or uncompensated.

2   The policyholder list will not contain any reference to a specific insurance company. Wherever available, it will comprise companies' electronic databases with the three criteria of family name, first name and the complete date of birth. It will also comprise companies' electronic databases containing only the family name, first name and either no date of birth or an incomplete date of birth.

3   Provisions will be made for the publication of a consolidated list of any policies issued by a German insurance company outside of Germany, where the information is available.

III.   List of Jewish policyholders in Germany derived from the 1938 asset declarations

The Foundation commits itself to generate an additional list of Jewish policyholders residing in Germany (mainly using 1938 asset declarations) to complement those already discovered through the ICHEIC archive research program. The Foundation will use its best efforts to supplement the 1938 asset declarations through research of other appropriate archives and records. Exhibit 2 sets out the additional archives which are intended to be searched for this purpose. The advisory group will recommend priorities for this effort.

IV.   Matching of the company policyholder list with the comprehensive list of Jewish residents who lived in Germany between 1933 to 1945

The Foundation will appoint a competent expert group to carry out the matching of the company policyholder list with the list of Jewish residents in Germany. The matching process will be conducted in Germany and will be monitored by the advisory group. The matching process should be done on the basis of three criteria: family name, first name, and date of birth where these are contained in both lists. If there is no complete date of birth available in one or other or both of the two lists, the matching will be done on the basis of a match between the family names and the first names in the two lists. The matching process will be carried out following the writ ten recommendations of the experts in the Berlin Meeting.

V. **Matching with ICHEIC Claims Database**

A procedure to match the ICHEIC database of submitted claims with the companies' policyholders list, while protecting the confidentiality of the companies' list, has been agreed as provided in Exhibit 3.

VI. **Publication of List of Policyholders in Germany**

1. The list to be published will have three components:

    (a) the match of the companies' policyholders list and the list of Jewish residents in Germany,

    (b) the list of Jewish policyholders described in III above, and

    (c) the match of the companies' policyholders list and the list of Righteous Gentiles compiled by Yad Vashem. One single comprehensive list to be published would be advisable. The list to be published will only contain the family name, the first name of the Holocaust victims, and year of birth and will not contain any statement regarding the actual status of the policy, i.e., whether the policy was paid or unpaid, compensated or uncompensated.

2. The list to be published will be made available on the ICHEIC website, with the warning appearing on the ICHEIC website, as set out in Exhibit

VII. **Claims Handling**

The lists, as published on the ICHEIC website, are to be used to assist potential claimants. The data on this list will be in an electronic format. All actual claims will be researched by the companies using all of their records, whether or not the names are in an electronic format.

Annex H

Exhibit 1

Sources for a list of names of Jewish citizens of the German Reich under the Nazi rule (1933–1945) discussed at the Berlin-Meeting on May 6-7, 2002

I) Part One

Archives and other sources suggested by ICHEIC:
Yaacov Lozowick, Yad Vashem (1)
Hadassah Assouline, Central Archives (2)
Yoram Mayorek (3)
Lawrence Weinbaum (4)

Name of archive	content
BEG (Bundesentschädigungsgesetz) (1)	
Israel Ministry of the Interior – Population Registry (1)	Capability of creating a databank with names of everyone who was born in Germany before a certain date and who immigrated to Israel
OFD West Berlin (resides in Potsdam) (1)	Files on property of Jewish families – 40,000 files (38,000 already digitized by Yad Vashem). Remaining 2,000 could be computerized
OFD East Berlin (resides in Potsdam) (1)	Property – between 12,000 and 20,000 files. Could create databank
OFD Staatsarchiv Hamburg (1)	Property – 11,000 files. Copies at Yad Vashem. Could create databank
Gesamtverzeichnis der Ausbürgerungslisten,1933-1938 (1)	List of people (mostly Jews) whose Germancitizenship was revoked, 10,000 names. Yad Vashem owns a copy. Could create databank
I 56-Archives of the Central British Fund for World Jewish Relief 1933-1960 (1)	20,000 names of emigrants. Yad Vashem owns a copy. Could create databank
Archival collection from lawyers whose clients were restitution seeking former German Jews	1,000 – 2,000 files. Could create databank.
OFD Staatsarchiv München (1)	11,500 files. „Steuerakten der ehemals rassisch Verfolgten". Could probably be computerized quickly.
Hessisches Hauptstaatsarchiv (1)	36-38,000 files "Landesamt für Vermögenskontrolle und Wiedergutmachung in Hessen". Could probably be computerized quickly.
OFD Landesarchiv Magdeburg (1)	At least 3,600 files. "Oberfinanzdirektion Mitteldeutschland". Could probably be computerized quickly.
OFP Hannover, Niedersächsisches Hauptstaatsarchiv (1)	6,600 files. Could probably be computerized quickly.

Name of archive	content
OFD Westfalen, Staatsarchiv Münster (1)	2,000 files. Could probably be computerized quickly.
OFD Leipzig(1)	At least 1,400 files. Could probably be computerized quickly.
YIVO New York. RG-247 National Coordinating Committee for Aid to Refugees coming from Germany (1)	Names of German emigrants. Could be computerized.
YIVO New York. RG-245.4 HIAS and HICEM Main offices, New York (1)	Could be computerized
YIVO New York. RG-245.5 HICEM Main Office in Europe (1)	Could be computerized
YIVO New York. RG-248 National Refugee Service 1938-1946 (1)	69 reels. Could be computerized
YIVO New York. RG 447 Carl Schurz Foundation-Oberlaender Trust Fund (1)	6 reels. Could be computerized.
American Joint Distribution Committee, New York (AJDC). Emigration Germany. File 658: Register of names of emigrants 1933-1938. (1)	Could be computerized
AJDC, New York, Emigration Germany, Files 674-676 HICEM (1)	Could be computerized
AJDC, New York. Emigration Germany. Files 683-688: Refugees -United States (1)	Could be computerized
Central Archives for the History of the Jewish People, Jerusalem. Centralverein deutsche Buerger juedischen Glaubens (2)	Lists of members
Central Archives, Jerusalem. Jewish marriage records from Germany (2)	
Central Archives, Jerusalem. Danzig community files (2)	Lists of taxpayers from 1929-1937
Central Archives, Jerusalem. Papers from Erwin Lichtenstein, Tel Aviv reparations lawyer (2)	1400 files of former Danzig residents
Central Archives, Jerusalem. Hamburg Jewish community papers(2)	3 files containing genealogical and tax lists for years 1922-1938.
Central Archives, Jerusalem. Darmstadt Jewish community papers (2)	Community membership and tax lists for years 1936-1940
Central Archives, Jerusalem. HIAS – papers of Far Eastern Jewish Central Information Bureau, Shanghai (2)	1000 pages of lists of refugees in Shanghai in 1943 and 1945

Israel State Archives, Jerusalem. Record group 11. Palestine Government Migration Dept. (3)	508 boxes of naturalization cases
Israel State Archives, Jerusalem. Record group 73, Ministry of the Interior, Population registration. (3)	Population census of November 1948 and personal files of deceased Israeli citizens, 1948-1980.
Central Zionist Archives, Jerusalem. Record group SP6 (3)	Personal Files of prospective immigrants
Central Zionist Archives, Jerusalem. Record group S6 (3)	Immigration Dept. of the Jewish Agency: various lists of immigrants
Central Zionist Archives, Jerusalem. Record group S7. Central Bureau for the Settlement of German Jews in Palestine (3)	Various lists of German-Jewish immigrants
Central Zionist Archives, Jerusalem. Record group S75. Youth Aliyah Department (3)	Card index of the pupils
National Archives, Washington D.C. Record group 265. The Office of Foreign Assets Control (3)	Return of the 1943 census of foreign assets owned by US residents.
London Metropolitan Archives. Archives of the Jewish Temporary Shelter (3)	
Jewish Refugees committee, London(3)	Personal files of Jewish refugees in GreatBritain
Association of Immigrants from Central Europe, Israel (4)	Records of German Jews who joined organization in 1930's

II   Part Two
Archives and other sources suggested by the Bundesarchiv (Federal Archives of the Federal Republic of Germany)

Sources, data base	Repository	Estim. number of names
Census data base 1939 (without Austria)	Bundesarchiv (Remerks:Rhine province (acc. to statistical information 33.779) and Thuringian (2.758) data not preserved)	276.205
Basic data for the first edition of the Memorial Book 1986	International Tracing Service, Bundesarchiv (Remeraks: Includes the time before 1939, but does not contain information on the territory of the former GDR)	495.220
Memorial Book 1986	Bundesarchiv (Remarks: Includes the FRG before German unity, East and West Berlin)	128.136
Jewish inhabitants of Thuringia	Bildungsring Geschichte Erfurt e.V., Prof. Wolf	4.000
Jewish inhabitants of Berlin	Foundation "Neue Synagoge Berlin-Centrum Judaicum"	179.854
Memorial Book Riga	Volksbund für Kriegsgräberfürsorge and Foundation "Neue Synagoge Berlin-Centrum Judaicum" (Remarks: Deportation to Riga)	31.770

Memorial Book Theresienstadt	Terezinska Indiciativa (Remarks:Deportation to Theresienstadt)	42.124
Emigrants to France 1933-1939	Published by Julia Franke, Berlin 2000	1.369
List of emigrants to Shanghai	Published by Armbrüster et al (Remarks: States only the age of the person in 1944)	7.800
Jews from Hamburg	Staatsarchiv Hamburg (Remarks: Information from Facts & Files)	10.000/2.000
Survivor Registry and other sources	U.S. Holocaust Memorial Museum (Remarks: Information from Facts & Files)	2.000
ICHEIC Research database, German entries	ICHEIC/Facts & Files (Remarks: Information from Facts & Files)	8.000/1.000
Databases for Memorial Books of German cities (Leipzig, Cologne)	Various Institutions (Remarks: Information needed most urgently for the territory of the former GDR)	
Total		**1.186.478/1.171.478**

General Remarks:

All databases which contain information in particular on life insurance policies of victims of the Holocaust in German archives are not included in this list, since for methodical accuracy the list of names and the research into information on life insurance policies should be prepared in two procedures. Insofar the Federal Archives agrees to the proposal of Facts & Files in principle.

All figures cannot be more than just rough estimates, since a major amount of names of the same person is contained in more than one record group or database. Attention is drawn to the publication of Heinz Boberach, Die Zahl der jüdischen Opfer des Nationalsozialismus aus dem Deutschen Reich. In: Beiträge zur rheinischen Landesgeschichte und zur Zeitgeschichte, Koblenz 2001.

Form the viewpoint of the Federal Archives special care should be taken of the Rhine province, this means information from the Central State Archives in Düsseldorf and Koblenz. Prof. Jersch-Wenzel will report on the situation in Polish archives insofar the former German territories east of the Oder and Neisse rivers are concerned.

If there is time for additional research we should follow the sound philosophy to consult library materials first (in particular the books available in the special library Germania Judaica administered by the University Library of Cologne) and then consult further archives at the regional and local levels.

Annex H
Exhibit 2
Archives to be searched to supplement the list of Jewish policy holders

Federal State	Archive	Location	Response		Name of collection and more detailed description	Rel ev ant	Quantity	Approx. no. of files
Baden-Württemberg	Staatsarchiv Freiburg	Freiburg	Have files relating to asset control and compensation	These contain some tax files, all are accessible	Regional Revenue Office, Freiburg	x	145 m	4,500
Baden-Württemberg	General-landesarchiv Karlsruhe	Karlsruhe	Have tax files		Tax offices have approx. 200 m of files Regional Office for Compensation has approx. 460 m of files	x	660 m	3,000
Baden-Württemberg	Staatsarchiv Ludwigsburg	Ludwigs-burg	Regional Revenue Office, Stuttgart		Regional Revenue Office, Stuttgart	x	100 m	3,000
Baden-Württemberg	Staatsarchiv Sigmaringen	Sigma-ringen	Have tax office files		Wü 126/2 (tax office, Biberach) T 1 Wü 126/7 (tax office, Horb) T 1	x		543
Bavaria	Staatsarchiv Amberg	Amberg	1,209 tax files of people who were persecuted on grounds of race		Tax files of people who were persecuted on grounds of race are held by the tax offices in Amberg, Cham, Neumarkt, Neunburg v. Wald, Regensburg, Schwandorf, Waldsassen, Weiden	x	1,209 files	1,209
Bavaria	Staatsarchiv Bamberg	Bamberg	Have asset control files from the Bavarian Regional Office for Property Administration and Compensation, 2,128 files. Tax files of 1,300 people who were persecuted on grounds of race from the Regional Revenue Office in Ansbach	Tax files are held in Coburg, property control files in Bamberg	Tax files of people who were persecuted on grounds of race in the regions of the tax offices in Bamberg, Bayreuth, Forchheim, Hof, Kulmbach, Lichtenfels, Wunsiedel	x	1,300 files	1,300
Bavaria	Staatsarchiv Coburg	Coburg	32 tax files of people who were perse cuted on grounds of race	Tax files of the Staatsarchiv Bamberg are kept in Coburg		x	32 files	32
Bavaria	Staatsarchiv Landshut	Landshut	24 tax files have survived	Are kept in a depot elsewhere	Tax files kept by Lower Bavarian tax offices relating to people who were persecuted or expelled by the Nazis	x	24 files	24
Bavaria	OFD Nuremberg	Nurem-berg	Property Sales Unit files		8,000 files of the Property Sales Unit are held at the Regional Revenue Office in Munich	x	8,000 files	8,000
Bavaria	Staatsarchiv Würzberg	Würzburg	Have forwarded tax files of people who were persecuted on grounds of race to Würzburg via the District Revenue Office in Ansbach and the Staatsarchiv in Nuremberg		Tax offices in Amorbach, Aschaffenburg, Bad Kissingen, Ebern, Gerolzthofen, Hammelburg, Hofheim i. Ufr., Kitzingen, Klingenberg, Lohr a.M., Marktheidenfeld, Schweinfurt and Bad Brückenau	x	600 files	600
Berlin	Landesarchiv Berlin	Berlin	Have confiscation files		Tax office Moabit-West	x	5,000 files	5,000
Brandenburg	Branden-burgisches Landeshaupt-archiv	Potsdam	No reply		40,000 files of the Property Sales Unit and Foreign Currency Office, 8 m of tax files	x	20,000 files	20,000

290

Federal State	Archive	Place	Response		Name of collection and more detailed description	Rel ev ant	Quanti ty	Approx. no. of files
Hamburg	Staatsarchiv der Freien und Hansestadt Hamburg	Hamburg	Tax office files with the "atonement" payment and punitive tax on Jews clearly indicated	Files on "atonement" payment by Jews, punitive tax on Jews, files on individual cases relating to the "Reichsflucht-steuer"	313-4 I tax administration I, 313-8 Regional tax office department I, 313-9 tax offices	x	36 files	36
Hesse	Hessisches Staatsarchiv Marburg	Marburg	Unrecorded income tax files, mainly of Jewish citizens, unrecorded files on real estate transactions and the punitive tax on Jews	Are stored in Wiesbaden	Tax offices in Eschwege, Korbach	x	2.5 m	200
Hesse	Hessisches Hauptstaats-archiv, Wiesbaden	Wies-baden	Tax office files with "atonement" payment and punitive tax on Jews clearly indicated		Land Property Control and Compensation Office in Hesse, tax office files, department 519/F Tax office Wiesbaden I Tax office Frankfurt-Stiftstrasse Tax office Frankfurt-Taunustor	x	14 m 880 files 3,000 files 306 files	9,000
Hesse	Hessisches Staatsarchiv Darmstadt	Darm-stadt	Have tax office files		Tax offices in Alsfeld, Bensheim-Heppenheim, Darmstadt, Friedberg, Fürth i. O., Giessen, Gross-Gerau, Lauterbach, Michelstadt, Offenbach a.M., Seligenstadt	x	8 m	500
Lower Saxony	Nieder-sächsisches Staatsarchiv in Aurich	Aurich	Have tax office files	Reference to compensation records		x	39.90 m, with some unexplained sets of data	2,500
Lower Saxony	Nieder-sächsisches Staatsarchiv in Bückeburg	Bücke-berg	48 tax office files	Reference to special inventory on the history of the Jews in Schaumburg	Files from the collection of the tax office in Rinteln (H44) on the punitive tax on Jews, also files on the administration of confiscated assets, forced sales, "Reichsfluchtsteuer", restitution claims and compensation	x	48 files	48
Lower Saxony	Nieder-sächsisches Hauptstaats-archiv in Hannover	Hanover	Have foreign currency files and Property Sales Unit files	Are mouldy, ask the Regional Revenue Office in Münster again whether they have any other files	Chief Regional Finance Officer of Hanover, Foreign Currency Office, emigration files (approx. 3,000 files), Regional Revenue Office of Weser-Ems, Property Sales Unit (files covering approx. 12,000 individual cases)	x	15,000 files	15,000
Lower Saxony	Nieder-sächsisches Hauptstaats-archiv in Hannover	Olden-burg	Tax office records only date back to 1950	Claims for the return of Jewish property available, 4 files on confiscated property	Very small number of individual files, Jewish businesses, claims for the return of Jewish property, confiscated assets, files on the whereabouts of Jewish property in Dalmenhorst, Oldenburg and Wilhelshaven	x	approx. 50 files	50
Lower Saxony	Nieder-sächsisches Staatsarchiv in Osnabrück	Osna-brück	Have tax office files	Referred to Staatsarchiv Oldenburg research project to collate all sources of Jewish history in the Weser-Ems region	Restitution. Tax office, Lingen. List of assets of 14 people, land sales, forced auctions	x		50

Federal State	Archive	Location	Response		Name of collection and more detailed description	Rel ev ant	Quantity	Approx. no. of files
North-Rhine/ Westphalia	Nordrhein-Westfälisches Staatsarchiv Detmold and Nordrhein-Westfälisches Personen-standsarchiv Westfalen-Lippe	Detmold	Have tax office files	Punitive tax on Jews and "Reichsflucht-steuer"	Files available –D 26 – tax offices from 1888 to 1984, 770 boxes = approx. 6,600 archive volumes from 1888 to 1984. Reference book D26 and accession book. Files on administrative office and personnel administration, income tax, turnover tax, business tax, corporation tax, capital transfer tax, emergency aid, wealth tax, tax on land acquisition, "Reichsfluchtsteuer", punitive tax on Jews and property lists from the tax offices in Bielefeld-Innenstadt, Bielefeld-Aussenstadt, Bünde, Detmold, Herford, Höxter, Lemgo, Lübbecke, Minden, Paderborn, Warburg and Wiedenbrück	x		3,000
North-Rhine/ Westphalia	Nordrhein-Westfälisches Hauptstaats-archiv Düsseldorf	Düssel-dorf	Tax files available	Punitive tax on Jews and "Reichsflucht-steuer", foreign currency files	Tax offices have 1,000 files; in particular, the tax office in Cologne Altstadt has files from the regional revenue office in Düsseldorf on "Reichsflucht" and currency control	x		1,500
North-Rhine/ Westphalia	Nordrhein-Westfälisches Staatsarchiv Münster	Münster	Tax files available	Files on punitive tax on Jews and "Reichsflucht-steuer"	Tax offices from 1936-1980. Have been organised at district level since 1919, with a subordinate authority of the Reich tax revenue responsible for collecting property and transport tax. Approx. 15,000 files (approx. 1,200 boxes), unregistered (B 155). Files not accessible for use. Tax matters concerning the following tax offices: Ahaus, Altena, Arnsberg, Bochum-Mitte, Bochum-Süd, Borken, Bottrop, Brilon, Coesfeld, Dortmund-Hoerde, Dortmund-Ost, Dortmund-Unna, Dortmund-West, Gelsenkirchen-Nord, Gelsenkirchen-Süd, Gladbeck, Hagen, Hamm, Herne-Ost, Herne-West, Ibbenbüren, Iselohn, Lippstadt, Lüdenscheid, Lüdinghausen, Marl, Meschede, Münster-Innenstadt, Münster-Aussenstadt, Olpe, Recklinghausen, Schwelm, Siegen, Soest, Steinfurt, Wanne-Eickel, Witten; files on punitive tax on Jews from Ahaus tax office (reference book B 155)	x	1,000 files	1,000

Federal State	Archive	Location	Response		Name of collection and more detailed description	Rel ev ant	Quantity	Approx. no. of files
North-Rhine/ Westphalia	Vermögens-abteilung der Oberfinanz-direktion Köln, Aussenstelle Münster	Münster	Referred to by the Staatsarchiv Münster	"Reichsflucht-steuer" and foreign currency files	Foreign currency unit and "Reichsfluchtsteuer"	x	90 m	1,800
Rhineland-Palatinate	Landeshaupt-archiv Koblenz	Koblenz	Tax files available	Punitive tax on Jews and "Reichsflucht-steuer"	1,946 files on confiscation and restitution, mainly concerning real estate; various other relevant file collections – see publication of the Regional Archive Department	x	2,000 files	2,000
Rhineland-Palatinate	Landesarchiv Speyer	Speyer	Tax files available	Punitive tax on Jews and "Reichflucht-steuer"	Return of Jewish property, punitive tax on Jews, files on individual cases, files on general tax assessment, enforcement files to secure claims by the tax administration on individual Jewish firms and private individuals	x	1,000 files	1,000
Saxony	Sächsisches Hauptstaats-archiv	Dresden		Punitive tax on Jews and "Reichflucht-steuer"	Some files are to be forwarded to Chemnitz	x		30
Saxony	Sächsisches Staatsarchiv Leipzig	Leipzig		Punitive tax on Jews and "Reichflucht-steuer"	Tax office Grimma	x	5 m	
Schleswig-Holstein	Landesarchiv Schleswig-Holstein	Schles-wig	Have foreign currency files and some tax files	Foreign Currency Office at the Regional Revenue Office in Nordmark	Only some tax files dating back to before 1945 are available, files may be used to obtain information about individuals or individual firms; information may also be obtained through the tax office	x		1,000
Thuringia	Thürin-gisches Staatsarchiv Gotha	Gotha	Have forwarded the tax files of people who were persecuted on grounds of race to Würzburg via the District Revenue Office in Ansbach and the Staatsarchiv in Nuremberg	Punitive tax on Jews and "Reichsflucht-steuer"	Files at the tax office in Eisenach and Nordhausen, Schleusingen	x	3 m	60
Thuringia	Thürin-gisches Staatsarchiv Rudolstadt	Rudol-stadt	Have tax office files		Electronic search assistance, tax files of the tax offices in Rudolstadt, Arnstadt and Saalfeld, no details as to whether these relate to Jewish property; it is only possible to make a targeted search for individuals and firms	x		50

ANNEX H

EXHIBIT 3

MATCHING

Principles of the ICHEIC – GDV Agreement

The matching process is undertaken to achieve our common goal of paying valid claims—and in particular to provide a process that assists in overcoming the obstacles in identifying and paying claims.

1. Named and unnamed company claims in the ICHEIC claimant database relating to policies likely to have been issued by German companies will be matched under the ICHEIC matching process against the comprehensive electronic list of insurance policies compiled by the BAFin, pursuant to Annex H of the Agreement among ICHEIC, the German Foundation and the GDV.

2. The confidentiality of the list of German companies' holocaust era insurance policies will be protected respecting all data protection regulations. The matches found will be used in the claims process, as described below.

3. All matches, as defined by the matching process, will be categorized into MT0 – MT10 by ICHEIC

4. All matches in categories MT0 – MT5 and MT7 will be reviewed by ICHEIC and divided into four categories: exact match, high probability match, possible match and no match.

5. ICHEIC will send exact matches under MT0 to the companies as part of the agreed claims handling process.

6. ICHEIC will send matches in categories MT1 – MT5 and MT7 that have been confirmed as high probability matches to the companies as part of the agreed claims handling process.

7. Where the ICHEIC matching process identifies more than one match for a specific policy, ICHEIC will send only the best of these matches to the company concerned, other than in exceptional circumstances (e.g., two claimants who are members of the same family).

8. Unless they can provide evidence that shows the match is invalid, the companies will treat exact matches in paragraph 5 as meeting the Relaxed Standards of Proof so far as the existence of a policy issued to the policyholder named by the claimant is concerned.

9. Matches in paragraph 6 above will be taken by the companies as providing strong evidence that the policyholder named by the claimant owned the policy in the match. If a company rejects the match, this fact and the reasons for the rejection will be disclosed to the claimant in the denial letter.

10. Once a match is found, the procedures for named company claims, including appeals, will apply.

11. Possible matches will be examined by ICHEIC to determine the feasibility of resolving if any are high probability matches if such examination is determined to be useful considering time, effort and cost.

12. In the event of a match as set out above, the company is entitled to reject the claim where it can show that the policy was paid or compensated in

accordance with the provisions of the Agreement between ICHEIC, the Foundation and the GDV.

13. The total number of matches to be sent to the companies under this process is not expected to exceed the total number of relevant claims received by ICHEIC and likely to have been issued by German companies.

14. ICHEIC will be responsible for the costs of performing the matching, prior to sending the matched policies to the companies.

15. The ICHEIC matching process will be performed in an efficient and cost effective manner and, if necessary, in Germany.

ANNEX H
Exhibit 4

IMPORTANT INFORMATION ABOUT THE LISTS

The International Commission on Holocaust Era Insurance Claims (ICHEIC) has compiled the following lists of names from several different sources, including but not limited to names received from insurance company members of ICHEIC, the Dutch SJOA Foundation and German insurance companies not belonging to ICHEIC and from various public archives. The names provided by German companies result from a collaborative effort between ICHEIC, the German Foundation "Remembrance, Responsibility and the Future" and the German companies.

The names on the published lists are those of people who had or may have had a life insurance policy of any kind (including education, dowry, endowment or pension/annuity policies) during the relevant period (1920-1945) and who are thought likely to have suffered any form of racial, religious or political persecution during the Holocaust.

The fact that a name appears on the published list is not a guarantee that the individual named or his or her heirs or beneficiaries are entitled to payment. This is for several reasons. For example, investigation and/or research of the claim might reveal that the claim has been settled, that it was paid by the insurer to beneficiaries or to the insured, that loans were taken out against the policy, that the insurance contract did not materialize or lapsed afterwards for reasons unconnected with the Holocaust, or that the claim was compensated or settled through post-war government restitution programs, in particular those of the Federal Republic of Germany.

By the same token, because the surviving records are incomplete, these lists are unlikely to include all the names of Holocaust victims who had insurance policies during the relevant period. People should not be discouraged from filing claims simply because their name or the names of family members do not appear on any published lists. Anyone who believes he or she has a valid life, education or dowry policy is encouraged to present the claim to ICHEIC.

ICHEIC is continuing its international efforts to locate and review sources of information from which lists can be compiled. This site should be re-checked periodically, since ICHEIC will publish these lists via the Internet as they become available.

ANNEX I

AUDIT OF GERMAN NON-MOU INSURANCE COMPANIES

1. The Bundesanstalt für Finanzdienstleistungsaufsicht (the BAFin) and the International Commission on Holocaust Era Insurance Claims (ICHEIC) have discussed the arrangements for auditing certain German insurance companies (not belonging to ICHEIC) as a part of the overall agreement among the German Foundation, ICHEIC and the GDV (the "Agreement") and have reached the understandings, set out in the rest of this Annex, on the following issues:

- companies to be audited;
- objectives and methodology of the audits;
- certification and reports by the BAFin;
- the role of the observer(s) appointed by ICHEIC to be members of the BAFin audit teams;
- a procedure for resolving any disagreements between the BAFin and the ICHEIC observer(s).

(a)   Companies to be audited

2.   The agreed objective is to audit those companies which are most likely to receive a significant number of "named company claims" from ICHEIC. Exhibit 1 contains a list of 8 non-MOU German companies which meet this criterion. ICHEIC and the BAFin will agree on the names of two more companies to be added to this list. The BAFin and ICHEIC will consult with each other if it appears for any reason that any changes should be made to this list.

(b)   Objectives and Methodology of the Audits

3.   The BAFin will conduct its audit on the basis of the standards set out in Exhibit 2 in accordance with the provisions of, and under the powers given to it by, Sections 81 and 83 of the German Insurance Regulatory Law.

4.   The BAFin will make a written assessment, giving its opinion on whether the companies satisfactorily meet each of the agreed standards set out in paragraphs 1–5 of Exhibit 2 in investigating all claims sent to them in accordance with the provisions of the Agreement.

5.   For the purpose of making its assessments in relation to Exhibit 2 the BAFin will make full use of the information about the companies' archives and records which it acquired from the enquiries and on-the-spot investigations it carried out in 1998 and 1999, though any changes in or additions to the archives and records which had occurred subsequently will be checked by the BAFin. The BAFin will supplement the enquiries made by it in 1998 and 1999 by further audits of how each company actually investigated claims in order to enable it to determine whether the standards in paragraphs 1 to 5 of Exhibit 2 have been met. The BAFin intends to conduct these audits by examining a statistically valid sample of both named company and unnamed company claims once 15% of such claims sent to it by ICHEIC through the GDV have been processed by each company.

(c) **Certification and Reports by the BAFin**

6. Subject to the results of the audit being agreed to be satisfactory by both the BAFin and the ICHEIC observer(s), the BAFin will provide ICHEIC with a certificate ("Testat") for each of the companies audited, stating that the named company complies with each of the agreed standards described in the five paragraphs set out in Exhibit 2. This certificate would be in the form of an assurance that:

    "Following its investigations the BAFin has determined that [name of company] is, in all material respects, in compliance with the standards ..."

7. If the BAFin finds that a company is not compliant in some material respect with one or more of the agreed standards in Exhibit 2 the BAFin will require the company immediately to remedy the defect(s) before issuing an opinion. If the BAFin and the ICHEIC observer(s) disagree as to whether a company is compliant, the procedure set out in paragraphs 11 to 23 below will apply.

8. In addition to the opinion the BAFin will supply ICHEIC with one anonymised report setting out what each company has done to comply with the agreed standards of Exhibit 2. Should the ICHEIC observer(s) have reasoned doubts, the BAFin will in good faith try to resolve the disagreement concerning the report before submitting it. This report will not, however, identify the companies concerned by name, if it contains information which was subject to the confidentiality requirements of Section 84 of the German Insurance Regulatory Law. The report will be made available to ICHEIC in both German and English.

(d) **Role of the ICHEIC Observer(s)**

9. ICHEIC has the right to choose and propose one—or if desired up to two— suitably qualified observer(s) to be included by the BAFin in any of the above-mentioned audits of the BAFin. The observer(s) must affirm to the President of the BAFin that they will maintain confidentiality according to Section 84 of the German Insurance Regulatory Law pertaining to the procedures in this agreement.

10. The observer(s) will:

    *   participate actively and fully throughout the audit. In particular, they will be able to put whatever questions they want to the insurance companies and to the BAFin and to contribute their views to the assessments of the companies' compliance with the standards;
    *   like all other members of the BAFin audit team, be provided with all information obtained in Holocaust-related enquiries carried out by the BAFin in 1998 and 1999 and needed for the preparation of the auditing of the company in question;
    *   participate in the preparation of the initial BAFin-questionnaire sent to a company in advance of an on-site investigation visit and in the formula-tion of the additional work to be done by the audit team, taking into account the results of the BAFin's earlier investigations.
    *   participate in the preparation of the reports and opinions referred to in paragraphs 4 to 8 above. In particular they will contribute to answering

the question whether the insurer is appropriately processing the claims with the legitimate interests of the victim in mind and is in compliance with the agreed standards, set out in Exhibit 2.

(e) Procedure for Resolving Disagreements Between the BAFin and an ICHEIC Observer

11. In the event that there is a disagreement between the ICHEIC observer(s) and the BAFin either regarding the adequacy of the audit procedures or on whether the company concerned complies with the agreed standards relevant for the claims processing, the ICHEIC observer(s) shall, in good time before the completion of the audit, set out in writing to the leader of the audit team the reasons for the disagreement and any proposals for resolving it. The ICHEIC observer(s) and the BAFin shall endeavour in good faith to resolve any such disagreement. If the disagreement cannot be resolved the ICHEIC observer(s) may appeal to the Appeal Panel (Panel).

12. The ICHEIC observer(s) shall, within four weeks after they and the BAFin have determined that they are unable to resolve the disagreement, notify the Panel in writing of his (their) intention to submit the disagreement to the Panel for resolution. The ICHEIC observer(s) shall then within a further four weeks from the date of the initial notification, file a written statement to the Panel, giving a full explanation of the facts and reasons which lead him (them) to consider that the company concerned may not be in compliance with the agreed standards. The Panel may on a reasoned request of the observer(s) allow a short extension of the four week deadline.

13. The Panel shall consider all appeals filed within the four week filing period (paragraph 12 above); the Panel may reject an appeal if it was not timely filed. The Panel and all other participants involved in this procedure shall strictly protect the confidentiality of all documents or other information received by them in connection with the appeal.

14. Copies of the observer's written statement shall be sent to the BAF in and the company concerned. The Panel shall invite the BAFin and the company concerned to file a written response to the observer's written statement within a period of four weeks.

15. The Panel shall provide the written statements of the ICHEIC observer(s) and of the company and of the BAFin to the Chairman of ICHEIC and to not more than 8 other ICHEIC representatives named by the Chairman and to a designated member of the board of the Foundation and shall invite them to present their views on each appeal.

16. To protect the confidentiality of the information in these documents the Panel shall require that:

- the recipients of the documents each sign a confidentiality undertaking;
- the documents (which shall be numbered) shall only be read in secure circumstances and that no copies shall be taken;
- the documents shall all be returned to the Panel on completion of the appeal procedure in each case.

17. The Panel shall review each appeal, based on ICHEIC's observer's report and on any responses received from the company and the BAFin and taking into account the views presented by the Chairman of ICHEIC and the member of the Board of the Foundation. The Panel may reject or accept the appeal in whole or in part, setting forth its reasoned decision in writing.

18. The Panel shall determine whether the auditing standards set out in Exhibit 2 have been complied with. If the Panel determines that additional documents, evidence or information is needed in order to properly evaluate if the agreed auditing standards were met, it may request such documents, evidence or information.

19. If a company fails to provide requested existing documents, evidence or information, the Panel may, after taking all relevant facts into account, render a decision as it seems just and fair in the circumstances.

20. If the Panel, when determining an appeal, has a substantial basis for believing that the company concerned has not complied with the agreed auditing standards, it shall notify the company concerned of its decision and of the measures it considers necessary to remedy the non-compliance. The company shall implement the measures considered necessary by the Panel as quickly as possible, informing the Panel, the BAFin, the Foundation, the Chairman of ICHEIC and the appellant observer(s) that it is doing so. The company shall inform the Panel, the BAFin, the Foundation, the Chairman of ICHEIC and the appellant observer(s) when the measures have been fully implemented.

21. The Panel shall also state whether it considers it necessary for the company concerned to reexamine any decisions which it has already taken on named claims where those decisions may have been affected by the company's non-compliance. If the Panel detects in the framework of deciding the observer's appeal that a company has not complied with the standards set out in Exhibit 2 in investigating a particular claim the Panel shall remedy this non-compliance by directing the company to make an award to the claimant or claimants concerned in accordance with the Appeal Guidelines.

22. The Panel shall notify the company concerned, the BAFin, the Foundation, the appellant observer(s) and the Chairman of ICHEIC of its decision in writing within 14 days of the date of the decision. The decision shall be kept confidential by all parties and persons involved in the appeal. The decision of the Panel is final and shall not be appealable to any court.

23. The BAFin may issue a "Testat" when both it and the ICHEIC observer(s) are satisfied that the company has complied with the Panel's decision.

ANNEX I

EXHIBIT

The audits shall be conducted according to Sections 81 and 83 of the German Insurance Regulatory law, on the basis of the standards set out in the following 5 paragraphs:

1. Whether the companies have established an accurate "family tree" identifying all their relevant companies and branches operating during the period 1920–1945. This "family tree" should cover all life insurance branch offices and subsidiaries of the company operating inside Germany or in other relevant territories occupied by the Third Reich in the period 1938–1945 and also any portfolio acquired from other companies which includes policies in force during the 1920–1945 period. Relevant companies should include any subsidiary or branch office where a control-relationship exists today or, in countries where nationalisation occurred, where control existed before nationalisation. The family tree should be authenticated by the supervisory authority.[1]

2. Whether the companies have made all reasonable efforts to find, secure and organise all relevant archive sites, containing archives and records relevant to policies in force in the period 1920–1945.[2]

3. Whether the companies have made all reasonable efforts to identify and secure all surviving relevant policy files and other company records. "Other company records" is to be widely interpreted as covering eg, name cards, life policy registers, reserving registers, correspondence, compensation files and any other document likely to contain details about the policyholders of life insurance policies, whether paid or unpaid, which were in force in the period 1920-1945.

4. Whether the companies have or have established electronic or manual databases which they can use to carry out an effective search of their records of relevant life insurance policies, wherever reasonably possibly solely on the basis of the policyholder names submitted by the claimants.

5. Whether the companies have developed fair and efficient systems and procedures for the investigation of all claims received in accordance with the provisions of the Agreement, with the investigation system described in a work-flow chart.[3] It is desirable that each claims file will contain a completed audit trail allowing auditors to validate, on a sample basis, whether the investigation has been carried out in accordance with the agreed claims handling procedures and with the other relevant provisions of the Agreement.

---

1. Since the BAFin has complete records of the past history of insurance company mergers and acquisitions they will be able to verify authoritatively whether the companies' "family trees" are accurate.
2. It is recognised that for those German companies which sold policies in occupied territories other than Germany—in particular in Eastern Europe—any records still in the hands of the companies may be incomplete and that records still held in Eastern Europe may not always be accessible.
3. It is recognised that each insurer can have different procedures in place for the investigation and handling of claims tailored to its individual circumstances.

ANNEX J

ICHEIC STAGE II PEER REVIEW AUDIT

Purpose: The second stage audit is to verify that MoU companies are processing actual claims received in accordance with agreed ICHEIC standards.

I.   Audit Structure

- One ICHEIC peer review auditor will conduct each company second stage audit.

- A statistically valid random sample of claims will be audited. (Estimated to be approximately 300- subject to change.)

- A first sample will be taken on instruction from ICHEIC after each company has made final decisions on a sufficient number of claims.

- Assuming a company is proven compliant in the initial samples, further sampling will be delayed until close to the end of the process, when a similar size sample will be taken on the remaining claims processed. (There will be further sampling as necessary.)

- In cases where the first sample identifies material or recurring problems in a company's decision-making process (which require corrective action or review of past decisions) or ICHEIC becomes aware from other sources of such problems, there may be a need for further interim samples.

II.   **Auditor's Reports**

- ICHEIC/Capita London Markets Services, Ltd. (CLMS) will, as a prior step, work together with the insurers to establish that

   1 all claims sent by ICHEIC/CLMS to date have been entered on each insurers' claims database; and
   2 that the CLMS database is up to date in recording the decisions made by the companies on these claims.

- Although audits may vary from company to company, the specific work of the auditor will include:

   1. review of the audited company's compliance with ICHEIC standards and decisions in its evaluation of claims;
   2. review of the accuracy of any necessary transfer by the company of the claim information received from CLMS to the company's claims database;
   3. determination of the inclusion of a completed company's audit trail (as approved for Audit Standard 5) showing that all appropriate agreed procedures in the company's work-flow chart, as agreed in the first stage of the audit, had been carried out in sequence;

302

4. repeat of the matching process for an agreed proportion of the claims and records; (For claims in the sample where no match has been found by the company and the claimant has no evidence, no further review by the auditor would be needed.)

5. repeat of the processing carried out by the company (including implementation of ICHEIC standards and decisions) to determine whether the auditor's results are the same as the company's in the case of any claims in the sample where either initial complete or partial matches were made by the company or matches were provided from CLMS or there is documentary evidence of a policy which the company has subsequently rejected; and

6. review of cases of named company claims in the sample to check whether the company's decision letter has:

- given reasons for the denial;
- included copies of any relevant documents found by the company during the investigation of the claim;
- included a valuation sheet in the case of offers;
- informed the claimant of his/her rights to an appeal and included and appeal form.

III. Letter of Engagement

- ICHEIC's letters of engagement with the peer review auditors will be based upon the guidelines in this Annex J and will be agreed within ICHEIC in accordance with ICHEIC procedures.

ANNEX K
ICHEIC – Monitoring Group – Terms of Reference

In order to ensure that the ICHEIC claims process successfully accomplishes the goals of the MOU, the following terms of reference describe the role of the ICHEIC Monitoring Group, which shall apply only to the MOU companies.

1. Lord Archer of Sandwell (or his successor) is the Chairman of the Monitoring Group.
2. The Monitoring Group consists of representatives appointed by the insurance companies, the US regulators, and the Jewish groups/the State of Israel.
3. The Monitoring Group will receive periodic reports from ICHEIC relating to problems or issues arising from the processing of claims.
4. The Monitoring Group will, from time to time, be charged by either the Chairman of ICHEIC or the Chairman of the Monitoring Group, with reviewing and verifying that all members of ICHEIC are complying with ICHEIC rules, procedures and decisions, including decisions of the Chairman, and are doing so as effectively and efficiently as possible.
5. The Chairman of ICHEIC or the Chairman of the Monitoring Group will direct the Monitoring Group to commence its review based upon:

   (a) information of a pattern of non-compliance by a company or companies; or
   (b) a concern relating to the consistency or effectiveness of claims processing.

   Such information or concerns may be identified by any member of ICHEIC, the appeals panel or the audit process.

6. All findings and recommendations shall be reported to the ICHEIC Chairman, who will forward a copy of the report to the German Foundation.

Index